FORMS OF THOUGHT

Forms of thought are involved whenever we name, describe, or identify things, and whenever we distinguish between what is, might be, or must be the case. It appears to be a distinctive feature of human thought that we can have modal thoughts, about what is possible or necessary, and conditional thoughts, about what would or might be the case *if* something else were the case. Even the simplest thoughts are structured somewhat like sentences, containing referential and predicative elements, and studying these structures is the main task of philosophical logic. This clear and accessible book investigates the *forms* of thought, focusing on and drawing out the central logical notions of reference, predication, identity, modality, and conditionality. It will be useful to students and other readers interested in epistemology and metaphysics, philosophy of mind and language, and philosophical logic.

E. J. LOWE is Professor of Philosophy at the University of Durham. His publications include *Subjects of Experience* (Cambridge, 1996), *The Possibility of Metaphysics* (1998), *An Introduction to the Philosophy of Mind* (Cambridge, 2000), *The Four-Category Ontology* (2006), *Personal Agency* (2008), and *More Kinds of Being* (2009). He is a General Editor of the series Cambridge Studies in Philosophy.

FORMS OF THOUGHT

A Study in Philosophical Logic

E. J. LOWE

CAMBRIDGE
UNIVERSITY PRESS

University Printing House, Cambridge CB2 8BS, United Kingdom

Cambridge University Press is part of the University of Cambridge.

It furthers the University's mission by disseminating knowledge in the pursuit of education, learning and research at the highest international levels of excellence.

www.cambridge.org
Information on this title: www.cambridge.org/9781107001251

© E. J. Lowe 2013

This publication is in copyright. Subject to statutory exception and to the provisions of relevant collective licensing agreements, no reproduction of any part may take place without the written permission of Cambridge University Press.

First published 2013

A catalogue record for this publication is available from the British Library

Library of Congress Cataloguing in Publication data

Lowe, E. J. (E. Jonathan)
Forms of thought : a study in philosophical logic / E.J. Lowe.
pages   cm
Includes bibliographical references (pages) and index.
ISBN 978-1-107-00125-1 (Hardback)
1. Logic.   1. Title.
BC71.L69 2013
160–dc23
2012041306

ISBN 978-1-107-00125-1 Hardback

Cambridge University Press has no responsibility for the persistence or accuracy of URLs for external or third-party internet websites referred to in this publication, and does not guarantee that any content on such websites is, or will remain, accurate or appropriate.

Contents

List of figures		*page* vii
List of tables		viii
Preface		ix
Acknowledgements		xii
1	Introduction	1
PART I	REFERENCE AND PREDICATION	
2	Individuation, reference, and sortal terms	11
3	Two styles of predication – dispositional and occurrent	31
4	Ontological categories and categorial predication	50
PART II	IDENTITY	
5	What is a criterion of identity?	69
6	Identity conditions and their grounds	94
PART III	MODALITY	
7	Identity, vagueness, and modality	119
8	Necessity, essence, and possible worlds	139

vi   *Contents*

PART IV   CONDITIONALITY

9   The truth about counterfactuals   163

10   Conditionals and conditional probability   182

Bibliography   205
Index   210

Figures

Figure 3.1	The ontological square, version I	*page*	34
Figure 3.2	The ontological square, version II		35
Figure 3.3	The ontological square, version III		36
Figure 3.4	The ontological square, version IV		38

Tables

Table 3.1 Logical symbolism for the four-category ontology   *page* 36

Preface

I have given this book the subtitle *A Study in Philosophical Logic* in recognition of Bertrand Russell. It was Russell who gave philosophical logic its name, in *Our Knowledge of the External World*, saying that its business is to extract our knowledge of the logical forms of propositions from its 'concrete integuments' and to 'render it explicit and pure' (see the passage quoted at the beginning of Chapter 1 of the present book). Although in practice that task must be approached by investigating the structure of sentences in natural language – since it is in such sentences that our thoughts are clothed and communicated – the underlying aim is to reveal the *forms of thought*, at least to the extent that thoughts are propositional in character and thus capable of standing in logical relations to one another.

Propositional thought is always complex and structured, even when it involves only 'simple' or 'atomic' propositions, and this is why propositional thoughts can always stand in logical relations to other such thoughts. Identifying the forms of atomic thoughts is, then, the first task of philosophical logic, and only having completed that should we endeavour to reveal the forms of more complex thoughts, including compound thoughts which contain subordinate thought-contents as proper parts. Atomic thoughts contain both referential and predicative constituents, so that an inquiry into the nature of *reference* and *predication* is an essential first step in philosophical logic. But some predications have a special importance from a logical point of view, especially predications of *identity* and predications of *necessity* and *possibility* – *modal* predications. That being so, an investigation of the notions of identity and modality is another essential step that philosophical logic must take. And where compound thoughts are concerned, the compounding relations between subordinate thought-contents need to be understood, the most important of these – in view of its intimate connection with logical inference – being *conditionality*. These, accordingly, are the central logical notions that will be discussed in this book: *reference, predication, identity, modality,* and *conditionality*. Much that needs to be said concerning the forms of thought can be said in terms of these notions. Other important logical notions that I shall *not* focus on in this book are those of *negation, existence,* and *truth* – and, although I have views about all of these three notions, I shall reserve a full examination of them for another occasion, discussing them only in passing in the present book.

However, a complicating factor for present purposes is that none of the logical notions that I do discuss in this book can be understood entirely independently of each other: for instance, there are intimate connections between reference and identity and between modality and conditionality. Hence, although different chapters of this book are primarily devoted to each of the five core notions mentioned above, not everything to be said about each notion will be confined to the chapters devoted to it. Even so, I have endeavoured to make each chapter of the book relatively self-standing, so that it is intelligible for a reader who does not have time to study the book as a whole and just wants to focus on one particular issue. As a consequence, some chapters inevitably include a certain amount of recapitulation of matters discussed more fully elsewhere; but I hope that readers will find this preferable to a much more extensive use of cross-reference between chapters, which would have required them to turn quite frequently to other chapters in the course of their reading in order to follow certain discussions or lines of argument.

I have noted already that this book does not pretend to offer a discussion of all the logical notions needed for a full characterization of the forms of propositional thought and an exhaustive account of all the logical relations in which propositional thoughts can stand to one another. But one omission may strike some readers as being strange, namely the lack of much discussion – save in Chapter 10 – of the *propositional attitudes*, such as belief. Now, it is undoubtedly true that important logical questions arise concerning the validity of logical inferences in which the conclusion and some of the premises are sentences involving propositional attitude verbs, because a sentence of the form '*S* believes that *p*' – for example – apparently provides a *non-extensional context* for the embedded sentence '*p*', in which co-referring terms cannot necessarily be substituted for one another *salva veritate*. However, while the notion of extensionality is undoubtedly a logical one – and one which I admittedly do not discuss in this book – it must surely also be acknowledged that the notion of belief as such is not a logical but a *psychological* one, and this, at root, is why I do not have much to say about it in this book. My assumption is that

Preface xi

philosophical logic, although it is centrally concerned with the nature of propositional *thoughts*, is concerned with them solely insofar as such thoughts have truth-evaluable *propositional contents*, and is not at all concerned with such thoughts qua psychological states of thinkers: that, rather, is a task for the philosophy of mind.

Of course, there are some interesting formal and semantic analogies between propositional attitude expressions and *modal* expressions – between, for instance, sentences of the form 'S believes that p' and sentences of the form 'It is possible/necessary that p'. However, I do discuss modality extensively in this book, especially in Part III, and even urge, in Chapter 9, that modal expressions in everyday language sometimes call for 'epistemic' interpretations. Nonetheless, I have serious doubts about the idea that there could be a logic *of belief* – 'doxastic' logic – on a par with modal logic, treating 'it is believed that' as a quasi-logical sentential operator on a par with 'it is necessary that'. Purely logical notions, such as the five core notions focused on in this book, are 'topic-neutral', since logic and reasoning are applicable to *any* subject matter, whether it be in the domain of the physical, the psychological, the social, or indeed the abstract (as in mathematics). This, incidentally, is not to deny that an important distinction may be drawn between *theoretical* and *practical* reasoning, with the former providing guidance concerning *what we should believe* in the light of the evidence available to us, while the latter provides guidance concerning *how we should act* in the light of our goals and needs. But the same purely logical notions are applicable on *both* sides of this divide. Theoretical reasoning, in my view, does not require a logic *of* belief, in the sense that a putative 'doxastic' logic would constitute this.

This is a book aimed primarily at professional philosophers and graduate students in philosophy, although I have tried to write it in a style that makes it clear and accessible also to middle- and upper-level undergraduate students of philosophy with a suitable background in logic, metaphysics, and the philosophy of language. It is partisan, in the sense that I resolutely defend certain controversial positions on the issues that I discuss, but I attempt to conduct this defence in a fair-minded spirit, giving due weight to the force of opposing views. Most of these positions I have defended in print previously, and the chapters of this book draw to varying extents on earlier work of mine. At the same time, I have naturally changed my opinions about many matters over the years and this book represents only my current views about the topics that it covers.

Acknowledgements

The chapters of this book draw in some measure on previously published papers of mine, as follows, and I am grateful in all cases to the publishers and editors concerned for permission to reuse the material in question in this way. Chapter 2: 'Individuation, reference, and sortal terms', in A. Raftopoulos and P. Machamer (eds.), *Perception, Realism, and the Problem of Reference* (Cambridge University Press, 2012), pp. 123–41. Chapter 3: 'Modes of exemplification', in B. Langlet and J.-M. Monnoyer (eds.), *Gustav Bergmann: Phenomenological Realism and Dialectical Ontology* (Frankfurt: Ontos Verlag, 2009), pp. 173–91. Chapter 4: 'Categorial predication', *Ratio* 25 (2012), pp. 369–86. Chapter 5: 'What is a criterion of identity?', *Philosophical Quarterly* 39 (1989), pp. 1–21. Chapter 6: 'How are identity conditions grounded?', in C. Kanzian (ed.), *Persistence* (Frankfurt: Ontos Verlag, 2008), pp. 73–89. Chapter 7: 'Identity, vagueness, and modality', in J. L. Bermúdez (ed.), *Thought, Reference, and Experience: Themes from the Philosophy of Gareth Evans* (Oxford University Press, 2005), pp. 290–310. Chapter 9: 'The truth about counterfactuals', *Philosophical Quarterly* 45 (1995), pp. 41–59. Chapter 10: 'Conditional probability and conditional beliefs', *Mind* 105 (1996), pp. 603–15, and 'What is conditional probability?', *Analysis* 68 (2008), pp. 218–23.

Some of the material in this book was first presented in public in the form of conference or research seminar papers, and I am grateful to the many people – too many to be named individually here – who offered criticisms and suggestions for improvement on those occasions. I am indebted to Hilary Gaskin and Anna Lowe of Cambridge University Press for all their expert advice, encouragement, and assistance. Finally, I am also very grateful to a number of anonymous readers for the Press who provided very helpful suggestions both concerning the original book proposal and regarding the penultimate draft of the manuscript.

CHAPTER I

Introduction

Some kind of knowledge of logical forms, though with most people it is not explicit, is involved in all understanding of discourse. It is the business of philosophical logic to extract this knowledge from its concrete integuments, and to render it explicit and pure.

Bertrand Russell (1914)

As I mentioned in the Preface, I have given this book the subtitle *A Study in Philosophical Logic* in recognition of Bertrand Russell, who coined the term 'philosophical logic' in the passage quoted immediately above.[1] It is unfortunate, in my view, that many philosophers now seem to have forgotten the origin of this term and, instead of using it in Russell's very useful sense, take it to mean instead something like *the philosophy of logic(s)*, which is at once broader and narrower than what, I think, Russell primarily had in mind: broader inasmuch as the philosophy of logic(s) is concerned, inter alia, with evaluating consistency and completeness proofs for various systems of formal logic – that is, with *metalogic* – and with adjudicating between different rival systems of formal logic (for instance, different formal systems of modal logic); and narrower inasmuch as the philosophy of logic(s) is less concerned with what may aptly be called *the logic of natural language*, as opposed to systems of formal logic which utilize artificial symbolic languages. As I understand Russell, the primary aim of philosophical logic is to reveal the *forms of thought*, to the extent that thoughts are propositional in character and thus capable of standing in logical relations to one another, and this requires it to focus on thought as it is most naturally expressed, in the shape of sentences of one or another natural language. As I explained in the Preface, it is in pursuit of this aim that I have singled out the focal topics of the book's remaining nine chapters – namely the central logical notions of *reference, predication,*

---

[1] Bertrand Russell, *Our Knowledge of the External World* (London: George Allen and Unwin, 1922), p. 53.

I

2   *Introduction*

identity, *modality*, and *conditionality*. It is my belief that much – though by no means all – that needs to be said concerning the forms of thought can be said in terms of these key notions.

I shall keep the rest of this Introduction brief, restricting it to a short outline of the contents of the remaining chapters of the book, but I refer readers once more to the Preface for a statement of my primary intentions and guiding thoughts in writing the book. The remainder of the book is divided into four Parts, dealing respectively with the topics of *reference and predication* (Chapters 2 to 4), *identity* (Chapters 5 and 6), *modality* (Chapters 7 and 8), and *conditionality* (Chapters 9 and 10).

I REFERENCE AND PREDICATION

In Chapter 2, 'Individuation, reference, and sortal terms', I argue – contrary to the adherents of most versions of the so-called 'direct' theory of reference – that singular reference to an individual cannot in general be secured by a thinker without that thinker's grasping, at least implicitly, a *criterion of identity* which that individual satisfies, where such a criterion is linked to a family of general terms of the 'sortal' variety. This is a claim that I have defended elsewhere, notably in my *Kinds of Being: A Study of Individuation, Identity, and the Logic of Sortal Terms* (Oxford: Blackwell, 1989) and more recently in my 'Sortals and the Individuation of Objects', *Mind and Language* 22 (2007), pp. 514–33. Here I argue afresh for the claim. My defence of the claim does not, however, commit me to the truth of a so-called 'descriptive' theory of reference, as such a theory would normally be understood. Moreover, I distinguish my version of the claim – which I call 'categorialism' – from a more demanding and consequently less credible version, called 'sortalism'. According to my version, singular thought about an individual is available only to a thinker who at minimum grasps – even if only implicitly and somewhat imprecisely – to which ontological *category* the individual in question belongs, thereby allowing that the thinker may be seriously in error concerning any *specific* sortal concept under which that individual falls.

Chapter 3 is entitled 'Two styles of predication – dispositional and occurrent'. In this chapter, I am concerned solely with what are sometimes called *material* predications, as opposed to *formal* predications. As I understand this distinction, predications of the latter kind predicate merely 'formal' properties and relations, such as *existence* and *identity*, of their subjects, whereas predications of the former kind predicate 'material' properties and relations – that is, genuine *universals* – of their subjects. The

Introduction 3

implication is that material predications, as I understand them, are *existence-committing*: they commit the person who makes such a predication to the existence of the relevant universal. Hence, this is a thoroughly antinominalist view where such predications are concerned. However, I also believe, in line with other previous work of mine, that material predications further subdivide exhaustively and exclusively into two sub-kinds: *dispositional* predications and *occurrent* predications. This is an idea extensively discussed in my previously mentioned book, *Kinds of Being*, and more recently in my *The Four-Category Ontology: A Metaphysical Foundation for Natural Science* (Oxford: Clarendon Press, 2006) and *More Kinds of Being: A Further Study of Individuation, Identity and the Logic of Sortal Terms* (Malden, MA and Oxford: Wiley-Blackwell, 2009), the latter being a revised and extended version of *Kinds of Being*. But my treatment of the topic in Chapter 3 goes considerably beyond these earlier treatments in important new ways. In it, I also take the opportunity to correct some misconceptions that critics of my position have fallen prey to.

In Chapter 4, 'Ontological categories and categorial predication', I return to two important topics involved, either explicitly or implicitly, in the preceding two chapters: the notion of an ontological *category* and the notion of *formal* predication. My view is that a predication in which an entity is said to belong to a certain ontological category is one of the formal kind, the implication being that ontological categories should not be thought of as being high-level *universals* and, correspondingly, that categorial concepts should be thought of as being 'formal' rather than 'material' ones. Strictly speaking, then, such categories should not be included in an inventory of *what there is*: they do not belong to the existential content of reality and are not 'entities' of any kind – although this in no way compromises the mind-independent truth of categorial predications. In the course of accommodating the notion of categorial predication, I criticize the ontological presuppositions of the type of formal predicate logic that contemporary philosophers have inherited from the founders of modern quantificational logic, notably Gottlob Frege and Bertrand Russell, and propose some major reformations. This carries further forward the task, begun in my *Kinds of Being*, *The Four-Category Ontology*, and *More Kinds of Being*, of constructing a system of formal logic which perspicuously reflects the neo-Aristotelian ontological presuppositions of my own preferred system of categorial ontology, which identifies *four* fundamental ontological categories – those of *individual substance, substantial kind, individual mode or accident*, and *universal attribute*.

4   *Introduction*

Here it is perhaps worth mentioning again that I regard *existence* as being a 'formal' property, in the same sense in which I take identity to be a 'formal' *relation*. I also contend that the notion of existence, like that of identity, is a primitive and unanalysable one. The existence predicate, I maintain, is a so-called 'first-order' predicate, not a 'second-order' one, as Frege, Russell, W. V. Quine and very many modern analytic philosophers suppose. (It is largely a matter of taste whether we say 'second-*order*' or 'second-*level*' here, so my choice of the former is not meant to be significant.) It is important in this connection not to confuse the claim, which is certainly still very widely held, that '– exist(s)' is not a *first*-order predicate, on a par with '– run(s)' or '– eat(s)', with the claim, often associated with Kant, that '– exist(s)' is not a predicate *at all*. The latter view is scarcely credible, if taken literally. The former view, however, arises from the widespread doctrine that the logical form of propositions ascribing existence is *quantificational* – so that, for instance, 'Tigers exist' should be understood to be logically equivalent to, or indeed analysable as, 'Something is a tiger'. Quantifier phrases, as they are standardly construed by philosophical logicians, have the logical status of *second*-order predicates – that is, predicates of (first-order) predicates. However, in my view, existence is *not* properly expressed by a quantifier – the tendentiously named 'existential' quantifier, standardly symbolized by '∃'. '– exist(s)' really *is* a first-order predicate, on a par, as far as logical syntax is concerned, with '– run(s)' and '– eat(s)'. Nonetheless, because the existence predicate is a formal rather than a material one, it would be wrong in my view to suppose that existence is a real *universal* – and hence wrong to suppose that existence is something that itself *exists*. There is nothing at all paradoxical in saying this: indeed, on the contrary, to say that *existence exists* should strike most philosophers as absurd.

2 IDENTITY

Chapter 5, 'What is a criterion of identity?', looks in more depth at the notion of such a criterion that was first introduced in Chapter 2. This chapter is based on my paper of the same title which appeared in *Philosophical Quarterly* 39 (1989), pp. 1–21. I have retained its original title for this chapter and have revised it only where it deviates from my current views on its topic, because it has been widely referred to in the intervening years and I therefore thought it appropriate to make it available, in a form as close as possible to its original one, in the present volume. The only significant way in which I have changed my mind about things said in the

Introduction 5

original version involves certain matters covered in Chapter 2, concerning the manner in which children might be equipped to form identity-judgements about perceptible material objects in their immediate environment. Accordingly, I have now brought what I say in Chapter 5 into line with what I say in Chapter 2 on the matters in question.

In Chapter 6, 'Identity conditions and their grounds', I advance from the more semantically oriented concerns of Chapter 5 to explicitly metaphysical ones, where questions of identity are at issue. Assuming, in line with the conclusions of Chapter 5, that entities of different kinds very often possess different *identity conditions* – determining, for instance, what possible changes they can intelligibly be supposed to persist through over time – the question arises as to the *source* or *ground* of these conditions. One view which I resolutely reject in this chapter is the idea that these conditions have a purely *conceptual* basis and are to that extent the workmanship of the human mind, as John Locke might have put it. Instead, I argue in favour of a metaphysically realist view of how identity conditions are grounded, according to which their source lies in the very *essences* of the entities concerned, with 'essence' being construed in a realist and broadly neo-Aristotelian fashion consonant with the neo-Aristotelian categorial ontology espoused in earlier chapters. A very important aspect of my own account of essence – whether or not it is faithful to Aristotle himself in this respect – is that I deny that essences are themselves *entities* of any kind. In other words, I take the concept of essence to be, in the terminology introduced earlier, a *formal* rather than a material one.

3 MODALITY

Chapter 7 is entitled 'Identity, vagueness, and modality'. In this chapter I challenge the widely held view that predications of identity can never be *vague* or *indeterminate* in respect of their truth-value and never be *contingent*, other than as a consequence of features of the language in which we express them – that is to say, that the source of such vagueness or contingency can never be *ontological*, as opposed to semantic or epistemic, in character. Here I focus on two very well-known attempts to uphold each aspect of this widely held view, namely Gareth Evans's attempted proof that there cannot be 'vague objects' and the alleged proof of the necessity of identity that is attributable, independently, to Saul Kripke and Ruth Barcan Marcus. These two supposed proofs are interestingly parallel in certain important respects and both, in my view, suffer from

6 *Introduction*

essentially the same underlying fault, which renders each of them subtly question-begging. The vagueness question is particularly important, from a metaphysical point of view, because if my opponents are correct it is difficult to see how our common-sense ontology of 'ordinary objects', such as tables and horses – Aristotle's 'primary substances' – could be held to reflect the true nature of mind-independent reality. Instead, we would seem to be driven to endorse a much more 'revisionary' and 'sparse' ontology, acknowledging the reality only of 'simple' material objects, such as the fundamental particles posited by physics, or indeed the reality only of a *single* material object – the physical cosmos as a whole – as some extreme ontological monists maintain that we should.

Chapter 8, 'Necessity, essence, and possible worlds', focuses solely upon the semantics, logic, and metaphysics of modality. Very commonly in recent times – thanks especially to the seminal work of Saul Kripke on the foundations of modal logic – the notion of a necessarily true proposition is explicated in the following way: such a proposition, it is said, is one that is *true in every possible world*. However, this explication is no clearer than the key notion of a 'possible world' upon which it draws. In this chapter, I argue that this notion is thoroughly obscure and really of no use at all in explicating either the notion of necessity or the metaphysical ground of necessary truth. Instead, I appeal for these purposes once more to a neo-Aristotelian notion of *essence*, building on recent work of mine on this theme in, for instance, my paper 'Two Notions of Being: Entity and Essence', in Robin Le Poidevin (ed.), *Being: Developments in Contemporary Metaphysics* (Cambridge University Press, 2008). The conception of essence that I defend is, as I say, a neo-Aristotelian one, in stark contrast with the current mainstream conception, which attempts to define essence in terms of necessity, rather than vice versa. In defending this approach, I consciously draw upon insights that are to be found in Kit Fine's important recent work on the topic of essence and modality, although my own views on these matters do not exactly coincide with his in every important respect.

4 CONDITIONALITY

In Chapter 9, 'The truth about counterfactuals', I develop a distinctive account of the logic and semantics of counterfactual conditionals which departs in important respects from all other existing accounts, most notably the highly influential account of David Lewis. Of course, the interpretation of conditionals quite generally is notoriously

Introduction 7

controversial – much more so than that, say, of conjunctive or disjunctive propositions. It is still hotly debated, for example, whether conditionals fall into two logically distinct classes – *indicative* conditionals and *subjunctive* conditionals – and equally hotly debated whether all indicative conditionals are so-called *material* conditionals. Another much-disputed question is whether the notion of conditionality, at least in the case of indicative conditionals, is explicable in terms of the notion of *conditional probability*, rather than vice versa – a matter to which I turn in the final chapter of the book. In the present chapter, I argue in defence of a *unified* theory of conditionals, embracing both indicatives and subjunctives, which explicates them in terms of a generalized notion of *necessity* – this notion admitting various more specific modal interpretations dependent on context. One very important implication of the account is that the *logic* of conditionals, including counterfactuals, is reducible to a variety of standard modal logic. This chapter is essentially a revised and updated version of my paper of the same title, 'The Truth about Counterfactuals', *Philosophical Quarterly* 45 (1995), pp. 41–59, although the system of conditional logic that I defend was first aired much earlier, in my 'A Simplification of the Logic of Conditionals', *Notre Dame Journal of Formal Logic* 24 (1983), pp. 357–66. As with Chapter 5, I thought it best to restrict revisions here to a necessary minimum, because the original paper has been quite widely referred to since it first appeared in 1995. One reason why I consider the work of this chapter to be particularly important is that it can be drawn upon to challenge a view that has recently gained some currency, according to which our knowledge of *modal* truths, quite generally, can be explicated in terms of our knowledge of counterfactual conditionals. I believe the very reverse of this to be the case, precisely because I consider the logic of conditionals to be reducible to a variety of modal logic.

As I have just indicated, Chapter 10, 'Conditionals and conditional probability', is ultimately motivated by the question whether the notion of *conditionality* – the notion canonically expressed by the logical connective 'if' – is explicable in terms of the notion of *conditional probability*, as the latter is standardly understood in the mathematical theory of probability. A positive answer to this question has been very ably defended by Dorothy Edgington, whose work consequently poses a serious threat to my own attempt to frame a unified theory of conditionals which draws instead upon *modal* notions and standard *modal* logic. In this chapter, I argue that Edgington's position is unsustainable and that, in fact, the correct

8 *Introduction*

direction of explanation is *from* the notion of conditionality *to* the notion of conditional probability, not vice versa. In the process of arguing for this, I subject the standard ratio-based definition of conditional probability to a number of criticisms and propose in place of it a definition of conditional probability which is framed in explicitly conditional terms – and hence in terms fully consonant with my own unified theory of conditionals.

PART I

Reference and predication

CHAPTER 2

Individuation, reference, and sortal terms

In this, the first substantive chapter of the book, I want to defend a thesis that I call *categorialism* regarding the individuation of objects, in the cognitive sense of the term 'individuation'.[1] Individuation in this sense – which is to be distinguished from individuation in the metaphysical sense[2] – is the *singling out of an object in thought*. According to categorialism, a thinker can single out an object in this way only if he or she grasps, at least implicitly, some categorial concept under which he or she conceives the object in question to fall – such a concept being one that supplies a distinctive *criterion of identity* for objects conceived to fall under it. Plausible examples of such categorial concepts would be the concepts of an *animal*, a *material artefact*, and (what I shall call, for want of a better term) a *geographical prominence*.

Categorialism, thus, is a more liberal doctrine than *sortalism* – the latter doctrine maintaining that an object can be singled out in thought only when conceived of as falling under some specific *sortal* concept, such as the concept of a *cat*, a *table*, or a *mountain*. As these everyday examples illustrate, categorial concepts are more abstract than any of the more specific sortal concepts that fall within their range of application: *animal*, for instance, is more abstract than either *cat* or *dog*, and *geographical prominence* is more abstract than either *mountain* or *island*. All sortal concepts falling within the range of application of the same categorial concept are, it seems clear, necessarily associated with the same criterion of identity, but they evidently differ with respect to the more specific *sortal persistence conditions* governing objects that fall under them. These sortal persistence conditions – which impose restrictions on what varieties of

---

[1] I have defended this thesis before: see, especially, my 'Sortals and the Individuation of Objects', *Mind and Language* 22 (2007), pp. 514–33. Here I want to strengthen and extend the arguments of that paper.
[2] For more on this distinction, see my 'Individuation', in M. J. Loux and D. W. Zimmerman (eds.), *The Oxford Handbook of Metaphysics* (Oxford University Press, 2003).

12   *Reference and predication*

natural change an object can be supposed to survive while continuing to fall under the relevant sortal concept – are for the most part discoverable only empirically, whereas criteria of identity proper are most plausibly classified as relatively a priori metaphysical principles.

In the present chapter, I shall offer some arguments in support of categorialism and then go on to inquire whether these arguments can be extended from the domain of singular thought to that of singular linguistic reference: that is, I shall inquire whether it can reasonably be contended that a speaker cannot successfully refer to an object by means of a proper name unless he or she grasps, at least implicitly, that the name's referent falls under a certain categorial concept, which supplies a criterion of identity for the referent. This contention conflicts, of course, with the assumptions of any purely 'direct' theory of reference, to the extent that it makes an object's known satisfaction of some broadly descriptive specification a necessary – albeit not a sufficient – condition for successful linguistic reference to that object.

I SORTAL, CATEGORIAL, AND TRANSCATEGORIAL TERMS

In what follows, I shall talk pretty much interchangeably of *terms* and *concepts*, except when it is important to distinguish between constituents of language and constituents of thought. For much of the time, however, it will be more convenient to speak of *terms*, as these are obviously more immediately identifiable, being words or phrases occurring in natural or formal languages. *Sortal* terms – a locution coined by John Locke[3] – are nouns or noun phrases denoting putative *sorts* or *kinds* of objects.[4] They are also sometimes called *substantival general terms*.[5] Familiar examples would be the terms 'cat', 'table', and 'mountain'. They differ from *adjectival* general terms, such as 'white', 'square', and 'steep', in having not only criteria of application but also criteria of identity associated with their use. This is reflected in the fact that such terms are *count nouns*, not merely in the purely grammatical sense, but also in the more robust sense that there are principles governing their correct use in counting or enumerating objects to which they apply. A *criterion of application* tells us to which objects a general term applies and thereby fixes its extension. A *criterion of*

---

[3] See John Locke, *An Essay Concerning Human Understanding*, ed. P. H. Nidditch (Oxford: Clarendon Press, 1975), III, III, 15.

[4] See also P. F. Strawson, *Individuals: An Essay in Descriptive Metaphysics* (London: Methuen, 1959), p. 168; and David Wiggins, *Sameness and Substance Renewed* (Cambridge University Press, 2001).

[5] See P. T. Geach, *Reference and Generality*, 3rd edn (Ithaca, NY: Cornell University Press, 1980).

identity tells us what conditions need to be satisfied by objects to which a general term applies if those objects are to be identical with one another. Since objects can be counted only if some principle is supplied determining whether or not certain objects to be included in the count are identical with or distinct from one another, criteria of identity are presupposed by principles for counting. For example, an instruction to count the cats living in someone's house only makes sense given a principled way to determine whether a cat encountered at one time and place in the house is, or is not, the *same* cat as a cat encountered at another time and place in the house. Clearly, different criteria of identity and principles for counting apply to objects of different sorts – for instance, to cats as opposed to mountains. Equally clearly, there are no criteria of identity or principles for counting that apply to *white* objects, say, or to *square* objects, purely insofar as those objects are white or square. After all, both cats and mountains can be white, but when we count white cats we apply different principles from those we apply when we count white mountains, and this reflects a difference between the criteria of identity associated with the sortal terms 'cat' and 'mountain'.

Sortal terms fall into *hierarchies of subsumption*. For instance, 'cat' is subsumed by 'mammal', which is in turn subsumed by 'vertebrate'. Equally, 'cat' itself subsumes, for instance, 'Siamese cat'. Every sortal term within a given hierarchy of subsumption is necessarily governed by the same criterion of identity. At the top of any given hierarchy of subsumption is a *categorial* term: in the case of the hierarchy to which 'cat' belongs, the term in question is 'animal' (or, perhaps, 'living organism'). This is the highest term in the hierarchy which shares the same criterion of identity of all the sortal terms below it in the hierarchy. Any general term that has a still more general criterion of application than this categorial term, in that it also applies to objects describable by sortal terms belonging to other hierarchies of subsumption, is a *transcategorial* term. Thus, for example, 'material object' is a transcategorial term because it applies to objects such as cats, but also to objects such as mountains, even though the sortal terms 'cat' and 'mountain' belong to different hierarchies of subsumption. Because a transcategorial term does not belong to any single hierarchy of subsumption, there can be no specific criterion of identity, or principle for counting, associated with its use. As we shall shortly see, it is important not to confuse the criterion of identity associated with a sortal term with another kind of principle governing such a term, namely one specifying the *sortal persistence conditions* of objects to which the sortal term applies. These are the conditions that an object must continue to satisfy if the

14 *Reference and predication*

sortal term is to continue to be applicable to it, and these conditions can very often differ for different sortal terms within the same hierarchy of subsumption, or subsumed by the same categorial term. Thus, for instance, the persistence conditions of cats cannot simply be identified with those of mammals in general and, equally evidently, cats and frogs, say, have different persistence conditions, even though 'cat' and 'frog' are both subsumed by the categorial term 'animal'. It is only because all animals share the same criterion of identity that we can make sense of narratives, whether fictional or scientific, in which an animal of one sort supposedly undergoes metamorphosis into an animal of another sort, while remaining one and the same individual animal. And it is because objects that are not describable by the same categorial term – such as cats and mountains – do *not* share the same criterion of identity that we cannot make sense of narratives in which, for example, an individual cat survives transmutation into a mountain. A cat could conceivably be replaced by a *cat-shaped* mountain, but the two could not conceivably be one and the same object: the cat could not continue to exist 'as' a mountain.

2 CRITERIA OF IDENTITY AND SORTAL PERSISTENCE CONDITIONS

Now, something more precise needs to be said concerning criteria of identity and sortal persistence conditions. A criterion of identity is a principle expressing a non-trivial logically necessary and sufficient condition for the identity of objects of a given sort or kind, φ.[6] Formally, such a principle may be stated as follows:

(CIφ) $\quad \forall x \forall y ((\varphi x \ \& \ \varphi y) \rightarrow (x = y \leftrightarrow R_\varphi xy))$

Or, in plain English: for any objects x and y, if x and y are φs, then x is identical with y if and only if x stands to y in the relation R_φ. To avoid triviality, we must insist that R_φ – which may be called the *criterial* relation for φs – is not simply the relation of identity itself. R_φ must, of course, be an equivalence relation defined on objects of the sort or kind φ – that is to say, it must be reflexive, symmetrical, and transitive, and either hold or fail to hold between any pair of objects of the sort or kind φ. A paradigm example of a criterion of identity is provided by the axiom of extensionality

---

[6] I shall say much more about criteria of identity in Chapter 5. See also my *More Kinds of Being: A Further Study of Individuation, Identity and the Logic of Sortal Terms* (Malden, MA and Oxford: Wiley-Blackwell, 2009), pp. 16–28.

Individuation, reference, and sortal terms　　15

of set theory, according to which if x and y are *sets*, then x is identical with y if and only if x and y *have the same members* – so that sameness of membership is the criterial relation for sets. But sets, of course, are *abstract* objects. It is rather harder to provide completely uncontentious examples of criteria of identity for concrete objects of any sort. This should not surprise us, since our grasp of such criteria is typically implicit rather than explicit and the criteria themselves are often open to question and revision in the light of philosophical argument. The criteria implicit in the everyday use of sortal terms are, moreover, often somewhat vague and shifting. This would be a defect in a formal language, such as the language of mathematics, but can hardly be complained about where everyday discourse is concerned.

Vagueness in our everyday criteria of identity has the consequence that some everyday questions of identity lack determinate answers, but the vast majority do not. Consider, for instance, the everyday criterion of identity for *mountains*, which is plausibly something like this:

(CI_M) For any objects x and y, if x and y are mountains, then x is identical with y if and only if x and y have the same peak.

Here we are taking mountains to be regions of terrain that are elevated above their surroundings and which possess a peak – that is, a highest point. It may be worried that the concept of a peak or highest point is in some sense more sophisticated than that of a mountain and that this somehow compromises (CI_M)'s claim to be a *criterion of identity* for mountains. However, in the first place, I would not wish to claim that anyone who grasps the concept of a mountain must have an *explicit* grasp of the concept of a peak; and, in the second place, it seems clear that the concept of a peak or highest point is at least implicitly presupposed by that of a mountain, whereas the reverse is plainly not the case, since many things other than mountains can possess a highest point. Undoubtedly, (CI_M) is a rather rough-and-ready definition that professional geographers might take issue with, but it will serve for purposes of illustration.

Now, (CI_M) is clearly incapable of resolving some questions of mountain-identity. For instance, if we have a region of terrain that is elevated above its surroundings but in which two approximately equally high points are unsurpassed by any other, with a saddle-shaped dip between them, (CI_M) doesn't really help us to decide whether what we have here is a single mountain or two mountains separated by a shallow valley. But this doesn't mean that (CI_M) is worthless as a criterion of identity for mountains, since in the vast majority of cases it does supply a

16   *Reference and predication*

determinate answer to questions of mountain-identity. The same lesson may be drawn by reflecting on the everyday criterion of identity for *animals*, which – to echo Locke[7] – is plausibly something like the following:

(CI$_A$) For any objects x and y, if x and y are animals, then x is identical with y if and only if x and y participate in the same life.

It may sometimes be hard to determine whether we have a case of two animals that are vitally connected to one another – as in a case of conjoined twins, or in a case of a mother and her unborn child – or just a single animal. And this is because the notion of 'sameness of life' is to a certain extent vague. But other cases are clear-cut: for instance, a rat and a flea that lives in its fur are clearly two distinct animals according to (CI$_A$), which is as it should be.

A further lesson that (CI$_M$) and (CI$_A$) serve to reinforce is a point mentioned earlier, namely that objects belonging to sorts that are governed by different criteria of identity cannot intelligibly be identified with one another, with the consequence that one cannot intelligibly suppose that – to use again our earlier example – a cat could survive a process of metamorphosis which left it existing 'as' a mountain. This is because cats, being animals, have their identity determined by the relation of *sameness of life*, but mountains are simply not living things and consequently cannot be identified with anything that is essentially alive. Here it may be objected that I am just assuming without argument that, indeed, any animal is *essentially* an animal and so essentially alive. I confess that I am indeed making this assumption, although it seems to me to be an entirely reasonable one. To reject it is to suppose, in effect, that 'animal' is not, after all, a categorial term. To suppose that an animal could survive being changed into a mountain is to suppose that the sortal terms 'animal' and 'mountain' are both subsumed by some single higher-level categorial term which supplies a common criterion of identity for both animals and mountains. But what could this putative categorial term be? It could not be 'material object', since that is pretty clearly transcategorial and supplies no single criterion of identity for any of the objects to which it applies. The term applies, after all, to anything that is both an object and composed of matter. But, it seems clear, there is no single criterion of identity governing all such objects – bearing in mind here that a genuine criterion of identity must supply a *non-trivial* criterial relation for the objects that it governs.

---

[7] See Locke, *An Essay Concerning Human Understanding*, II, XXVII, 4.

Individuation, reference, and sortal terms 17

If this claim – that 'material object' is a transcategorial term – is not immediately obvious to some philosophers, I suspect it is because they may be prone to confuse it with another term which is, pretty clearly, a categorial term, namely 'hunk of matter'. A hunk of matter – or what Locke called a 'body', 'mass', or 'parcel' of matter – is a quantity of matter collected into a cohesive whole, which can remain intact under the impression of an external force and undergo motion as a result. Borrowing from Locke's account,[8] it is not too difficult to state a plausible criterion of identity for hunks of matter, as follows:

(CI_H) For any objects x and y, if x and y are hunks of matter, then x is identical with y if and only if x and y are composed of the same material particles bonded together.

(CI_H) has the plausible implication that if some material particles are removed from a certain hunk of matter, then what remains is, strictly speaking, a *different* hunk of matter. The fact that we do not always speak strictly in such circumstances is not to the point, since most ordinary speakers can readily be persuaded to agree that they are speaking loosely if they say that the loss of a few particles leaves us with just the *same* hunk; otherwise, indeed, unscrupulous dealers could exploit purchasers of gold ingots without threat of challenge, by regularly rubbing off a few gold particles between receiving their fee and delivering the goods. Here it may be objected that the purchasers are only interested in buying a certain *quantity* of gold, not a particular piece or hunk of it. However, a 'piece' of gold *just is* a certain quantity of gold gathered together into a connected whole, so the distinction has no bearing on the case. Even so, we should once again acknowledge a certain amount of harmless vagueness in (CI_H), arising from the fact that it is not always perfectly clear whether or not a certain 'material particle' (itself a somewhat vague term) is 'bonded' to others in a certain hunk of matter with sufficient cohesion to qualify as being a material *part* of that hunk.

This much, in any case, is perfectly clear: that no *animal* is to be identified with any *hunk of matter*, nor is any *mountain* to be so identified, despite the fact that animals and mountains are both material objects. The truth, rather, is that, at any time at which it exists, an animal *coincides* with a certain hunk of matter, as does a mountain. Thus, if Oscar is a certain cat existing now, then Oscar now coincides with a certain hunk of matter: but Oscar is not *identical* with that hunk, because if some material particles are

---

[8] See Locke, *An Essay Concerning Human Understanding*, II, XXVII, 3.

18 *Reference and predication*

removed from it a different hunk of matter will then coincide with Oscar, but Oscar will remain the same cat, provided that the removal of those particles does not terminate Oscar's life. Similarly, Mount Everest presently coincides with a certain very large hunk of matter. But if that hunk of matter were to be transported intact to Australia, this would not be a way of moving Mount Everest to Australia. Rather, it would be a way of *destroying* Mount Everest, since the removal process would have left the Himalayas without that elevated region of terrain that is Mount Everest.

So far in this section, I have said a good deal about criteria of identity, but nothing yet about sortal persistence conditions. Sortal persistence conditions are the conditions that an object of a given sort must comply with in order to continue to exist *as an object of that sort.* Clearly, the criterion of identity governing a given sort of objects must be complied with by any such object if it is to continue to exist *at all,* but this is not enough for its persistence as an object *of that sort,* since its compliance with the criterion of identity is compatible with its 'metamorphosis' into an object of another sort governed by the same criterion. A simple example to illustrate this point is the following. Mount Everest is, obviously, currently a mountain: but if sea levels were to rise dramatically, it could be transformed into an *island.* Mountains and islands are different sorts of 'geographical prominence' – to coin a phrase for the categorial term applicable to them both – since an island is necessarily surrounded by water, whereas a mountain (a terrestrial mountain, at any rate, as opposed to an undersea one) is necessarily *not.* A slightly more controversial example involving animals is provided by the case of a caterpillar and the butterfly into which it is eventually transformed. It is apparently the case that, in the chrysalis stage, the internal structure of the caterpillar is completely destroyed and reorganized, making this unlike the simple development of an amphibian, for example, from its larval to its adult phase. Nonetheless, throughout the metamorphosis of the caterpillar into the butterfly, the same *life* continues, making the butterfly the same animal as the caterpillar, even if it is not, in the relevant sense, the same *sort* of animal. This example is, of course, a scientific one which has a basis in empirical fact. But fictional examples of a similar kind are familiar from folklore, as in the story of the frog prince, in which a human being is transformed into an amphibian. We can make sense of this story, even while dismissing it as pure fiction, because we can intelligibly suppose the prince and the frog to participate in the same uninterrupted life.

Sortal persistence conditions, to the extent that they go beyond the demands of criteria of identity, are only discoverable by empirical means.

Individuation, reference, and sortal terms 19

But in order to discover those conditions empirically, we must first be able to grasp the relevant criteria of identity. For example, it is only because we already know or assume that sameness of life is the criterial relation for animal identity that we can then go on to determine whether, when a caterpillar is transformed into a butterfly, this is to be classified as an individual's surviving a change of *sort* or merely as its surviving a change of *phase* within the same sort. Consequently, criteria of identity, although they obviously do not lack empirical content, have the status of 'framework principles' rather than mere empirical discoveries. Revising or amending a criterion of identity is, thus, more in the nature of a methodological or indeed a philosophical exercise than is revising or amending an account of the sortal persistence conditions governing a sort or kind, at least where natural kinds are concerned. A great deal more can and should be said about such matters, but enough has now been said for the purposes of the present chapter.

3 TWO NOTIONS OF INDIVIDUATION

At the beginning of this chapter, I said that I would be defending a certain thesis regarding the individuation of objects, which I call *categorialism*. But in order to make this thesis clear, it is first necessary to distinguish between two different, albeit related, notions of *individuation*. The notion of individuation with which I am chiefly concerned at present is a purely *cognitive* notion. Individuation in this sense is a kind of cognitive *achievement*, namely *the successful singling out of an object in thought*. Categorialism is, then, the doctrine that a thinker can single out an object in this way only if he or she grasps, at least implicitly, some categorial concept under which he or she conceives the object in question to fall. When a thinker thus singles out an object in thought and has a specific thought about *that very object*, we have a case of singular, or *de re*, thought about that object. And it seems clear that at least sometimes thinkers do have such singular thoughts. I shall have much more to say about such thoughts shortly. Before that, however, I need to say something about the other notion of individuation.

In addition to the notion of individuation in the cognitive sense, we have the notion of individuation in the *metaphysical* sense. Individuation in this sense has nothing to do with thinkers or thoughts – except, of course, when we are talking about the metaphysical individuation of thinkers and thoughts themselves, for these, like objects of any other kind, are subject to principles of individuation. A principle of individuation, in the metaphysical sense, is a principle telling us how objects of a certain sort are singled out *in reality*, as opposed to how they are singled out *in thought*. Such a principle tells us what makes an object of a certain sort the very individual that it is, as opposed to any other individual of the same or indeed of any other sort. Unsurprisingly, then, a principle of individuation is closely related to a criterion of identity, although the two notions do not perfectly coincide. A criterion of identity for objects of a sort φ tells us what it takes for such objects to be the same φ or different φs. But it doesn't necessarily tell us what makes such an object the particular φ that it is. For example, our criterion of identity for mountains, (CI$_M$), tells us that mountain A is the same mountain as mountain B if and only if A and B have the same peak. But it doesn't appear that a particular mountain, such as Mount Everest, is *individuated* by its peak – not, at least, by its peak alone. To know *which mountain* Mount Everest is, we need to know not only which peak is its peak, but also, and more importantly, its geographical extent. Only when we know that do we know where Mount Everest 'begins' and other mountains in the region 'leave off'. That is to say, only then do we know how Mount Everest is singled out in reality from other surrounding mountains, and indeed from the air moving about it and the animals living on its slopes.

I have just spoken of knowing *which* mountain Mount Everest is. Someone who does know this can certainly individuate Mount Everest in the cognitive sense – can single that mountain out in thought and have singular thoughts about that very mountain. So, a thinker's knowledge of the principle of individuation governing an object, which is intimately bound up with its criterion of identity, is clearly at least *part* of a sufficient condition for that thinker's being able to single out that object in thought. The example of sets may provide a useful illustration once more. A set, it seems clear, is individuated – in the metaphysical sense – by its members, so that in this case, at least, there is a coincidence between the criterion of identity for sets and their principle of individuation. However, in order to know *which* set a given set is, it does not suffice merely to know that this set, like any other set, is individuated by its members. What *does* suffice is to know not only this but also *which objects* are in fact the members of the set in question. We may call a set's members its *individuators*. And the point of the example is to show that a *sufficient* condition for a thinker's being able to single out an object in thought is his or her knowing not only the object's principle of individuation, but also its individuators. Mere knowledge of the object's individuators does not suffice, without knowledge that *they are* its individuators, which requires knowledge of the

Individuation, reference, and sortal terms 21

object's principle of individuation. A child might know which objects are the members of a certain set – for instance, that 2, 3, 5 and 7 are the members of the set of prime numbers smaller than 10 – but without its knowing that these numbers are what individuate that set, it is doubtful whether the child could really be said to know *which* set that set is, since it might be under the mistaken impression that another set could have these same members.

However, I want to make it quite clear that I am not presuming at this point that a thinker can single out an object in thought *only if* he or she knows *which* object it is and knows this by knowing not only its principle of individuation but also what its individuators are. I am merely saying that knowledge of the latter kind *suffices* for a thinker's ability to single out an object in thought. I also believe that thinkers certainly do sometimes have knowledge of this kind and are, in virtue of it, able to single out certain objects in thought. The question, however, is whether such know- ledge is *necessary* for that achievement and, if not, what condition *is* necessary. Categorialism maintains that *one* necessary condition is the thinker's grasp – which may only be implicit – of a categorial concept under which he or she conceives the object in question to fall.

4 OBJECT PERCEPTION AND SINGULAR THOUGHT

The case discussed in the previous section, of a thinker's singling out in thought a particular set – the set of prime numbers smaller than 10 – is special in that the object in question is an *abstract* object, and hence not one that can be perceived by the senses. It may well be supposed that singling out in thought an abstract object like this is particularly demanding intellectually, for precisely this reason. By the same token, it may be supposed that if an object can be *perceived* by a thinker, the thinker's perception of the object provides him or her with a way of singling it out in thought which is intellectually much less demanding – so much so that in cases like this categorialism is a most implausible doctrine. Of course, this presumes that categorialism does not extend beyond thought to perception itself: that is, it presumes that it is false to maintain that a subject cannot even *perceive* an object without grasping some categorial concept under which he or she conceives the object in question to fall. But *perceptual* categorialism, as we may call this more extreme doctrine, is a most implausible thesis. It would imply, for instance, that animals lacking categorial concepts – as, quite plausibly, many higher mammals do – cannot perceive objects in their environment.

22

Reference and predication

For my own part, I am content to deny perceptual categorialism. I favour a *causal* theory of object perception according to which – to a first approximation – a subject S perceives an object O if and only if certain features of S's perceptual experience, discriminable by S, are differentially causally dependent on certain properties of O.[9] A feature F of S's experience is *differentially* causally dependent on a property P of O just in case variations in P would cause corresponding variations in F. So, for example, by this account I currently *see* a brown wooden table standing in front of me if, say, variations in its shape, orientation, or hue would give rise to corresponding variations in certain features of my current visual experience, discriminable by me. If variations in properties of the table would give rise to *no* variations in my current visual experience, or only to variations indiscriminable by me, then, I think, I do *not* see the table. This account of object perception imposes no direct epistemic requirement on such perception: a subject is not required, by this account, to know *what* object he or she perceives, nor even *that* he or she is perceiving an object. At most the account defines object perception in such a way that a subject's perception of an object makes it *possible* for the subject to know what he or she is perceiving, and that he or she is perceiving it, provided that he or she meets certain other requirements for such knowledge, yet to be specified. For instance, it might be insisted, as a minimum requirement, that a subject cannot know what he or she is perceiving, or that he or she is perceiving it, unless he or she is *attending* to the object in question. I should also make it clear that, in saying that the relevant variations in the subject's experience should be *discriminable* by the subject, I am not smuggling in an epistemic requirement on object perception. For I do not require the subject to be able to form *discriminatory judgements* regarding features of his or her perceptual experience – only to be *sensitive* to relevant variations in his or her perceptual experience. A subject could be tested for such sensitivity without being asked whether or not he or she could notice any experiential difference of a relevant kind. This is still only a rather sketchy account of object perception, but it will suffice for the discussion that is to follow.

Categorialism is likely to be challenged on the basis of examples such as the following. A subject, S – perhaps an infant or a young child – is confronted with an object, O, which S sees. Perhaps, furthermore, S directs his or her *attention* towards O and, as O moves, S *tracks* O's movement with his or her eyes, continuing to direct his or her attention towards O.

[9] See my *Subjects of Experience* (Cambridge University Press, 1996), pp. 102–17.

Individuation, reference, and sortal terms 23

Now let the question be asked: can S, in virtue of this sort of perceptual connection with O, have singular thoughts specifically *about* O – thoughts about O such as that *it is white* or that *it is furry*? Of course, we must presume that S can indeed *think* and, moreover, can have thoughts of the *form* 'X is white' and 'X is furry'. Our question is only whether, in order to have such singular thoughts about O in particular, all that is necessary in addition to these general cognitive capacities is that S should have the kind of perceptual connection with O that has just been described. A good many theorists would, I am sure, answer this question positively. But a *categorialist* would not. A categorialist will insist that, unless S conceives of O in a certain way, even if only implicitly, and is broadly *correct* in so conceiving of O, S's perceptual connection with O does not enable S to have singular thoughts about O. The conceptual requirement in question is this: S must, at least implicitly, conceive of O as falling under a certain categorial concept. This requirement will be met if, say, S conceives of O as being an *animal*. Thus, if S is perceptually connected with O in the described fashion, S conceives of O as being an animal, and O *is* an animal, then S is thereby put in a position to have singular thoughts about O. But it is not necessary that S should *explicitly* conceive of O as being an animal. It suffices that S should conceive of O as being some specific *sort* of animal, such as a *cat*. And in that case it is not necessary that O should actually *be* a cat, only that it be *some* kind of animal. Thus S can be mistaken about what sort of animal O is and still be put in a position to have singular thoughts about O. But, according to categorialism, S cannot be put in a position to have singular thoughts about O, even if S is perceptually connected with O in the described fashion, if S either fails, even implicitly, to conceive of O as falling under any categorial concept at all or else misconceives the putative object of his or her perception as being something falling under a categorial concept which does not apply to O.

It seems to me that this contention is susceptible of *proof*, or at least to the nearest thing to proof that is normally available in questions of philosophy. Let us suppose that O is, in fact, a *cat*. That is to say, let us suppose that S is perceptually connected to a certain cat in the described fashion: S *sees* the cat, S directs his or her *attention* towards the cat, and S *tracks* the cat's movements with his or her eyes, continuing to direct his or her attention towards the cat. Call the cat in question 'Oscar'. But let us also suppose that S does not conceive of Oscar as *being a cat*, nor indeed as falling under *any* sortal or categorial concept. Then the anti-categorialist is presented with the following difficulty. As we have already observed, whenever a certain animal exists in a certain place at a certain time, it coincides with a certain *hunk of matter*, which is numerically distinct from the animal in question. Now, the perceptual connection that S has with respect to Oscar, the cat, S will very likely *also* have with respect to a certain hunk of matter – namely the hunk of matter composing Oscar during the perceptual episode in question. I say 'very likely' because, of course, it is at least possible that *different* hunks of matter should compose Oscar at the beginning and end of the episode – if, for example, Oscar should lose some hair or ingest some food during the course of that episode. However, let us set aside this possibility for the time being and return to it later, since it will turn out to be an important one.

The problem for the anti-categorialist is now to explain why S's perceptual episode should put S in a position to have singular thoughts specifically about *Oscar*, as opposed to the hunk of matter – call it 'Hunk' – that, as we are now supposing, composes Oscar throughout the episode. If the anti-categorialist maintains, in the light of this challenge, that S is put in a position to have singular thoughts about *both* Oscar *and* Hunk, then another problem arises: what makes one of those thoughts specifically a thought about *Oscar* and another specifically a thought about *Hunk*? A genuinely singular, or *de re*, thought must determinately be a thought about a particular, uniquely identifiable object. I am not insisting that the *thinker* of the thought must be able to *identify* that object – to do so would clearly be question-begging in the present context – only that there must be *some* determining factor which makes the thought in question a thought about the particular object in question. But, as far as I can see, the anti-categorialist has no resources with which to say what this determining factor could be, since in a case such as that just sketched two *different* objects are symmetrically related to the thinker in the only way that the anti-categorialist requires for singular thought about them. By contrast, the categorialist has a tie-breaker for this kind of situation. According to categorialism, what makes *Oscar* the object of one of S's thoughts is the fact that S conceives of one of the objects being perceived as being a *cat* – or at least as being an *animal* or some *sort* of animal – and is correct in doing so.

A discussion is now needed of the more complicated case in which, say, Oscar loses some hair or ingests some food as it moves through S's field of view. If S continues to track *Oscar*, can't the anti-categorialist maintain that *this* is why S is put in a position to have singular thoughts specifically about Oscar? For, of course, in this case there is no *single hunk of matter* that S is tracking. Moreover, the anti-categorialist may now go on to claim that the original example, in which Oscar does not change in material

Individuation, reference, and sortal terms

composition, only presents a special case of this more complicated one. The anti-categorialist may urge that what puts S in a position to have singular thoughts specifically about Oscar in *all* such cases, complicated or simple, is a fact expressible by the *subjunctive conditional* that S *would* continue to track Oscar *if* Oscar were noticeably to lose or gain some appropriate component matter, such as some hair or some food. However, far from this suggestion serving to aid the anti-categorialist cause, I think that it effectively concedes victory to categorialism. For recall that I insisted only that S should at least *implicitly* conceive of the object of perception – in this case, Oscar – as falling under some categorial concept which does in fact apply to that object, namely, *animal*. I don't require S to be able to *articulate* this concept or its associated criterion of identity explicitly. But if S is demonstrably capable of perceptually tracking a particular animal through various changes to its material composition which are specifically permitted by the criterion of identity for *animals*, but *not* by the criteria of identity governing other categorial concepts, including that of *hunk of matter*, then this provides strong evidence that S *does* in fact possess an implicit grasp of the categorial concept of an animal. And bear in mind here that not just *any* change of material composition is compatible with the continuing existence of an animal.

Indeed, we can now see more clearly why it is *categorial* concepts that are crucial to the capacity for singular thought about objects encountered in perception, for it is precisely these concepts that are most intimately tied to *criteria of identity*. In cases in which two initially coinciding objects, such as a cat and a hunk of matter, go their separate ways in the course of some extended perceptual episode, the *correct* way to track those different objects will be determined precisely by their respective criteria of identity – whence it is reasonable to conclude that subjects who *succeed* in correctly tracking those objects exhibit at least an implicit grasp of the criteria of identity governing those objects, and thereby an implicit grasp of the categorial concepts under which they fall and which determine those criteria of identity. In short, the very perceptual tracking considerations that the anti-categorialist is prone to regard as *defeating* the claims of categorialism in fact serve to *support* those claims, when these considerations are given their proper scope.

What if it should turn out that S – who, remember, we have supposed to be an infant or young child – doesn't consistently and comprehensively track Oscar in *all* kinds of circumstances, in accordance with the criterion of identity for animals, but still clearly does so in certain limited kinds of circumstances? Suppose, for instance, that S tracks Oscar successfully

26 *Reference and predication*

through the loss of some hair and the ingestion or excretion of food matter, or through changes in the dispositions of Oscar's limbs and tail, but that *S* fails to do so through periods in which Oscar is curled up and asleep. Then I think we should say that *S* hasn't *fully* grasped, even only implicitly, the *adult* concept of an animal and its associated criterion of identity, perhaps because *S* doesn't yet understand that an animal can still be alive when it is asleep. But I still think that *S* is evincing the implicit grasp of *some* categorial concept with an associated criterion of identity – a concept which we might describe as being an infantile precursor to the fully fledged adult concept of an animal (a precursor concept which might well be *innate* in humans). And we may deem that this grasp is sufficient for *S* to have singular thoughts about Oscar, at least with respect to the limited kinds of circumstances in which the infantile criterion does not significantly come apart from the adult one in terms of its implications for the identity of the tracked object. A suitably nuanced version of categorialism should certainly be prepared to admit such qualifications as these to its basic doctrine.

5 CATEGORIALISM AND LINGUISTIC REFERENCE

From this point forward, I am going to assume that categorialism is correct. But categorialism is a thesis about *singular thought*, not about *linguistic reference*. Even so, it may – indeed, I think it *does* – have important implications for linguistic reference. According to currently dominant 'causal', or 'direct', or 'anti-descriptivist' theories of reference, all that is required for a speaker's use of a proper name or natural kind term, *N*, to be referentially successful – that is, for the speaker to use *N* to refer successfully to *N*'s referent – is that the speaker's use of *N* should stand in the right kind of causal-historical relation to a 'reference-fixing' event in which *N* was first introduced into the speaker's speech-community.[10] The 'right kind' of causal-historical relation consists, supposedly, in a chain of usage-acquisition, where each speaker *S* in the chain – apart, of course, from the first – uses *N* with an intention to refer to *the same thing* as did the speaker *S'* from whom *S* acquired the use of *N*. The first speaker in the chain is the person who first introduced *N* into the speech-community. According to this sort of account – which, to be fair, has only been sketched in a very bare-bones way here – successive speakers

---

[10] The *locus classicus* for this sort of view is, of course, Saul A. Kripke, *Naming and Necessity* (Oxford: Blackwell, 1980).

Individuation, reference, and sortal terms   27

in the chain of acquisition do not need to associate with *N* any *descriptive information* which applies to *N*'s referent in order to be able to use *N* successfully to refer to that referent. Hence, in particular, it is not the case, on this view, that the referent of *N*, as used by a given speaker, is determined by a certain *definite description* which the speaker associates with *N*.

Now, I am happy to concede that there may be a relatively attenuated and anodyne notion of 'reference' for which this sort of account is broadly acceptable. But if categorialism is a correct doctrine concerning singular thought, such an account of linguistic reference cannot be the whole story. This is because we must acknowledge that, at least sometimes, speakers use sentences containing proper names and natural kind terms to express *singular thoughts*. Suppose that some friends of my neighbours have acquired a new pet cat, which they decide to call 'Oscar'. And suppose that I overhear a conversation between my neighbours and their friends during the course of which they say, amongst other things, that Oscar is white and beautiful, but never say anything that reveals, either explicitly or implicitly, that Oscar is *a cat*. According to the causal-historical theory of linguistic reference, I am now in a position to refer successfully to *Oscar*, provided I use the name 'Oscar' with the intention to refer to whatever it was that my neighbours and their friends were referring to when they used the name in the conversation that I overheard. The *only* constraint on my referential success with the name 'Oscar' is supposed to be that I should intend to use it to refer to *the same thing* that my neighbours and their friends were using 'Oscar' to refer to. But 'thing' is not a categorial term: it is a *transcategorial* term, like 'object'. It carries with it no specific *criterion of identity*. Consequently, this supposed 'constraint' on my successful use of the name 'Oscar' is very slim indeed. As far as I am concerned, Oscar might be almost *any kind of thing whatever*. Indeed, if I were honest I would have to confess that I have *no idea* what kind of thing Oscar is. Now, as I say, I am relatively content to acknowledge that there is *some* sense in which I am referring to Oscar, even when I say that I have no idea what kind of thing Oscar is. But the more important question, I think, is whether, in the scenario just sketched, I can intelligibly be said to be able to use the name 'Oscar' in sentences to express *singular thoughts* about Oscar. I don't see how I can, given that categorialism is a correct doctrine concerning singular thought. For categorialism requires that, in order for me to have a singular thought about Oscar, I must at least conceive of Oscar as falling under some categorial concept, and *correctly* so conceive of him – so that, since Oscar is in fact a cat, I must at least conceive of Oscar

28   *Reference and predication*

as being an *animal* of some sort. But in the envisaged scenario I do *not* conceive of Oscar in this way, nor do I conceive of Oscar as falling under any other categorial concept.

Here it may be urged that this just shows that categorialism must be *wrong*, on the grounds that I can at least use the sentence 'I have no idea what kind of thing Oscar is' to express a singular thought of mine about Oscar. But that response is question-begging in the present context, given that I have just spent a good deal of time *defending* categorialism. Merely to *assert* that such a sentence may be used to express a singular thought about Oscar is no rebuttal of my previous arguments. At most it can be demanded of me that I give a plausible account of what sort of thought such a sentence *could* be supposed to convey, assuming the truth of categorialism. But this is surely not difficult. The obvious answer, which I think is a plausible one, is that 'I have no idea what kind of thing Oscar is' is implicitly *metalinguistic*. The thought that I am conveying by it is the thought that *I have no idea what kind of thing the referent of the name 'Oscar' is*. Here it might be objected that this only postpones the problem, because I have just replaced the name 'Oscar' by the singular noun phrase 'the referent of the name "Oscar"'. But, of course, even by the lights of the causal-historical theory of reference, this definite description should not be assimilated to a proper name. Rather, we can explain its standard use in terms of something like Russell's theory of descriptions; that is, in *quantificational* terms. Indeed, another way of expressing the thought conveyed by my use of the sentence 'I have no idea what kind of thing Oscar is' would be something like this: *the name 'Oscar' refers to something, but I've no idea what kind of thing it is*. And, of course, the 'it' in 'I've no idea what kind of thing it is' is not playing a *referential* role, but rather the role of a *variable of quantification*, bound by the preceding quantifier 'something'.

So, my contention is that, when a speaker uses a sentence containing a proper name or natural kind term to express a singular thought about the referent of that name or natural kind term, he or she must at least possess implicit knowledge of what *categorial* concept the referent falls under. This knowledge will obviously be *descriptive* knowledge, of a certain kind, about the referent. But in saying this I am not simply returning to the 'descriptive theory of reference', which causal-historical accounts of reference sought to overturn. For I am not contending that the descriptive knowledge of the referent that the speaker must possess in order to use the proper name or natural kind term in sentences expressing singular thoughts about the referent must be descriptive knowledge which determines precisely *which* thing is that referent. On the other hand, nor am

Individuation, reference, and sortal terms 29

I arguing against the latter view. Rather, at this point I would rather keep an open mind about the matter.

Another important application of categorialism to the theory of linguistic reference concerns the notion of a 'reference-fixing event', of the kind involved, according to the causal-historical account of reference, when a proper name or natural kind term is first introduced into a speech-community. Let us return to the story of my neighbours' friends' pet cat. It was said that the friends decided to call their new pet cat 'Oscar'. But to do that, they needed to have *singular thoughts about Oscar*. It may be that they first *saw* Oscar in a pet shop and, looking at him, decided there and then to call him 'Oscar'. Perhaps one of the friends said to the other, 'Let's buy him and call him "Oscar"'. But this required the friend to use the pronoun 'him' in a sentence expressing a singular thought about *the cat in front of them*. Consequently, according to categorialism, this friend had to conceive of that cat at least as being an *animal* of some sort.

What, though, if these people were seriously mistaken about the nature of the shop they had entered. Suppose that they thought it was a china shop and that what they were looking at was a very lifelike *china ornament* of a cat (perhaps Oscar was fast asleep at the time). Wouldn't they still have succeeded in having singular thoughts about *that cat* and have succeeded in naming him 'Oscar'? It might appear that common sense is on the side of those who answer this question positively, but we need to think the matter through more carefully. What entitles us to assume that what the friends would have succeeded in deciding to call 'Oscar' was *the cat* that they were looking at, given that they didn't conceive anything that they were looking at to *be* a cat? It won't do to answer here that the thing that they *were* looking at was in fact a cat, because this presumes that there was just *one* thing that they were looking at. But, as was remarked in an earlier section, whenever an *animal* of any sort is located at a certain place at a certain time, it coincides with a certain *hunk of matter*, which is distinct from the animal in question. So there were – at least – *two* things that the friends were looking at, a *cat* and a *hunk of matter* coinciding with that cat. Why, then, should we suppose that, despite their mistake, they succeeded in calling *the cat* 'Oscar' rather than *the hunk of matter*? To this it may be replied that they certainly didn't intend to be naming a *hunk of matter*. So the suggestion is that, by default, what they succeeded in naming was *the cat*. But that suggestion is question-begging in the present context, for it assumes that they did indeed succeed in naming *something* – and yet whether they did so is precisely the question now at issue. In any case, how can something be named *by default* in this supposed fashion?

Reference and predication

How can an intention *not* to name one thing somehow bring it about that *another* thing is named?

The suggestion that, in the scenario just described, my neighbours' friends succeeded in naming *a cat* 'Oscar', despite being under the impression that they were naming a *china ornament*, also faces the following difficulty. Suppose that the friends never discovered their mistake, because they were suddenly called away and never managed to return to the shop. And suppose that, later, reminiscing with my neighbours about the incident and expressing their regret at not having been able to make their purchase, they passed the name 'Oscar' on to my neighbours. And suppose that my neighbours also believed that 'Oscar' was the name of a certain china ornament that their friends had intended to purchase. According to preceding arguments of this section, my neighbours are not in a position to express singular thoughts about *the cat* that their friends actually saw, when using sentences containing the name 'Oscar'. And that seems right. If they say such things as 'Oscar would probably have been broken by now, because our friends are so clumsy with ornaments', it surely makes no sense to suppose that they are expressing such thoughts about a certain *cat*. But if that is the right thing to say about my neighbours' use of the name 'Oscar' – that it simply *fails to refer* – then it is surely also the right thing to say about their friends' use of it, even though it was they who introduced the name in the first place. Certainly, this is the verdict of categorialism and I consider it to be a virtue, not a failing, of the doctrine that this is so.

Finally, I should note that although I have been concentrating on the reference of *proper names* in this section, I intend all of its lessons to apply also to *natural kind terms*, although the adjustments to the account that would be needed to extend it to these would take up more space than the present chapter allows.

CHAPTER 3

Two styles of predication – dispositional and occurrent

In the preceding chapter, I devoted a considerable amount of discussion to *categorial* terms and concepts, although my focus was exclusively on categories of *objects*. Here I want to expand this discussion much more widely to embrace other categories of entities, including *properties*. Now, in recent years, I have been developing a neo-Aristotelian system of categorial ontology which I call *the four-category ontology*.[1] In this system, *exemplification* – understood as a formal ontological relation between particulars and universals – is not regarded as a *primitive* formal ontological relation but, rather, as having two different species, the *dispositional* and the *occurrent*, each of which is analysable with the aid of two formal ontological relations which *are* regarded as primitive: *instantiation* and *characterization*. Corresponding to this ontological distinction with regard to exemplification, there is a logical distinction to be drawn between dispositional and occurrent *predication*. In the present chapter, I want to develop this line of thought in greater detail and at the same time clear up some difficulties that a number of my critics have claimed to find in my account of these matters.

Before proceeding, I should mention that the distinction between dispositional and occurrent predication appears to be clearly marked in natural language by certain syntactic differences, so that my ontological distinction between dispositional and occurrent *exemplification* is partly intended to explicate these syntactic differences. Most notably, verb-phrases in natural language exhibit not only differences of *tense*, but also differences of what grammarians call *aspect*. For instance, the verbs in the sentences 'This chemical substance *dissolves* in water' and 'This chemical substance *is dissolving* in water' are both present-tensed, but the first has a 'habitual' aspect whereas the second has a 'continuous' aspect. We

---

[1] See especially my *The Four-Category Ontology: A Metaphysical Foundation for Natural Science* (Oxford: Clarendon Press, 2006).

31

32   *Reference and predication*

understand the first as attributing a *habitude* or *disposition* to the subject of the sentence and the second as attributing an *ongoing activity* to that same subject – an activity which constitutes the *manifestation* or *exercise* of the disposition in question. Indeed, the first sentence may be paraphrased as 'This chemical substance is water-soluble', in which a *dispositional adjective* is explicitly used to describe the subject – such adjectives typically being formed from the stem of a verb plus a suffix of the form '-able', '-ible', or '-uble', as in 'breakable', 'fusible', and '(dis)soluble'. It is also notable that when the subject of a sentence whose verb has the 'habitual' aspect is a *kind* of thing or stuff – rather than a particular instance of such a kind – as in 'Sodium chloride dissolves in water', the sentence in question expresses what philosophers of science would call a *lawlike generalization*, or *natural law* (in this case, a chemical law). These points will all be seen to be highly relevant to the discussion that follows.

I THE FOUR-CATEGORY ONTOLOGY AND ITS LOGIC

The four basic ontological categories of my system are these: (1) substantial universals, (2) non-substantial universals, (3) substantial particulars, and (4) non-substantial particulars – or, less long-windedly and more memorably, *kinds, attributes, objects,* and *modes*.[2] The latter terminology, although convenient, is, I concede, not entirely perspicuous. For one thing, the term 'attribute' might be thought to embrace only *monadic* universals, whereas I am happy to include relational universals in my ontology. For another, the terms 'object' and 'kind' both have common uses in metaphysics that are much broader than mine are intended to be. Thus 'object' is sometimes used as a synonym for the all-purpose term 'entity', while 'kind' is often used as an alternative to 'type', in the sense in which the latter figures in the so-called 'type–token distinction'. (In other words, 'type' is often used in a way in which it is pretty much interchangeable with 'universal', thus ignoring entirely my own distinction between substantial and non-substantial universals.) Finally, 'mode' may strike many as archaic-sounding in comparison with the currently more fashionable term 'trope' – although I would urge that the former is in fact more, rather than less, perspicuous than the latter, since it is

---

[2] I should perhaps stress, if it is not already sufficiently obvious, that the *basic* ontological categories of which I am now speaking lie at a much higher level of abstraction than the categories that were the chief concern of Chapter 2, such as the category of *animals* and the category of *material artefacts*. The latter categories are only *sub*-categories of the basic category of *substantial particulars*, inasmuch as all individual animals and material artefacts qualify as 'individual substances'.

Two styles of predication – dispositional and occurrent   33

appropriately suggestive of the idea that properties, whether they are universals or particulars, are rightly to be thought of as *ways* of being. (The term 'trope' has, furthermore, a standard literary use which has no connection whatever with its current use in metaphysics – a fact that can only serve to render the latter use confusing.)

Since, however, *any* choice of terminology in this area of metaphysics is bound to involve some departure from common usage, it may help at this point if I supply some everyday examples of items that at least *appear* to fall into the four categories that I have in mind when I present my ontological system. I must stress that these can only be taken, at this stage at least, to be *apparent* examples because, although I certainly want to defend the four-category ontology as a foundation for metaphysical inquiry, I do not want to be committed without argument to supposing that everyday language and thought provide us with incontestably correct illustrations of its applicability to the real world. We should be prepared to allow that the four categories are best illustrated, in fact, only by entities postulated in advanced scientific theories, rather than by those assumed in our 'common-sense' ontology. So, with this caveat in mind, here are some putative examples of the four categories. A particular *table*, *rock*, or *dog* would, then, be an example of something belonging to the category of *object*, as I conceive of it. Such items are more traditionally known as *individual substances*. Corresponding examples of the category of *kinds*, as I conceive of it, would be the kinds *table*, *rock*, and *dog* of which the foregoing objects are, respectively, particular instances. Examples of the category of *attribute* would be the properties, conceived as universals, of *brownness*, *hardness*, and *furriness* that are exemplified, respectively, by those objects. And, finally, examples of the category of *mode* would be the particular instances of those universals possessed by those objects: the table's particular brownness, the rock's particular hardness, and the dog's particular furriness.

At least implicitly, I have already drawn on both of my aforementioned primitive formal ontological relations – *instantiation* and *characterization* – in introducing and describing the foregoing examples. For, first of all, both kinds and attributes are *instantiated* by, respectively, the objects and modes that are their particular instances – for example, the kind *table* by particular tables and the attribute *brownness* by particular brownnesses. And, second, in my terminology, to say that an object *possesses* a mode of a certain attribute is just another way of saying that that mode *characterizes* – or, if one prefers an older expression, *inheres in* – the object in question. Indeed, I want to go further and say that, likewise, characterization is a relation in

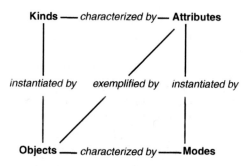

Figure 3.1. The ontological square, version 1

which, at the level of universals, *attributes* stand to *kinds*. I shall say much more about this in due course, but already we have the materials to construct, in Figure 3.1, a version of *the ontological square*: a diagram that is enormously useful for the purposes of depicting the formal ontological relationships in which items belonging to the four different categories stand to one another.

It may be observed that the *upper* level of the ontological square, occupied by kinds and attributes, is the level of *universals*, while the *lower* level of the square, occupied by objects and modes, is the level of *particulars*. Similarly, we can call the *left-hand* side of the square, occupied by kinds and objects, the side of *subjects* and the *right-hand* side of the square, occupied by attributes and modes, the side of *properties* – subjects being entities that *are characterized* in various ways and properties being entities that *characterize* in various ways. Indeed, using this terminology, we could speak of the four fundamental ontological categories depicted in the square, beginning at the bottom left-hand corner and proceeding clockwise around it, as being those of *particular subjects, universal subjects, universal properties* and *particular properties*. In that case, however, it should be clearly understood that the expressions 'universal', 'particular', 'subject' and 'property' do not themselves signify ontological categories as such but are, rather, *cross-categorial* terms, just as the all-purpose ontological term 'entity' is. Figure 3.2 is another version of the ontological square depicting this aspect of the four-category ontology.

At this point, it will be useful for me to introduce some logical symbolism, for in what follows we shall be concerned quite as much with the *logic* as with the metaphysics of the four-category ontology. Standard first-order predicate logic with identity deploys only a single class of constants and variables – *objectual* ones – and a way of representing

Two styles of predication – dispositional and occurrent 35

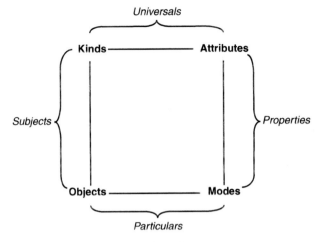

Figure 3.2. The ontological square, version II

explicitly only a single formal ontological relation, *identity*. In a logic that is capable of representing perspicuously all of the metaphysically important features of the four-category ontology, we need, however, *four* different classes of constants and variables, together with ways of representing explicitly *three* different primitive formal ontological relations – not just identity, but also *instantiation* and *characterization*.

So this is what I propose. We shall use, as is already customary, lower-case letters from the beginning of the Roman alphabet, a, b, c, ... as *object constants* and lower-case letters from the end of the Roman alphabet, x, y, z, ... as *object variables*. For *kind constants* we shall use lower-case letters from the beginning of the Greek alphabet, α, β, γ, ..., and for *kind variables* we shall use lower case letters from the end of the Greek alphabet, φ, χ, ψ, ... For *attribute constants* we shall, in mimicry of existing custom, use the upper-case Roman letters F, G, H, ... and for *attribute variables* we shall use upper-case letters from the end of the Roman alphabet, X, Y, Z, ... Finally, for *mode constants* we shall use the lower-case Roman letters f, g, h, ..., while for *mode variables* we shall use the lower-case Roman letters r, s, t, ... As for the three primitive formal ontological relations, we shall, as is customary, represent *identity* by the equality sign, '=', and supplement this with the slash, '/', to represent *instantiation*. Finally, we shall represent *characterization* by simple *juxtaposition* of appropriately chosen constants or variables. Thus, for example, 'a/β' and 'f/G' say, respectively, that object a instantiates kind β and that mode f instantiates

Table 3.1. *Logical symbolism for the four-category ontology*

	Objects	**Kinds**	**Attributes**	**Modes**
constants	a, b, c, …	α, β, γ, …	F, G, H, …	f, g, h, …
variables	x, y, z, …	φ, χ, ψ, …	X, Y, Z, …	r, s, t, …

Instantiation: a/β, f/G
Characterization: af, βG

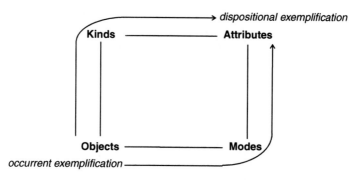

Figure 3.3. The ontological square, version III

attribute *G*, while '*af*' and 'β*G*' say, respectively, that object *a* is characterized by mode *f* and that kind β is characterized by attribute *G*.

The foregoing proposals are presented in more convenient tabular form in Table 3.1.

Since I do not regard *exemplification* as being a primitive formal ontological relation, I do not need an undefined symbol to represent it. Exemplification, as Figure 3.1 implies, is a relation between *objects* and *attributes*. Or, more exactly, there are two different relations of exemplification between objects and attributes, corresponding to the two different routes from the bottom left-hand corner of the ontological square (the *object* corner) to the upper right-hand corner (the *attribute* corner). For reasons which will become more apparent in due course, I call these two different species of exemplification *dispositional* and *occurrent* exemplification, which may be depicted on the ontological square as in Figure 3.3.

Using the expressions '**D**[*a*, *F*]' and '**O**[*a*, *F*]' to say, respectively, that object *a* exemplifies attribute *F dispositionally* and that object *a* exemplifies

Two styles of predication – dispositional and occurrent   37

attribute *F occurrently*, I propose that we may define these two species of exemplification as follows:

$$\mathbf{D}[a, F] =_{df} \exists\varphi(\varphi F \,\&\, a/\varphi)$$
$$\mathbf{O}[a, F] =_{df} \exists r(ar \,\&\, r/F)$$

In other words, an object *a* exemplifies an attribute *F dispositionally* just in case *a* instantiates some kind that is characterized by *F*, while an object *a* exemplifies an attribute *F occurrently* just in case *a* is characterized by some mode that instantiates *F*.

2 CROSS-CATEGORIAL ONTOLOGICAL DEPENDENCIES

Before I say any more about the crucial issue of the two different species of exemplification, I want to present yet another version of the ontological square, this time one which represents the metaphysically significant relationships of *ontological dependency* that are characteristic of entities belonging to the four different ontological categories.[3] First of all, then, I need to point out that, true to the Aristotelian spirit in which the ontological square is conceived, the four-category ontology embodies an *immanent realist* view of universals, according to which it is an essential feature of any universal that it has particular instances, which provide the ground of its existence. According to this view, there are, then, no *uninstantiated* universals and every universal stands in a relationship of existential dependence to its particular instances. I shall call the relationship in question *weak existential dependence*. I call it 'weak' for the following reason: although, according to this view, a universal must *have* particular instances, which constitute the ground of its existence, a universal does not depend for its very *identity* on the particular instances that it happens to have, which is a purely *contingent* matter. Thus, for example, although the attribute brownness (assuming there to be such an attribute) must have particular instances in the form of the particular brownnesses of various brown objects, that very same attribute could have existed even if *those* particular brownnesses had not, provided that *other* particular brownnesses had existed – for example, if other objects had been brown.

Next, I want to say that the *modes* of an object stand to that object in another relationship of existential dependence, which I shall call *strong existential dependence* – 'strong' because in this case the modes *do* depend for their very identity on the object that they characterize. Thus, for example, what distinguishes one particular brownness from another exactly resembling

---

[3] For more on the notion – and the varieties – of ontological dependence, see my *The Possibility of Metaphysics: Substance, Identity, and Time* (Oxford: Clarendon Press, 1998), Chapter 6.

brownness is, precisely, *the object that possesses it*, or in which it 'inheres' – the implication of this being that modes cannot be 'transferred' from one object to another and cannot exist 'unattached' to any object. Clearly, since one object must possess many different modes, whereas the same mode cannot be possessed by many different objects, the relationship of strong existential dependence between modes and their object is a *many–one* relation.

Finally, I want to say that a kind stands in a *one–many* relationship of strong existential dependence with its various attributes: that is, that one kind must be characterized by many different attributes and that it depends for its very identity on the attributes that characterize it (or, at least, on those of its attributes that are 'part of its essence', if a distinction may be drawn between these and its 'accidental' attributes). Thus, for example, I would want to say that the kind *electron* depends for its identity on the specific attributes of *charge*, *spin*, and *rest mass* that characterize that kind of fundamental physical particle. (Electrons carry unit negative charge, have a spin of one-half and have a certain specific rest mass, differing from all other kinds of fundamental physical particle in at least one of these respects.)

Figure 3.4, then, is a version of the ontological square which represents the foregoing relationships of ontological dependency between items located at the different corners of the square, where a *solid*-headed arrow signifies *strong* existential dependence and an *open*-headed arrow signifies *weak* existential dependence.

It will be noticed that, in Figure 3.4, each corner of the ontological square differs from every other corner in respect of the number and type of arrows that proceed from or lead to it. The *object* corner has two arrows, one of each type, leading to it. The *kind* corner has two arrows, one of each type, proceeding from it. The *attribute* corner has one solid-headed arrow leading to it and one open-headed arrow proceeding from it. And the *mode* corner has

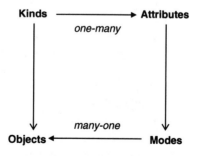

Figure 3.4. The ontological square, version IV

Two styles of predication – dispositional and occurrent   39

one open-headed arrow leading to it and one solid-headed arrow proceeding from it. Thus *objects* are represented as being the *least dependent* of all entities, in keeping with another Aristotelian sentiment, namely that *individual substances* are ontologically more basic than entities belonging to any other ontological category, insofar as they constitute the ultimate ground of all being. Moreover, because the four corners of the ontological square can be unambiguously identified in terms of the number and type of arrows leading to or proceeding from them – in other words, because the four categories can be unambiguously differentiated from one another in terms of the characteristic relationships of ontological dependency in which their members stand to the members of the other categories – the four-category ontology is not subject to the kind of objection that Frank Ramsey and others have raised against simpler systems of categorial ontology which appeal merely to the subject–property or universal–particular distinctions.[4] This objection is that the advocates of these systems cannot explain, in a non-question-begging way, what distinguishes each of the categories in such a system from another category in the same system and thus what renders each category *unique*. We could call this *the problem of categorial uniqueness* – and the important point is that the four-category ontology has the distinct advantage over some of its apparently more parsimonious rivals of being able to solve it.

Incidentally, before I move on from the subject of the ontological square, here is a useful mnemonic to remind one of the order of its four corners, starting, in appropriately Aristotelian fashion, with the bottom left-hand *object* corner: *OcKhAM* – *O*bjects, *K*inds, *A*ttributes, and *M*odes. There is some irony in this mnemonic, of course. William of Ockham himself, who did not favour realism concerning universals, would certainly not have approved of the four-category ontology. And, indeed, many present-day ontologists would no doubt attempt to wield Ockham's notorious *razor* against my system, accusing me of multiplying entities beyond necessity. However, one of the objectives of my work on the four-category ontology has been precisely to show how that ontology, while it is undoubtedly richer than many of its popular rivals – such as the pure trope ontology, the ontology of objects and attributes, and the ontology of objects and modes, each of which limits itself to only one or two corners of the ontological square – deserves our allegiance on account of its superior capacity to resolve a wide range of metaphysical problems, such as the problem of categorial uniqueness, which we have just discussed, and

---

[4] See F. P. Ramsey, 'Universals', in his *The Foundations of Mathematics and Other Logical Essays* (London: Kegan Paul, 1931). For further discussion, see my *The Four-Category Ontology*, Chapter 7.

40 *Reference and predication*

the so-called *inference problem* concerning the relationship between laws of nature and particular matters of fact. This latter problem, indeed, is the one that I shall focus on next.

3 LAWS OF NATURE AND THE INFERENCE PROBLEM

As I have already indicated, in my view all *kinds* are *characterized* by certain *attributes* – and *laws of nature*, by my account, consist precisely in such facts of characterization solely involving universals.[5] All *objects*, on the other hand, are characterized by *modes* that *instantiate* certain attributes – and it is in their being so characterized that particular *occurrent* facts or states of affairs consist. By contrast, particular *dispositional* facts or states of affairs consist in objects instantiating *kinds* that are characterized by certain attributes – in other words, they consist in objects being subject to certain laws governing the kinds to which they belong. What Bas van Fraassen and others call 'the inference problem' does not afflict this account of laws, as it does those of David Armstrong, Michael Tooley, and Fred Dretske – accounts which, like mine, locate laws in the domain of universals.[6] The complaint, as it applies to Armstrong's theory, is just this. According to Armstrong, a law of nature (at least, in the simplest sort of case) consists in the obtaining of a second-order relation of natural *necessitation*, N, between first-order universals or attributes – for example, F and G – which may be represented by a statement of the form '$N(F, G)$' ('F-ness necessitates G-ness', as we might express it in English).[7] And then he contends, crucially, that '$N(F, G)$' entails the corresponding universal generalization concerning particulars, '$\forall x(Fx \rightarrow Gx)$' (in plain English, 'Everything that is F is G' or 'All Fs are Gs'). But now the problem is that no account is provided of how '$N(F, G)$' entails '$\forall x(Fx \rightarrow Gx)$', since there appears to be no appropriate formal relationship between two sentences of these forms.

As I have just remarked, the inference problem does not arise for my account of laws. This is because, according to my account, what laws entail regarding the domain of particulars are solely *dispositional*, not occurrent, facts or states of affairs – and such entailments are formally valid in the system of sortal logic that I endorse. In the simplest case, a law has the form 'βF', where 'β' denotes a kind and 'F' an attribute. A corresponding particular dispositional fact has the form '$\exists \varphi(\varphi F \,\&\, a/\varphi)$', where, as was explained earlier, 'φ' is a variable ranging over kinds, 'a' denotes an object, and '$/$' signifies the formal

---

[5] See further my *The Four-Category Ontology*, especially Part III.
[6] See Bas C. van Fraassen, *Laws and Symmetry* (Oxford: Clarendon Press, 1989), Chapter 5.
[7] See D. M. Armstrong, *What Is a Law of Nature?* (Cambridge University Press, 1983).

Two styles of predication – dispositional and occurrent 41

ontological relation of instantiation. (The quoted formula here expresses, thus, the fact that a is disposed to be F – in other words, that a exemplifies F dispositionally. Recall here our earlier definition of '$D[a, F]$' as being equivalent to '$\exists\varphi(\varphi F \ \& \ a/\varphi)$'.) The crucial point, then, is that 'βF' entails '$\forall x(x/\beta \rightarrow \exists\varphi(\varphi F \ \& \ x/\varphi))$' – and thus, via the definition of '$D[a, F]$', entails '$\forall x(x/\beta \rightarrow D[x, F])$' – the proof of which is elementary: see Proof [1] in the Appendix at the end of this chapter. In other words, if the law that kind β is characterized by attribute F obtains, then it follows that every object instanti-ating β has the disposition to be F. But, crucially, it does *not* follow that every such object is *occurrently F*. Laws, then, fully determine how objects are *disposed* or *tend* to appear or behave, but not how they *actually* appear or behave. Consequently, they do not entail universal regularities (Humean 'constant conjunctions') amongst such appearances or behaviour, in the way that the Armstrong–Tooley–Dretske account of laws proposes and which critics like Van Fraassen profess – rightly, I think – to find mysterious.

4 CONDITIONAL LAWS AND THE PROBLEM OF IDIOSYNCRATIC DISPOSITIONS

However, some further complications now need to be discussed, in the light of criticisms of my system alluded to earlier. As some critics have pointed out, it seems implausible, at first sight, to suppose that *every* particular dispositional fact is grounded in some law governing a kind to which the object possessing the disposition belongs.[8] After all, objects of the *same* kind often seem to have different and sometimes even entirely idiosyncratic dispositions. For instance, a particular dog, Fido, might conceivably be the only dog in the world disposed to drink whisky: but it is clearly not a law governing canine behaviour that *dogs drink whisky*. This apparent difficulty can, however, be overcome by recognizing the irreducibly *conditional* character of many laws. That is to say, the funda-mental form of many laws is not, as we have hitherto been supposing, simply something like 'βF', but rather something like '$\beta(G \rightarrow F)$'.

Consider the following simple example. A body of frozen water – a piece of ice – is *not* disposed to evaporate, but a body of boiling water *is*. (Change the example if you do not like it: I use it purely for illustrative purposes.) Yet both are bodies of the same kind – *water*. Ice and boiling

---

[8] Amongst the people who have raised this point, either in print or in correspondence, are Ryan Wasserman, Ludger Jansen, and David S. Oderberg. I am particularly indebted to David Oderberg in this regard.

water are not, after all, different *kinds* of stuff, just the same kind of stuff in different physical forms. The change that happens when ice melts is a *phase* change, not a *substantial* change. Consequently, however, we should not affirm it as a law governing the kind water that *water evaporates* – rather, what we should affirm is that *water evaporates if, or when, it is boiling*, and this is consistent with our also affirming that *water does not evaporate if, or when, it is frozen*. Both laws apply at all times to any body of water, whether or not it happens to be frozen or boiling (or indeed neither). What entitles us to say that a piece of ice is *not* disposed to evaporate, whereas some boiling water *is*, is not, then, that they instantiate different kinds governed by different unconditional laws, but rather that the single kind that they both do instantiate – water – is governed by two different *conditional* laws, and that while one of these bodies of water happens to satisfy the antecedent condition of one of these laws, the other body happens to satisfy instead the antecedent condition of the other law.

Casually speaking, we may indeed say that the sentences 'Boiling water evaporates' and 'Frozen water does not evaporate' express laws. But it is at least potentially misleading to express the laws in question in those ways, since the complex sortal terms 'boiling water' and 'frozen water' are not denotative of *different kinds*. We do better to express the laws in question conditionally, as earlier: 'Water, when it is boiling, evaporates' and 'Water, when it is frozen, does not evaporate'. An adequate system of sortal logic will reflect this by admitting logical operations on predicates as well as on whole sentential formulas.[9]

So how do the foregoing considerations enable us to deal with the example of Fido, the dog that is idiosyncratically disposed to drink whisky? They do so in the following way. It is surely reasonable to suppose that Fido's peculiar condition is *lawfully explicable*, rather than just being *miraculous*. Presumably, Fido – perhaps on account of some feature of his past experience or training – has some property, X, such that it is a law that *dogs, if they have X, drink whisky*. Fido just happens to be peculiar in being the only dog to have X.[10]

---

[9] See further my *More Kinds of Being: A Further Study of Individuation, Identity and the Logic of Sortal Terms* (Malden, MA and Oxford: Wiley-Blackwell, 2009), Chapter 11. Note especially, in this connection, that '$\beta(G \rightarrow F)$' must *not* be taken to be logically equivalent to '$\beta G \rightarrow \beta F$': for example, 'Water evaporates if, or when, it is boiling' is plainly not equivalent to 'If water boils, then water evaporates'.

[10] Note that I am assuming here that Fido's peculiarity is not the upshot of some genetic mutation, because in that case there might well be grounds for saying that Fido differs *in kind* from other dogs

Two styles of predication – dispositional and occurrent 43

It will be helpful at this point to introduce a distinction between *essential* and *accidental* dispositions – and to say that Fido possesses only an accidental disposition to drink whisky. Our earlier definition of '$D[a, F]$' is, in these terms, really only a definition of *essential* dispositionality. So let us make that explicit by using the formula '$D_E[a, F]$' to say that a is *essentially* disposed to be F, defining this exactly as we earlier defined '$D[a, F]$':

$$D_E[a, F] =_{df} \exists\varphi(\varphi F \ \& \ a/\varphi)$$

Then let us use the formula '$D_A[a, F]$' to say that a is *accidentally* disposed to be F, defining this as follows:

$$D_A[a, F] =_{df} \exists X(O[a, X] \ \& \ {\sim}D_E[a, X] \ \& \ \exists\varphi(\varphi(X \rightarrow F) \ \& \ a/\varphi))$$

In other words, we say that a is *accidentally* disposed to be F just in case there is some attribute, X, such that a occurrently exemplifies X – but is not essentially disposed to be X – and for some kind, φ, that is instantiated by a, it is a law that φs are F if they are X. Drawing on the preceding definition of essential dispositionality, we can simplify this to:

$$D_A[a, F] =_{df} \exists X(O[a, X] \ \& \ {\sim}D_E[a, X] \ \& \ D_E[a, (X \rightarrow F)])$$

That is to say, a is accidentally disposed to be F just in case a occurrently exemplifies some attribute, X, such that, although a is *not* essentially disposed to be X, a *is* essentially disposed to be F *if it is* X.

Here it may be asked why I include the conjunct '${\sim}D_E[a, X]$' in the *definiens* of '$D_A[a, F]$'. The answer should be evident. It is plausible to suppose that '$D_E[a, X]$' and '$D_E[a, (X \rightarrow F)]$' together entail '$D_E[a, F]$', so that without this conjunct our definition would allow an object a to be *both* essentially *and* accidentally disposed to be F, which seems absurd. In fact, this entailment holds only under certain assumptions – notably, under the assumptions that an object cannot instantiate more than one kind and that two laws of the form 'βG' and '$\beta(G \rightarrow F)$' together entail one of the form 'βF'. See Proof [2] in the Appendix for a proof that the entailment holds under these particular assumptions, which I shall take to be correct for present purposes.

This, however, raises a further question. It might be supposed, prima facie, that '$O[a, F]$' entails '$D_E[a, F]$' – that if an object a exemplifies an attribute F occurrently, then a is *essentially* disposed to be F, rendering our

and that he belongs to a kind, φ, such that it is a law that φs drink whisky. I am grateful to Frédéric Nef for raising this issue in conversation.

44 *Reference and predication*

definition of '$D_A[a, F]$' inconsistent. Clearly, we must for this very reason deny that such an entailment holds – and, indeed, it seems reasonable to maintain instead that '$O[a, F]$' entails only the *disjunction* '$D_E[a, F] \vee D_A[a, F]$': that if an object *a* is occurrently *F*, then *a* is *either essentially or accidentally* disposed to be *F*. But aren't we now faced with a regress problem? For, if the latter entailment holds, then, clearly, given our original definition of accidental dispositionality, so does the following: '$D_A[a, F]$' entails '$\exists X(D_A[a, X]$ & $\exists \varphi(\varphi(X \rightarrow F)$ & $a/\varphi))$'. The implication seems to be that an object can possess one accidental disposition *only on condition of possessing another one*.

Fortunately, it seems clear that this potential regress is not inevitably infinite. For notice that we *don't* have it that '$D_A[a, F]$' entails '$\exists X(X \neq F$ & $D_A[a, X]$ & $\exists \varphi(\varphi(X \rightarrow F)$ & $a/\varphi))$'. So it is not in fact strictly true, given our assumptions so far, that an object can possess one accidental disposition only on condition of possessing *another* one. We can, then, have a case in which '$D_A[a, F]$' is true even though the following is also true: '$\forall X((D_A[a, X]$ & $\exists \varphi(\varphi(X \rightarrow F)$ & $a/\varphi)) \rightarrow X = F)$'. In such a case, it would clearly follow that this is true: '$D_A[a, F]$ & $\exists \varphi(\varphi(F \rightarrow F)$ & $a/\varphi)$', which is equivalent to '$D_A[a, F]$ & $D_E[a, (F \rightarrow F)]$'. For a proof of this, see Proof [3] in the Appendix. However, there is no contradiction lurking here, because '$D_A[a, F]$ & $D_E[a, (F \rightarrow F)]$' is not at all absurd, in constrast with '$D_A[a, F]$ & $D_E[a, F]$'. For, presumably, it is a merely trivial logical truth that any object *a* is essentially disposed to be *F if it is F*. In other words, our definitions of accidental and essential dispositionality allow that *sometimes*, at least, it is true that an object *a* is accidentally disposed to be *F* simply because a truth of the following form obtains: '$O[a, F]$ & $\sim D_E[a, F]$' – for this certainly entails the *definiens* of '$D_A[a, F]$', given the triviality of the aforementioned truth. See again the Appendix, Proof [4], for a proof of this. In other, and presumably more usual, cases, of course, '$D_A[a, F]$' will be true even though '$O[a, F]$' is not true.

5 CONDITIONAL LAWS AND THE PRINCIPLE OF INSTANTIATION

Finally, I want to point out that an important advantage of recognizing the prevalence of conditional laws is that it renders more plausible the *principle of instantiation* that is central to a neo-Aristotelian immanent realist view of universals like mine – especially for those philosophers, such as Armstrong and myself, who not only adhere to this principle but also hold that we

Two styles of predication – dispositional and occurrent   45

should decide *which* universals to admit into our ontology largely by seeing which universals science invokes in the laws that it postulates to explain empirical phenomena. According to the principle of instantiation, every existing universal must have, at least at some time and some place, *a particular instance*: there are no *uninstantiated* universals. Now, for a *conditional* law of the form '$\beta(G \to F)$' to obtain, the principle of instantiation requires only that each of the universals β, F, and G should have instances – *not* that there should be an instance of β that also occurrently exemplifies either G or F. For example, the principle allows that it may be a law that *water, when it is boiling, evaporates* – that *boiling water evaporates* – without requiring there to exist, at any time or place, *a body of water that is boiling*. Imagine, thus, a universe in which water exists but temperatures never rise high enough to reach its boiling point. Provided that *some* liquids sometimes actually boil and evaporate in this universe, it can still be true, consistently with the principle of instantiation, that *water, if or when it is boiling, evaporates*.

Now, clearly, many laws are expressed by sentences which do not reveal their underlying conditional form – 'Ice does not evaporate' is a simple example of this. 'Water boils' is, of course, another – for this must be taken as an elliptical way of stating the conditional law that water boils if, or when, its temperature and the atmospheric pressure reach certain levels (for instance, when its temperature reaches a hundred degrees Celsius at sea-level pressure).[11] But it may well be that *very many more laws than we intuitively suppose* are really conditional in form, thereby reducing considerably the number of universals that we need to include in our ontology and, correspondingly, reducing the burden that is imposed by the principle of instantiation. Here, then, is another example of how the four-category ontology, despite being – or, rather, *in virtue of* being – more complex than some of its rivals, can deal better than they do with certain long-standing metaphysical problems.

---

[11] Note, indeed, that if we held 'Water boils' to be a law, then, given our previous assumption that 'Water, if it is boiling, evaporates' is a law, we would be committed – via the principle that 'βG & $\beta(G \to F)$' entails 'βF' – to holding that 'Water evaporates' is a law, which we have already denied to be the case. This confirms that 'Water boils' should be taken to be an elliptical expression of a law which is really conditional in form.

Appendix: proofs

The simple proofs included in this appendix all use the familiar *tree* method of proof,[12] whereby it may be shown that a set of premises, Γ, entails a proposition p by assuming Γ and $\sim p$ and showing that a logical inconsistency must result. An 'x' at the foot of a branch indicates that it contains such an inconsistency – that is, that the branch includes both a certain proposition and that proposition's negation – and if all branches terminate in this way the proof is complete.

[1] Proof that 'βF' entails '$\forall x(x/\beta \rightarrow \exists\varphi(\varphi F \,\&\, x/\varphi))$'

$$\beta F$$
$$\sim\forall x(x/\beta \rightarrow \exists\varphi(\varphi F \,\&\, x/\varphi))$$
$$|$$
$$\exists x\sim(x/\beta \rightarrow \exists\varphi(\varphi F \,\&\, x/\varphi))$$
$$|$$
$$\exists x(x/\beta \,\&\, \sim\exists\varphi(\varphi F \,\&\, x/\varphi))$$
$$|$$
$$a/\beta \,\&\, \sim\exists\varphi(\varphi F \,\&\, a/\varphi)$$
$$|$$
$$a/\beta$$
$$\sim\exists\varphi(\varphi F \,\&\, a/\varphi)$$
$$|$$
$$\forall\varphi\sim(\varphi F \,\&\, a/\varphi)$$
$$|$$
$$\forall\varphi(\varphi F \rightarrow \sim a/\varphi)$$
$$|$$
$$\beta F \rightarrow \sim a/\beta$$
$$|$$

$$\sim\beta F \qquad\qquad\qquad \sim a/\beta$$
$$\text{x} \qquad\qquad\qquad\qquad \text{x}$$

---

[12] See, for example, Colin Howson, *Logic with Trees* (London: Routledge, 1997).

Two styles of predication – dispositional and occurrent   47

[2] Proof that '$\mathbf{D_E}[a, G]$ & $\mathbf{D_E}[a, (G \to F)]$' entails '$\mathbf{D_E}[a, F]$'

$$\mathbf{D_E}[a, G] \ \& \ \mathbf{D_E}[a, (G \to F)]$$
$$\sim\!\mathbf{D_E}[a, F]$$
$$|$$
$$\exists\varphi(\varphi G \ \& \ a/\varphi)$$
$$\exists\varphi(\varphi(G \to F) \ \& \ a/\varphi)$$
$$|$$
$$\sim\!\exists\varphi(\varphi F \ \& \ a/\varphi)$$
$$|$$
$$\beta G \ \& \ a/\beta$$
$$\gamma(G \to F) \ \& \ a/\gamma$$
$$|$$
$$\beta G$$
$$a/\beta$$
$$a/\gamma$$
$$|$$
$$\beta = \gamma \qquad \text{(i)}$$
$$|$$
$$\beta(G \to F) \ \& \ a/\beta$$
$$|$$
$$\beta(G \to F)$$
$$|$$
$$\beta G \ \& \ \beta(G \to F)$$
$$|$$
$$\beta F \qquad \text{(ii)}$$
$$|$$
$$\beta F \ \& \ a/\beta$$
$$|$$
$$\exists\varphi(\varphi F \ \& \ a/\varphi)$$
$$\text{x}$$

Notes

(i) This line follows from the preceding two, given, as was proposed in the main text, that an object cannot instantiate more than one kind.

48 *Reference and predication*

(ii) This line follows from the preceding one, given, as was proposed in the main text, that two laws of the form 'βG' and '$\beta(G \to F)$' together entail one of the form 'βF'.

[3] Proof that '$\mathbf{D_A}[a, F]$' and '$\forall X((\mathbf{D_A}[a, X] \,\&\, \exists\varphi(\varphi(X \to F) \,\&\, a/\varphi)) \to X = F)$' together entail '$\exists\varphi(\varphi(F \to F) \,\&\, a/\varphi)$'

$$\mathbf{D_A}[a, F]$$

$$\forall X((\mathbf{D_A}[a, X] \,\&\, \exists\varphi(\varphi(X \to F) \,\&\, a/\varphi)) \to X = F)$$

$$\sim\exists\varphi(\varphi(F \to F) \,\&\, a/\varphi)$$

$$|$$

$$\exists X(\mathbf{O}[a, X] \,\&\, \sim\mathbf{D_E}[a, X] \,\&\, \exists\varphi(\varphi(X \to F) \,\&\, a/\varphi)) \quad \text{(i)}$$

$$|$$

$$\mathbf{O}[a, G] \,\&\, \sim\mathbf{D_E}[a, G] \,\&\, \exists\varphi(\varphi(G \to F) \,\&\, a/\varphi)$$

$$|$$

$$\mathbf{O}[a, G]$$

$$\sim\mathbf{D_E}[a, G]$$

$$\exists\varphi(\varphi(G \to F) \,\&\, a/\varphi)$$

$$\mathbf{D_A}[a, G] \qquad\qquad \mathbf{D_E}[a, G] \qquad \text{(ii)}$$
$$\qquad\qquad\qquad\qquad\qquad \text{x}$$

$$(\mathbf{D_A}[a, G] \,\&\, \exists\varphi(\varphi(G \to F) \,\&\, a/\varphi)) \to G = F$$

$$\sim(\mathbf{D_A}[a, G] \,\&\, \exists\varphi(\varphi(G \to F) \,\&\, a/\varphi)) \qquad\qquad G = F$$

$$\exists\varphi(\varphi(F \to F) \,\&\, a/\varphi)$$
$$\text{x}$$

$$\sim\mathbf{D_A}[a, G] \qquad\qquad \sim\exists\varphi(\varphi(G \to F) \,\&\, a/\varphi)$$
$$\text{x} \qquad\qquad\qquad\qquad \text{x}$$

Two styles of predication – dispositional and occurrent   49

Notes

(i) This line follows from '$\mathbf{D_A}[a, F]$', given the definition of the latter in the main text.

(ii) This line follows from '$\mathbf{O}[a, G]$', given, as was contended in the main text, that '$\mathbf{O}[a, G]$' entails '$\mathbf{D_E}[a, G] \vee \mathbf{D_A}[a, G]$'.

[4] Proof that '$\mathbf{O}[a, F]$ & $\sim\mathbf{D_E}[a, F]$' entails '$\exists X(\mathbf{O}[a, X]$ & $\sim\mathbf{D_E}[a, X]$ & $\exists\varphi(\varphi(X \to F)$ & $a/\varphi))$' – the *definiens* of '$\mathbf{D_A}[a, F]$'

$$\mathbf{O}[a, F] \ \& \ \sim\mathbf{D_E}[a, F]$$
$$\sim\exists X(\mathbf{O}[a, X] \ \& \ \sim\mathbf{D_E}[a, X] \ \& \ \exists\varphi(\varphi(X \to F) \ \& \ a/\varphi))$$
$$\mid$$
$$\exists\varphi(\varphi(F \to F) \ \& \ a/\varphi)$$
$$\mid$$
$$\mathbf{O}[a, F] \ \& \ \sim\mathbf{D_E}[a, F] \ \& \ \exists\varphi(\varphi(F \to F) \ \& \ a/\varphi)$$
$$\mid$$
$$\exists X(\mathbf{O}[a, X] \ \& \ \sim\mathbf{D_E}[a, X] \ \& \ \exists\varphi(\varphi(X \to F) \ \& \ a/\varphi))$$
$$\text{x}$$

CHAPTER 4

Ontological categories and categorial predication

I have said a good deal in previous chapters about the notion of an ontological category, but now I want to examine more closely the forms of sentence that we deploy in speaking about such categories. When we say of something that it 'is an object', or 'is an event', or 'is a property' – just to cite a few examples – we are engaging in what I propose to call *categorial predication*: we are assigning something to a certain *ontological category*. Ontological categorization is clearly a type of classification, but it differs radically from the types of classification that are involved in the taxonomic practices of empirical sciences, as when a physicist says of a certain particle that it 'is an electron', or when a zoologist says of a certain animal that it 'is a mammal', or when a meteorologist says of a certain weather phenomenon that it 'is a hurricane'. Classifications of the latter types presuppose that the items being classified have already been assigned to appropriate ontological categories, such as the categories of *object, species,* or *event.* But what do categorial predications *mean*? How are their *truth-conditions* to be determined and how can those truth-conditions be known to be satisfied? Do they have *truthmakers*? Questions like these are amongst those that will be addressed in the present chapter. As in the preceding chapter, my most important guiding light in such matters will be Aristotle, although what follows is in no sense intended to be an exercise in the scholarly exegesis of Aristotelian texts.

I FANTOLOGY; OR, 'ONTOLOGY LITE'

Most philosophers today who have been brought up in the analytical tradition have been exposed, at a formative period of their thinking, to the formalism of first-order predicate logic with identity. This has equipped them with a certain conception of reference and predication which is, from the point of view of serious ontology, extremely thin and superficial. It is a view which embodies – to invoke Barry Smith's apt

Ontological categories and categorial predication

term – all the myths of 'Fantology': the idea that the most basic form of atomic proposition is one that may be symbolized as 'Fa', where 'F' is the predicate and 'a' is a singular term, or 'individual constant' (the logical counterpart of a proper name).[1] The only further elaboration of this that is countenanced is to admit *relational* predicates with any finite number, n, of 'places', giving us as the most general form of an atomic proposition '$R^n a_1 a_2 \ldots a_n$'. And the only 'relation' that is given any special formal recognition is the dyadic relation of *identity*, with its own dedicated symbol, '$=$', as in '$a_1 = a_2$'. Sometimes, a formal recognition is also accorded to the monadic *existence* predicate, as in '$E!a$', but this is generally analysed in terms of the particular (or, more tendentiously, 'existential') quantifier, '$\exists$', together with identity, as being equivalent to '$\exists x(x = a)$'. And that, basically, is the sum total of the formal machinery of standard first-order predicate logic that serves to represent anything remotely 'ontological' in character: it is 'ontology lite'.

One point I am aiming to make here is that there are many more ontological distinctions that we need to be able to make that go beyond either the distinction between object (or 'individual') and property or that between existence and identity. It just isn't good enough to say, with W. V. Quine, that the fundamental question of ontology is 'What is there?', and that its most concise answer is 'Everything'.[2] Ontology is concerned above all with the *categorial* structure of reality – the division of reality into fundamental *types* of entity and their ontological relations with one another. The object/property distinction is very probably *one* such distinction that any system of categorial ontology should recognize, and identity is *one* such relation, but very plausibly there are many others besides these.

Note that, on the now standard view – basically Quine's, which is a development of Frege's and Russell's – we do not even get an 'ontological commitment' to *properties and relations* out of 'first-order' languages, since the latter do not involve quantification into predicate position. For that we need, supposedly, a *second*-order language, where we can say things of the form '$\exists F(Fa)$' and the like. But this then apparently treats 'properties' (the 'values' of second-order variables) as second-order *objects*, of which yet higher-order properties may further be predicated. So, on this view, the

---

[1] See Barry Smith, 'Of Substances, Accidents and Universals: In Defence of a Constituent Ontology', *Philosophical Papers* 26 (1997), pp. 105–27, and 'Against Fantology', in M. E. Reicher and J. C. Marek (eds.), *Experience and Analysis* (Vienna: HPT & ÖBV, 2005).

[2] See W. V. Quine, 'On What There Is', in his *From a Logical Point of View*, 2nd edn (Cambridge, MA: Harvard University Press, 1961).

52   *Reference and predication*

object/property distinction is really just a *relative* one, with an nth-order *object* being an $(n-1)^{th}$-order *property*, for all $n > 1$. Hence *all* entities are 'objects' on this view, but there are different 'orders' of objects, starting with first-order ones which are not 'properties' of anything. And maybe we can even discern an echo here, however weak, of the Aristotelian notion of a 'primary substance', which is not 'said of' anything – of which much more anon. (Quine himself, of course, was sceptical about including 'properties' in our ontology – at least, properties conceived as 'universals', as opposed to items identifiable as *sets* of first-order objects – on the grounds that he could see no principled way to *individuate* them, rendering them vulnerable to his dictum 'No entity without identity'.)

The next pernicious aspect of the 'standard' view is this: it accommodates no notion of 'property' other than as *something* – though exactly *what* is often left obscure – that 'corresponds' to a *predicate*, as in '*Fa*', where '*F*' supposedly expresses a 'property' of *a*. This is despite the fact that we know that, on pain of contradiction, not *every* predicate can denote or express a property – this simply being a consequence of one version of Russell's paradox. Take the predicate '– is non-self-exemplifying', which seemingly applies, for example, to the first-order property of *being green* (a 'first-order' property because it is a property of first-order *objects*, such as *apples* and *leaves*). 'Being green (greenness) is not *green*' certainly seems to be true, whence it seems that we can conclude that 'Being green is *non-self-exemplifying*' is also true. If the example is not liked, another can easily replace it. But we know that there can be no (second-order) *property* (property of a first-order property) of *being non-self-exemplifying*, since if there were it could plainly be *neither* self-exemplifying *nor* non-self-exemplifying, giving us a contradiction.

We are also now in the territory of Frege's notorious paradox of the concept (that is, first-order property) *horse*, which he contended was *not* an object because it is not 'saturated' – the apparent implication being that the *object* that we *do* denote by the singular term '(the property of) being a *horse*' is not what is expressed by the predicate '– is a horse'.[3] The best that the standard view can do at this point, it seems, is to say that for every 'property' of order n – 'property' in the sense of *semantic value of a predicate* – there is a corresponding *proxy*-object of order $(n + 1)$, which is the semantic value of a corresponding singular term. If that is right, then it turns out that the object/property distinction isn't even straightforwardly

---

[3] See Gottlob Frege, 'On Concept and Object', in *Translations from the Philosophical Writings of Gottlob Frege*, 2nd edn, ed. and trans. P. T. Geach and M. Black (Oxford: Blackwell, 1960).

Ontological categories and categorial predication 53

relative, as was suggested earlier. Rather, we have a series of *objects* of ascending 'orders' and, *distinct but in parallel with that*, a series of corresponding 'properties'. The scheme is something like the following – where, listed in each column of the table, are typical expressions whose semantic values are the 'objects' and 'properties' of successively higher 'orders':

	Objects	Properties
1st order	'Dobbin'	'– is a horse'
2nd order	'Being a horse'	'– is a first-order property'
3rd order	'Being a first-order property'	'– is a second-order property'
4th order	'Being a second-order property'	'– is a third-order property'
Et cetera		

This scheme is organized so as to enable us, supposedly, to assign appropriate 'semantic values' to the semantically interpretable parts (subjects and predicates) of sentences such as the following:

(1) Dobbin is a horse
(2) Being a horse is a first-order property
(3) Being a first-order property is a second-order property
   Et cetera

Of course, as well as affirming, for example, (2) – 'Being a horse is a *first-order property*' – we are *also* supposed to be able to affirm 'Being a horse is a *second-order object*', since the foregoing table displays that alleged fact by listing 'Being a horse' in the second row under the 'Objects' column. One might suppose that this would entitle us to conclude that *a first-order property is (identical with) a second-order object*: but that is problematic, given Frege's contention that the object/property (or object/concept) distinction is mutually exclusive, on the ground that properties, but not objects, are 'unsaturated' entities. This just shows how intractable the 'paradox' is, at least given Fregean assumptions.

But what, really, are the 'semantic values' of predicates – *properties* – supposed to *be*? On one view – not Frege's, clearly, but maybe Quine's – they are just the 'extensions' of those predicates: the sets of things to which they apply, such as the set of all (actually existing) horses in the case of the predicate '– is a horse'. This would make the semantic value of that predicate an *object*, however, since sets are pretty clearly objects by any

54 *Reference and predication*

reasonable account. On another view – neither Frege's nor Quine's – the semantic value of such a predicate is instead a certain kind of *function*: namely, a function from 'possible worlds' to sets of objects existing in those worlds.[4] Thus the semantic value of the predicate '– is a horse', on this view, is a function from possible worlds to the sets of *horses* existing in those worlds (and Quine would reject the view because he rejects 'possible worlds'). This, in the current technical jargon, assigns an *intension*, rather than just an *extension*, as the 'semantic value' of this predicate. But, fairly evidently, a 'function', at least as this is normally understood by mathematical logicians, is itself just a special kind of set-theoretical entity and so a certain kind of *abstract object* – not the kind of 'unsaturated' entity that Frege took properties (or 'concepts') to be. However, these entanglements take us too far from our current purpose, save to illustrate once more the baroque qualities of 'Fantology' and its insouciance about questions of serious ontology. Its adherents exhibit no genuine interest in understanding the real *nature* of properties, if such entities there be.

However, one important further application of the foregoing scheme of objects and properties of different 'orders' is worth mentioning, and it concerns the notion of *existence*. As was indicated earlier, 'Dobbin exists' is standardly analysed as '$\exists x(x = \text{Dobbin})$', and here '$\exists x(x = -)$' may be regarded as denoting or expressing a *first*-order property – the property, possessed by Dobbin and indeed by all other existing objects, of *being identical with something*. But we can, supposedly, also *re-parse* '$\exists x(x = \text{Dobbin})$' by treating the expression '$= \text{Dobbin}$' as being, in effect, a sign for the quite different first-order property of *being identical with Dobbin*. This being done, '$\exists x(x -)$' may then be taken to express the *second*-order property of *having at least one (first-order) instance*, which is here being predicated of the first-order property of being identical with Dobbin. Thus re-parsed, '$\exists x(x = \text{Dobbin})$' should really be understood as having the logical form '$G_2(F_1)$', with 'F_1' denoting the first-order property of being identical with Dobbin and 'G_2' the second-order property of having at least one instance, so that the whole sentence may be re-translated into (rather barbaric) English as 'Being identical with Dobbin has at least one instance'.

---

[4] Frege himself does, in his own way, treat properties ('concepts') as functions, but as functions from objects to *truth-values*, and he accordingly regards functions as 'unsaturated' entities: see 'Function and Concept', in Geach and Black (eds.), *Translations from the Philosophical Works of Gottlob Frege*. Russell speaks instead of 'propositional functions', conceived as functions from objects to *propositions*: see 'Propositional Functions', in Bertrand Russell, *Introduction to Mathematical Philosophy* (London: George Allen and Unwin, 1919). But neither view is any more attractive than the views now under discussion in this paragraph.

Ontological categories and categorial predication

But once again, of course, the singular term 'being identical with Dobbin' now has to be taken to denote a second-order *object*, not the first-order *property* that is the semantic value of the predicate '– is identical with Dobbin', at least if we follow Frege in these matters.

Now, at this point I want to cry out that all of this is completely *insane* from an ontological point of view that aspires to any seriousness, being driven entirely by the constraints of a particular style of logical formalism and the ramshackle ontology that typically accompanies it. We need to sort out our *ontology* properly first, and only then shape our formal logic to fit it, not vice versa. And the first step towards sanity here is to abandon the idea that there is something special and sacrosanct about the 'atomic' logical form '*Fa*' – Fantology. Fantology, which originates from the systems of formal logic newly developed by Frege and Russell around the beginning of the twentieth century, does implicitly rest on certain onto-logical assumptions, but on rather weak and ill-thought-out ones – assumptions which seemed to matter little when they were overshadowed by the sheer *logical* power of those formal systems. It weakly reflects, thus, the *object/property* distinction, whose historical roots lie in traditional Aristotelian substance ontology – ultimately, in fact, in Aristotle's early work, the *Categories*.[5] But in the *Categories*, Aristotle does not assume a simple dichotomy between 'substance' (or 'object') and 'property'. Rather, he introduces a more complex *fourfold* ontological scheme by way of two key formal notions: those of 'being *said of* a subject' and 'being *in* a subject'. Somewhat obscure though these notions may initially seem to be, on further investigation they in fact bear rich ontological fruit and valuable insights into the proper relations between logic and ontology. It is a worthwhile project, then, to try to clarify them in terms rather more familiar to present-day metaphysicians, whereupon a comparison between Fantology and traditional Aristotelian categorial ontology will prove to be quite revealing.

2 ARISTOTELIAN CATEGORIAL ONTOLOGY AND ITS LOGICAL FORMALIZATION

I turn now to the foregoing task: that of explicating the 'being said of'/ 'being in' distinction and its application by Aristotle in his characteriza-tions of the most basic ontological types figuring in his fourfold categorial scheme, these types being (1) *primary substance*, (2) *secondary substance*,

---

[5] See Aristotle, *Categories and De Interpretatione*, trans. J. L. Ackrill (Oxford: Clarendon Press, 1963).

56 *Reference and predication*

(3) *property* or *attribute* and (4) *individual accident* or *mode* (to use some familiar Scholastic nomenclature).[6] First of all, then, being *said of* is clearly indicative of *predication*, while being *in* is indicative of what would, long after Aristotle's time, come to be called *inherence*. Now, Aristotle's *primary substances* in the *Categories* are described by him as being *neither said of nor in* a subject – in other words, they are not *predicable* of anything, nor do they exist 'in' anything as ontological ingredients or constituents. Being neither 'of' nor 'in' other things, they are thus in neither sense ontologically *dependent* beings, and this indeed is why primary substances are taken by him to be the entities that are ontologically most fundamental. By contrast, Aristotle's *secondary* substances – the species and genera of primary substances – are, according to him, 'said of' but not 'in' a subject, thus sharing one kind of ontological independence with primary substances but not another. Thus, for example, in affirming that Dobbin *is a horse*, we are predicating *the species horse* of the primary or individual substance Dobbin. But, on Aristotle's view, this species isn't 'in' the individual substance, as an ontological 'constituent' of the latter – that is, as some entity numerically *distinct* from that substance but one which, nonetheless, somehow helps to *constitute* it as the particular substance that it is. Next, we have items in the category 'both said of and in a subject', which gives us a contrast between the predicate '– is a horse' and, say, the predicate '– is warm-blooded'. The latter expresses a *property* or *attribute* of Dobbin, which he shares with all other individual substances of the same species (all other horses) – shares, it seems, as an ingredient or constituent in his *nature or being* (his 'essence').[7] Finally, there are the items that are '*in* a subject but not *said of* a subject', which are generally taken to be a primary substance's 'individual accidents' or 'modes' – items such as the *particular* whiteness of Dobbin, as opposed both to the *universal* whiteness that he shares with all other white primary substances and to the particular whitenesses of *other* white primary substances.

It will be noted that all *predicables* belong either to the category of secondary substances or to the category of attributes and that all items in

---

[6] I use a slightly different terminology for these categories in Chapter 3 – a terminology that I personally prefer – but here I am more concerned to be faithful to the nomenclature of Aristotle and his Scholastic successors.

[7] Here I am, for the sake of simplicity, glossing over an important distinction between properties in the strictest sense, which are necessarily shared by all primary substances of the same species – by all individual horses, for instance – and what might be called 'general accidents', which are shared by some but not all such primary substances, an example being Dobbin's whiteness (since not all horses are white). I take it that, for the Aristotelian, both warm-bloodedness and whiteness are 'in' Dobbin, but only the former is *necessarily* 'in' *all* individual horses.

Ontological categories and categorial predication 57

these categories are *universals* rather than particulars – all *particulars* belonging either to the category of primary substances or to the category of modes. Thus, on this account, although modes are in one sense 'properties' of primary substances, they are not *predicable* of them, which may sound odd to the ears of present-day metaphysicians. And yet it does seem to be borne out by what we actually *say* in English and other natural languages. When, for instance, we say that Dobbin *is white*, we are making no reference to his *individual* whiteness, even if it is *because* this individual whiteness 'inheres' in him that whiteness (the universal) is predicable of him. (Incidentally, it is precisely because present-day metaphysics is equivocal about the status of 'properties', sometimes treating them as universals and sometimes as particulars in the guise of 'tropes', that I generally prefer to use the term 'attribute' to denote items that are 'both said of and in a subject'.)

Much more can and should be said about all this, but already we can see that we have here a much richer ontology than anything that is offered by Fantology and one that is, despite being categorially more complex, ontologically far less baroque and extravagant. For example, we have no grounds now for believing in a potentially infinite hierarchy of 'orders' of objects and properties. Thus warm-bloodedness is *said of* a subject – it is a 'predicable' – but is not *itself* a subject, in the relevant sense of 'subject'. Of course, the *word* 'warm-bloodedness' can be made the *grammatical* 'subject' of a *verb*: but that is not the *ontological* conception of a subject, which is that of a *substance* (whether primary or secondary). So, the sentence 'Warm-bloodedness is a property of horses', say, shouldn't be understood as predicating the (pseudo-)property or attribute of *being a property of horses* of the (pseudo-)subject *warm-bloodedness*. Rather, it is just a roundabout way of saying 'Horses are warm-blooded', which expresses a general truth about the secondary substance or species *horse*, holding in virtue of that species' *essence*. To regard warm-bloodedness as a *subject* – a quasi-substance – would simply and literally be a *category mistake*, on the Aristotelian view. Thus, on this approach, we need have no truck with 'second-order logic' (at least as it is ordinarily conceived) and other such formal monstrosities. And we aren't faced with Frege's hideous 'paradox' of the concept *horse*. For that paradox is really just an artefact of an impoverished logical formalism and its misconceived ontological assumptions.

So, what would a *better* logical formalism look like? First of all, if we are going to follow the Aristotle of the *Categories*, we shall obviously need *four* distinct classes of 'material' (that is, non-formal or non-logical) expressions, not just the *two* ('*F*' and '*a*') of standard first-order predicate logic, in order

58   *Reference and predication*

to denote (1) primary substances, (2) secondary substances, (3) properties or attributes, and (4) individual accidents or modes. Let us then adopt the following notation for this purpose:[8]

(1) $a, b, c, \ldots$ denote primary substances
(2) $\alpha, \beta, \gamma, \ldots$ denote secondary substances
(3) $F, G, H, \ldots$ denote attributes
(4) $f, g, h, \ldots$ denote modes

Again, if we are going to follow the Aristotle of the *Categories*, we need *different* devices for expressing 'saying of' (predication) and 'being in' (inherence), in place of the *single* device for expressing 'predication' that we find in standard first-order logic. And indeed I am happy to follow Aristotle here too, partly for purposes of illustration, but also because I largely agree with him.[9] So, to this end, let us simply use *post*-positioning to represent *predication*, as in standard first-order logic, giving us, for example, 'βa' and 'Fa' as ways to symbolize 'Dobbin is a horse' and 'Dobbin is warm-blooded' respectively (where 'β' = 'horse', 'a' = 'Dobbin' and 'F' = 'warm-blooded'). And let us additionally use *pre*-positioning to represent *inherence*, giving us, for example, 'af' and 'aG' as ways to symbolize 'This whiteness is in Dobbin' and 'Whiteness is in Dobbin' respectively (where 'f' = 'this whiteness', 'a' = 'Dobbin' and 'G' = 'white(ness)'). Note that, with this scheme, we can represent 'Dobbin is white' and 'Whiteness is in Dobbin' as 'Ga' and 'aG' respectively, reversing the positions of 'G' and 'a'. But, very plausibly, two such sentences are *logically equivalent*, even if they are not synonymous, so that for logical purposes we may discard formulas of the form 'aG' as superfluous. Here is the scheme laid out in tabular form, followed by the formation rules for constructing 'atomic' sentences:[10]

---

[8] Compare Table 3.1 of Chapter 3, which adopts the same symbolism.

[9] See my *The Four-Category Ontology: A Metaphysical Foundation for Natural Science* (Oxford: Clarendon Press, 2006). Although I broadly follow Aristotle in that book, I do not there deploy his being said of/being in distinction, preferring instead to make use of a three-way distinction between instantiation, characterization, and exemplification. I still prefer the latter approach – which I adopt also in Chapter 3 – but am using this opportunity to explore further an approach that is closer to Aristotle's own.

[10] It should be noted, incidentally, that these formation rules differ from those provided in Table 3.1 of Chapter 3, since in that chapter I was appealing to my own preferred formal ontological relations of instantiation, characterization, and exemplification, instead of employing Aristotle's *being said of/being in*, or *predicable/inherent* distinction.

Ontological categories and categorial predication

1. Subjects	2. Predicables	3. Inherents
Primary substances	Secondary substances	Attributes
$a, b, c, \ldots$	$\alpha, \beta, \gamma, \ldots$	$F, G, H, \ldots$
Secondary substances	Attributes	Modes
$\alpha, \beta, \gamma, \ldots$	$F, G, H, \ldots$	$f, g, h, \ldots$

Rule 1. Any item in column 1 can have something in column 2 *predicated* of it, this being represented by *post*-positioning the former item to the latter: thus, 'βa', 'Ga', '$\alpha\beta$' and 'Fa' – as in 'Dobbin is a horse', 'Dobbin is white', 'Horses are mammals' (or 'A/The horse is a mammal') and 'Mammals are warm-blooded', where 'β' = 'horse', 'a' = 'Dobbin', 'G' = 'white', 'α' = 'mammal' and 'F' = 'warm-blooded'. (Note that the definite or indefinite article in 'A/The horse is a mammal' is logically redundant and would not, of course, have any equivalent in Latin and many other languages.)

Rule 2. Any item in column 1 can have something in column 3 *inherent* in it, this being represented by *pre*-positioning the former item to the latter: thus, 'aG', 'af', 'αF' and 'βf' – as in 'White(ness) is in Dobbin', 'This whiteness is in Dobbin', 'Warm-blooded(ness) is in mammals' and 'This whiteness is in horses', where 'G' = 'white(ness)', 'a' = 'Dobbin', 'f' = 'this whiteness', 'F' = 'warm-blooded(ness)', 'α' = 'mammal' and 'β' = 'horse'. As implied above, we take 'warm-blooded' and 'warm-blooded*ness*' to be equivalent for onto-logical purposes, the difference in form being merely a grammatical peculiarity of English. And, once more, we take 'White(ness) is in Dobbin' and 'Warm-blooded(ness) is in mammals' to be logically equivalent, respectively, to 'Dobbin is white' and 'Mammals are warm-blooded', rendering formulas of the forms 'aG' and 'αF' redundant for logical purposes. The only odd case is the last, 'This whiteness is in horses', for how, it might be asked, can a *mode* 'inhere' in a *species*? One answer might be that it does so just as long as *some* individual member of the species, such as Dobbin, has this whiteness inhering in it. Alternatively, we might simply want to exclude this last case as not well formed and restrict accordingly the second formation rule just stated (Rule 2).

Observe that these formation rules give us just the following *six* types of 'atomic' sentences: Fa, αb, $G\beta$, $\alpha\beta$, af and αg. The first type predicates an

60 *Reference and predication*

attribute of a primary substance, the second predicates a secondary substance of a primary substance, the third predicates an attribute of a secondary substance, the fourth predicates a secondary substance of another secondary substance, the fifth expresses the inherence of a mode in a primary substance and the sixth expresses the inherence of a mode in a secondary substance. (For reasons just explained, the first type also serves to express the inherence of an attribute in a primary substance and the third type also serves to express the inherence of an attribute in a secondary substance.) As just mentioned, we might want to exclude the sixth type and allow only the first five. There is nothing sacrosanct, of course, about this notation, and others could have been used quite as well. But it is interesting to note that, if we restrict our attention to just the first five types, we can see that the four basic classes of 'material' terms occur in them with the following frequencies: secondary substance terms (α, β) *four* times, primary substance terms (a, b) *three* times, attribute terms (F, G) *two* times and mode terms (f, g) just *once*. Whether that rather neat distribution has any significance is hard to say. In saying that just these types of atomic sentences are well formed, other combinations of terms are by implication excluded, such as 'GF' and '$f\beta$': one attribute cannot be predicated of or inhere in another attribute, nor can a mode be predicated of a secondary substance or a secondary substance inhere in a mode.

Of course, this gives us, so far, only a way to represent formally 'atomic' propositions. There is a lot more expressive power that we still need to cater for in order to express, for instance, truths of *existence* and *identity*. Here we may follow existing practice, however, and use the symbols 'E!' and '=' respectively for these purposes. But we also need *quantifiers* – at least a *particular* and a *universal* quantifier – although for this purpose too we may as well again follow existing practice and use the symbols '∃' and '∀'. However, we shall *not* adopt the usual assumption that existence can be 'analysed' in terms of '∃' and '='. And another appropriate diversion from standard practice would be to favour so-called *restricted* quantifiers for most purposes. For instance, in order to represent the sentence 'Some (individual) horses are white', we shall use a formula such as '$(\exists x: \alpha x)(Fx)$', where '$\alpha$' = 'horse' and '$F$' = 'white'. Similarly, in order to represent the sentence 'Some (species of) mammals are viviparous', we shall use a formula such as '$(\exists \varphi: \beta \varphi)(G\varphi)$', where '$\beta$' = 'mammal' and '$G$' = 'viviparous'. (It will be noticed, incidentally, that I am here adopting the convention of using $x, y, z, \ldots$ as variables ranging over primary substances and $\varphi, \chi, \psi, \ldots$ as variables ranging over secondary substances.)

Ontological categories and categorial predication 61

My reason for favouring restricted quantifiers for these purposes emerges most clearly in the case of universal generalizations. Consider, for instance, the true sentence 'All (species of) mammals are warm-blooded'. This I prefer to represent by a formula such as '$(\forall\varphi: \beta\varphi)(H\varphi)$', where '$\beta$' = 'mammal' and '$H$' = 'warm-blooded'. This, I think, is greatly preferable to a formula such as '$\forall\varphi(\beta\varphi \rightarrow H\varphi)$', which uses *unrestricted* quantification over secondary substances. In fairly plain English, the difference is, very roughly, between 'Any mammalian species is warm-blooded' and 'Any species, if it is mammalian, is warm-blooded'. But one problem with the latter formulation arises when we consider what sort of sentence qualifies as an *instance* of this sort of generalization. The sort of sentence that qualifies is one such as 'If (the species) mountain is mammalian, then it is warm-blooded' – or, more colloquially, 'If mountains are mammals, then they are warm-blooded' – which I would represent by a formula such as '$(\beta\gamma \rightarrow H\gamma)$', where '$\gamma$' = 'mountain'. The latter clearly *is* entailed by '$\forall\varphi(\beta\varphi \rightarrow H\varphi)$', by an application of the logical rule of universal instantiation. But the *antecedent* of 'If mountains are mammals, then they are warm-blooded' – 'Mountains are mammals' – is very hard to make any sense of. Indeed, it seems to constitute a *category* mistake: not, indeed, one involving the four *most basic* categories of the Aristotelian scheme, but one involving two different *sub*categories of secondary substances. Mammals (that is, mammalian *species*, such as the horse and the rabbit) belong to the subcategory of *biological* species, whereas mountains belong to the subcategory of *geological* species – and it apparently makes no sense even to entertain the 'thought' that mountains are mammals; that is, that a species of geological structure is a species of living organism. No such absurdity is entailed by my preferred formula, '$(\forall\varphi: \beta\varphi)(H\varphi)$'. This, *in conjunction with* a formula of the form '$\beta\gamma$', entails one of the form '$H\gamma$'. For instance, 'All (species of) mammals are warm-blooded' together with 'The horse is a (species of) mammal' entails 'The horse is warm-blooded'. But the additional premise here, 'The horse is a (species of) mammal', is evidently perfectly uncontentious and indeed just expresses an essential truth about horses.

I noted above in passing that I follow the convention of using $x, y, z, \ldots$ as variables ranging over primary substances and $\varphi, \chi, \psi, \ldots$ as variables ranging over secondary substances. For the sake of completeness, however, we need also variables ranging over *attributes* and *modes*.[11] But in saying

---

[11] Such variables are provided for in Table 3.1 of Chapter 3, but again it must be remarked that Table 1 of Chapter 3 employs different formation rules for constructing atomic sentences from those now being utilized.

62 *Reference and predication*

this we must be careful to remember that the latter are not *subjects* (that is, they are not *substances*, either primary or secondary). We can have *names* for them and *variables* ranging over them, but that should not lead us to treat them as quasi- or pseudo-substances, which is the implicit mistake of those philosophers and logicians who think that 'second-order' logic, by quantifying into predicate position, incurs ontological commitment to a new class of 'objects', over and above the 'first-order' objects that are the supposed values of 'first-order' variables. This, I think, is just a horrible ontological muddle on their part. *Properties*, in the form of both attributes (universal properties) and modes (particular properties), should certainly be accorded a place in any sensible ontology, but it is wrong to *reify* or *hypostatize* them. This is because they are essentially 'inherent' entities, always being 'in' a subject (substance) – or, as we might otherwise put it, always being only *aspects* of substances, or '*ways* substances are', never substances in their own right.

Note, incidentally, that the formal logical language sketched above is in fact only classifiable as a '*first*-order' language in the standard sense, despite the fact that it includes names for and variables ranging over properties, in the shape of both attributes and modes. This is because it does *not* involve 'quantification into predicate position' in the standard sense. (Moreover, in model-theoretic terms, it does not invoke a domain which includes *all subsets* of the domain of first-order objects quantified over by a standard first-order language and hence a domain whose cardinality is necessarily greater than that of the latter, even if there are infinitely many such first-order objects; a domain of quantification for a formalized language like mine could perfectly well include only a denumerable infinity of entities, so long as it included some entities belonging to each of the four basic ontological categories.) Now, the latter phenomenon – quantification into predicate position – is exemplified in a formula of so-called 'second-order' logic such as '$\exists F(Fa)$'. But, in standard predicate logic, the 'F' in 'Fa' is supposed to represent a *predicate*, understood as an 'incomplete' expression such as '– is white'. By contrast, 'Fa' in my formalization of Aristotelian categorial ontology serves to express the proposition that the attribute F(ness) inheres in, or is predicable of, the primary substance a. 'F' and 'a' here are thus to be thought of as two *terms*, each *naming* an entity belonging to a certain ontological category. In standard predicate logic, 'F' is not a *term* in this sense at all, since it doesn't serve to *name* any entity but just represents what remains of a complete predicative sentence when a name is removed from it – as, for example, '– is white' is what remains when the name 'Dobbin' is removed from the sentence 'Dobbin is white'.

Ontological categories and categorial predication 63

Another way to make this point is to say that, in the standard formalism, the 'F' in 'Fa' has an implicit 'is' of predication *built into it*, whereas in my formalism 'F' simply denotes a certain *attribute* and its predicability of a is represented formally not by a further symbol (although this could certainly be done), but rather by means of the post-positioning convention whereby 'a' is placed immediately after 'F'.

3 CATEGORIAL PREDICATION: ITS FORM, MEANING, AND USE

I come now properly to the most important topic of this chapter, *categorial predication*, for which the preceding two sections have provided a necessary preliminary. The system of formal logic whose language I have been constructing is meant to be one which respects and reflects certain fundamental categorial distinctions of an ontological nature. But now we have to consider how we can speak *explicitly* of such categorial distinctions, by extending the expressive power of our formalized language. So far, these categorial distinctions have been only *implicit* in the language, being embodied in our choice of *symbol* types and our ways of representing predication and inherence. A *categorial* statement, however, will be one which explicitly assigns some entity to a specific ontological category; and in our present system, of course, we have *four* such categories: those of *primary* and *secondary substance, attribute* and *mode*. (But we should again recall that these are just the *basic* categories of the system, which need by no means exclude further *sub*categories of these basic ones.)

So consider, for example, a statement such as 'Dobbin is a primary substance', or 'The horse is a secondary substance (species)'. On the face of it, the expression '– is a primary substance' is a *predicate*, which *says something* of Dobbin. (That, as we have seen, is at least the now standard conception of what a 'predicate' is.) But on our currently preferred *Aristotelian* view of predication, *predicables* are what are 'sayable' of subjects. So, does there exist a *predicable* that is said of Dobbin by the statement 'Dobbin is a primary substance'? If so, then that predicable will have to be either a *secondary substance* or else an *attribute*: for these and only these are things that may be 'said of' a subject. One suggestion, then, might be that there is a species (or, rather, a very high-level *genus*) – that of *primary substance* – which can be 'said of' Dobbin, very much as the species *horse* and the genus *mammal* can be 'said of' Dobbin. An alternative suggestion is that there is a highly abstract *attribute* – that of *being a primary substance* – which can be 'said of' Dobbin, very much as the attributes *being warm-blooded* and *being herbivorous* can be 'said of'

64 *Reference and predication*

Dobbin. But neither suggestion is preferable to the other and both are in fact unattractive (and perhaps even incoherent).[12]

The solution is to reject *both* suggestions. This, however, requires us to recognize a certain ambiguity in the notion of 'saying of' or predication. In one sense – the sense hitherto to the fore in our discussion of the Aristotelian system – the notion of predication is a *relational* one. In this sense, in predication *one* thing is 'said of' *another* thing, with each of these things belonging to an appropriate ontological category. For example, an *attribute* is said of a *substance*, either primary or secondary. Or a *secondary substance* is said of a *primary substance*. Or *one* secondary substance is said of *another* secondary substance. But then there is and must be another, *non*-relational notion of 'saying of' or predication, where this includes assigning an item to a certain ontological category. (Another plausible case is that of predicating *existence* of something, since it is highly doubtful that existence is properly conceived as a *property* or *attribute* of anything; if it were, then it ought to make sense to say that *existence exists*, and yet it scarcely does seem to make sense to say this.)

One characteristic of a statement involving categorial predication is that if it is 'formally correct', then it should be *necessarily true*. A perspicuous formalized language should respect this requirement. Suppose, thus, that we introduce the formal ontological predicates 'P', 'S', 'A' and 'M' into the formalized language that was developed in section 2. These are to express, respectively, the English predicates '– is a primary substance', '– is a secondary substance', '– is an attribute' and '– is a mode'. Then, to distinguish *categorial* predication from (what we might aptly call) *material* predication (which we have chosen to express by the device of post-positioning), let us use *superscription* for the former. Thus, for example, 'Dobbin is a primary substance' will be formalized as 'a^P', where 'a' represents 'Dobbin'. And then our point is that such a statement will be necessarily true if and only if it is *well formed*, as it is in this case: that is, it will be necessarily true if and only if the categorial superscript matches the symbol-type to which it is attached. In the present case, 'a' is a symbol for an individual or primary substance and hence matches the superscript 'P'. By contrast, a formula such as 'F^P', representing a statement such as 'Whiteness is a primary substance', is just *not well formed* in this system and hence *necessarily false*.

---

[12] Consider, thus, the proposal that 'primary substance' denotes a *genus* to which all primary substances belong. Then it turns out that, since all genera belong to the category of *secondary* substance, the sentence 'Primary substance is a secondary substance' must be in some sense true. But I find it very hard to make any clear sense of this.

Ontological categories and categorial predication 65

But how, it might now be asked, could there be any real *use* for such statements of categorial predication, given that the categorial distinctions are already built into the symbolism of the formalized language (as they are not, perhaps, in a natural language such as English)? The answer is that we want our language to be capable of talking about *pure ontology*. For that, we need also names and variables which are *categorially neutral*, in order to say things such as 'Every primary substance has at least one mode inherent in it'. Thus, using 'e' (for 'entity') as a new type of ontologically neutral variable, we could express the last-mentioned sentence formally in this manner: '$\forall e_1(e_1{}^P \rightarrow \exists e_2(e_2{}^M \ \& \ e_1e_2))$'. (Here we are using unrestricted quantifiers, of course, and the proposal would be that these are *only* to be used in statements of pure ontology; note also that, in the formula just stated, 'e_1e_2' must be construed as expressing *inherence* rather than predication, given the formation rules and the typing of e_1 and e_2 as P and M respectively.) Statements of pure ontology would all be like this and in this way we could envisage the construction of a formal, axiomatizable *theory* of pure ontology, which would constitute an a priori science analogous to various branches of pure mathematics. In the formal theory of pure ontology, no *specific* entity of any category would be referred to, such as *Dobbin* or *whiteness*: all statements would concern the categories themselves and relationships obtaining between their members purely in virtue of their categorial status, as in the case of the sample statement cited above. Of course, for present purposes I am assuming that the 'correct' formal theory of pure ontology will be a characteristically 'Aristotelian' one, of the kind sketched earlier. But that assumption is not vital to the notion of pure ontology as such. Indeed, one can envisage alternative (or even just *different*) systems of pure ontology, just as there are different branches of pure mathematics. (Some systems of ontology, for instance, include the basic category of *event*, whereas in the 'Aristotelian' ontology there is no room for such entities save in the guise, perhaps, of modes of primary substances.) However, one should not take the analogy with pure mathematics too far, since the latter consists of theories which do make reference to *specific* entities of certain types, such as the natural numbers, whereas pure ontology is perfectly general or 'topic-neutral' in its subject matter.

To repeat an earlier point of great importance, categorial predications are – as Wittgenstein might at one time have remarked – true, when they are true, simply in virtue of their 'logical grammar'. Thus, 'a^P' can be seen to be true simply by inspection of its logical form. In that sense, such a truth has and requires no 'truthmaker', if by a 'truthmaker' we mean some *entity* which, by existing, *makes* it true. 'a^P' doesn't even require the existence of the primary or individual substance a to make it true: thus, 'Dobbin is a primary substance' can be known to be a true – indeed, a *necessarily* true – categorial predication *whether or not* Dobbin is known to exist. I do want to allow, of course, that from 'a^P' we may validly infer '$\exists e(e^P \ \& \ e = a)$', and vice versa. Thus, I am happy to allow that 'Some primary substance is (identical with) Dobbin' is just a long-winded way of saying 'Dobbin is a primary substance'. But recall that I am rejecting the claim that 'Some primary substance is (identical with) Dobbin' is logically equivalent to 'Dobbin *exists* and is a primary substance' or, more generally, that '$\exists e(e^P \ \& \ e = a)$' is logically equivalent to '(E!a & a^P)'. Dobbin's existing is no doubt logically equivalent to some *existing* primary substance's being (identical with) Dobbin, but not just to *Dobbin's being a primary substance*, since the latter is just an a priori truth arising from an ontological necessity concerning the correct ontological categorization of any such item as Dobbin is *conceived* to be, whether or not Dobbin actually *exists*.

PART II
Identity

CHAPTER 5

What is a criterion of identity?

In Chapter 2, I made extensive appeal to the notion of a *criterion of identity*, in connection with our ability to individuate and refer to particular objects both at a time and across time. However, the complaint is often heard that, while the phrase 'criterion of identity' is frequently *used* in contemporary philosophical writings, relatively rarely is any attempt made to spell out its intended meaning at all precisely, or to defend the cogency of the notion that it is supposed to convey.[1] There may also seem to be a suspicious dearth of specific and plausible *examples* of such criteria in the literature. Since, as I have already made clear, I consider the notion of a criterion of identity to be a vitally important one, both for the philosophy of logic and language and for metaphysics, I want, in this chapter, to try to dispel some of the obscurity and to allay some of the suspicions that have beset this notion.[2] Two particularly important issues that I shall address are these: first, in stating a criterion of identity for individuals of a given sort, is it legitimate to quantify over a domain including precisely individuals *of that sort*? In short, are 'impredicative' criteria of identity acceptable? And, second, must it be the case that criteria of identity for at least *some* sorts of individuals can be stated, at least in principle, in terms which involve neither reference to nor quantification over individuals of *any* sort? The thought behind a positive answer to this second question would be that putative criteria of this kind are needed to underpin our most primitive

---

[1] See, for example, P. F. Strawson, 'Entity and Identity', in H. D. Lewis (ed.), *Contemporary British Philosophy, Fourth Series* (London: George Allen and Unwin, 1976), reprinted in his *Entity and Identity and Other Essays* (Oxford: Clarendon Press, 1997).

[2] In this chapter, I shall in part – but only in part – be covering the same territory as I did earlier in Chapter 2. But here I shall be approaching the notion of a criterion of identity with much greater emphasis on its history and its logical involvements, thereby extensively supplementing the characterization of this notion that I provided in Chapter 2, with a view to making its philosophical credentials more secure. Another important difference between the present chapter and Chapter 2 is that, in the present chapter, I lay no emphasis, as I did in Chapter 2, on the distinction between *sortal* and *categorial* terms, focusing here almost exclusively on the former.

69

70 *Identity*

acts of reference to individuals and thus ultimately ground our very understanding of the notions of individuality and reference. My answers to these two questions will be 'yes' and 'no' respectively.

I should mention that my discussion of criteria of identity in this chapter will keep a much closer eye on the history of this topic than was the case in Chapter 2, as well as looking in much more depth at certain logical problems to which the notion of a criterion of identity appears to give rise, including questions concerning the *logical form* of such criteria, which has certainly been subject to much debate.

I THE FREGEAN THESIS

Gottlob Frege is usually given credit for introducing the notion of a criterion of identity into philosophical discourse, on the strength of certain sections of the *Grundlagen*.[3] My own feeling is that this accolade – while warranted in regard to terminology – fails to do justice to John Locke, who grasped the key point that that in which identity 'consists' for things of one sort (say, parcels of matter) may not be the same as that in which it 'consists' for things of another sort (say, living organisms).[4] What assuredly *can* be credited to Frege, however, are *first* a certain very general thesis apparently tying the sense of any singular term to a criterion of identity, and *second* one very specific and frequently exploited example of such a criterion. In fact, though, both the scope of the thesis and the significance of the example are open to debate.

Frege's general thesis – to which I shall hereafter refer as the 'Fregean thesis' – is framed by him in the following words:

If we are to use the symbol *a* to signify an object, we must have a criterion for deciding in all cases whether *b* is the same as *a*, even if it is not always in our power to apply this criterion.[5]

---

[3] See Gottlob Frege, *Die Grundlagen der Arithmetik* (1884), translated as *The Foundations of Arithmetic* by J. L. Austin (Oxford: Blackwell, 1953), §§62 ff. The implication in question may be found in Michael Dummett, *Frege: Philosophy of Language*, 2nd edn (London: Duckworth, 1981), pp. 73 and 545.

[4] See John Locke, *An Essay Concerning Human Understanding*, ed. P. H. Nidditch (Oxford: Clarendon Press, 1975), II, XXVII. 'Consist' is Locke's own choice of word: see §9.

[5] Frege, *The Foundations of Arithmetic*, §62. The word which Austin translates as 'criterion' is *Kennzeichen*. By contrast, Ludwig Wittgenstein uses the word *Kriterium* throughout the *Philosophical Investigations*, which may cast some doubt on the close affinity mooted by Dummett in *Frege: Philosophy of Language*, p. 73. Of course, precisely what Wittgenstein himself meant by 'criterion' is the subject of a vast secondary literature, to which I have no wish to contribute here.

What is a criterion of identity? 71

The reason why I say that the intended scope of this thesis is debatable is that §62 of the *Grundlagen*, in which it appears, is the first of a group of sections introduced by the heading 'To obtain the concept of Number, we must first fix the sense of a numerical identity', and §62 itself opens with the question 'How, then, are numbers to be given to us, if we cannot have any ideas or intuitions of them?' – all of which might suggest that the thesis in question is intended to be restricted to symbols used to signify *abstract* rather than concrete, perceptible objects. One commentator who certainly does *not* interpret the intended scope of the thesis in this narrow way, however, is Michael Dummett, who expressly regards it as intended to apply to *all* significant singular terms, and indeed endorses the thesis under this liberal interpretation.[6]

2 FREGE'S EXAMPLE OF DIRECTIONS AND PARALLELISM

Before examining the content and merits of the Fregean thesis, we need to look at the oft-cited illustrative example of a criterion of identity that Frege deploys – the example concerning parallelism and the directions of lines. In §64, Frege remarks,

> The judgement 'line *a* is parallel to line *b*' . . . can be taken as an identity. If we do this, we obtain the concept of a direction, and say: 'the direction of line *a* is identical with the direction of line *b*'.

What Frege appears to be suggesting, in the light of the general thesis just enunciated by him, is that in order to use an expression of the form 'the direction of line *a*' to refer to an *object* (a *direction*), we need at least to supply a logically necessary and sufficient condition for the truth of identity statements in which such expressions flank both sides of the identity sign – a condition which, moreover, can be expressed without reference (either explicit or implicit) to *directions*. He is further saying that just such a condition can be specified in terms of the *parallelism* of the lines whose directions are to be identified. Generalizing, this provides us with the following model of a criterion of identity, where '$f()$' is a functional expression, 'x' and 'y' are individual variables, and 'R' expresses a certain equivalence relation defined over the domain to which the values of those variables belong:

(A) $\forall x \forall y (f(x) = f(y) \leftrightarrow Rxy)$

---

[6] See Dummett, *Frege: Philosophy of Language*, pp. 73 ff. and 545 ff.

72   *Identity*

Now, one problem with this model is that it seems to be applicable only in the case of a special class of singular terms – those formed by means of functional expressions like 'the direction of'. (Other examples might be 'the shape of' and 'the colour of', the former indeed being explicitly mentioned by Frege himself.) Proper names, strictly so called, clearly do not belong to this class – for example, 'London' and 'Napoleon'. Neither do certain other sorts of singular terms, such as personal pronouns. Surprisingly, however, this has not prevented some writers from trying to force all criteria of identity into the mould of Frege's example, even though it is not clear that Frege himself would have endorsed this. An instance of this approach may be found in a paper by Timothy Williamson.[7] Thus we find Williamson supposing that the form of a criterion of *personal* identity is to be extracted from the schema (A) by allowing the variables 'x' and 'y' to range over *person-stages* and stipulating that '$f(x)$' means 'the person of whom x is a stage'. But what reason at all have we to suppose that persons must be like directions in being objects to which we need (primarily, at least) to refer by means of functional expressions? Directions are, if you will, *essentially* directions *of* something – in Frege's treatment, they are directions of *lines*. But persons are not – or, at any rate, are not at all obviously – essentially persons *of* anything at all. Indeed, the supposed parallel between 'the direction of line x' and 'the person of whom x is a stage' seems entirely spurious, even if one countenances – as I do not – such objects as 'person-stages'. For an expression of the latter form is, on the contrary, more naturally assimilable to one such as 'the line of which x is the direction'. In short, what is being overlooked is a certain *order of ontological dependency* seemingly implicit in Frege's discussion of the example of directions: the parallelism of lines can provide a criterion of identity for the *directions* of lines only because directions are ontologically – and indeed conceptually – dependent on lines, in a way in which lines are not on directions.[8] But this immediately raises a difficulty for anyone seeking to extend schema (A) to names of what we might, in an Aristotelian vein, call (primary) *substances*, since these – assuming them to

---

[7] See Timothy Williamson, 'Criteria of Identity and the Axiom of Choice', *Journal of Philosophy* 83 (1986), pp. 380–94.

[8] This might perhaps be questioned, at least when directions are thought of in a perceptual, subject-centred way (as when one compares the directions of two objects as seen from a certain location). Obviously, however, Frege is not thinking of directions in this sense. But, in any case, the real issue is not whether Frege was right about directions but whether the account that he gives of them, right or wrong, can legitimately be extended to objects such as persons.

What is a criterion of identity? 73

exist – are precisely objects standing in no such relationship of ontological dependency with other objects.[9]

3 A RETURN TO THE FREGEAN THESIS

Having seen something of the limitations of Frege's best-known example of a criterion of identity, we may return to the general Fregean thesis that a singular term can be significantly employed only in association with some criterion of identity – where by a 'criterion of identity' let us not, on account of the limitations just adverted to, presume exclusively to mean a principle conforming to schema (A) above, but merely, as Frege himself puts it, a rule 'for deciding in all cases whether *b* is the same as *a*', where '*a*' and '*b*' are certain singular terms.

Unfortunately, this looser and more informal characterization of a criterion of identity threatens to be altogether *too* liberal. Thus it is likely to be objected that, understood in this light, the Fregean thesis is almost trivially true, since it may be urged that Leibniz's principle of the identity of indiscernibles provides just such a rule – and provides it for all singular terms, quite irrespective of their logical form and of the nature of the objects that they designate.[10] However, whatever else emerges from Frege's discussion of criteria of identity, it does at least emerge that such criteria, as *he* understands them, certainly *are* to be conceived of as very often differing for singular terms designating objects of different sorts, and most importantly are expected to cast light on the meaning of certain *general* terms describing those objects – general terms such as 'number', 'direction', and 'shape'. This is a feature of Frege's treatment which I shall explore more thoroughly a little later.

Now, this semantic connection between singular and general terms is evident in the case of the examples expressly discussed by Frege, because in their case a species of singular term is explicitly formed with the aid of a general term – for example, 'the direction of line *x*' with the aid of the general term 'direction'. When the Fregean thesis is advanced as applying *universally* to singular terms, however, the connection must be assumed in

---

[9] For more on this conception of substance, see my *The Possibility of Metaphysics: Substance, Identity, and Time* (Oxford: Clarendon Press, 1998), Chapter 6.

[10] Baruch Brody argues along very much these lines in his *Identity and Essence* (Princeton University Press, 1980), Chapters 1–3. Brody contends that Leibniz's principle (coupled with the standard logical axioms of identity) provides all that we could need by way of a criterion of identity, and accordingly dismisses attempts to frame distinctive identity criteria for different sorts of things. Naturally, I regard this contention as being entirely misconceived, for reasons which will become plain.

74　　　　　　　　　　　　　　　　*Identity*

many cases to be only implicit. Thus adherents of the full-blown thesis will typically urge, say, that the proper name 'Napoleon' is semantically linked to the sense of the general term 'man' (or perhaps 'person') – the linkage being provided precisely by the *criterion of identity* associated with the proper name 'Napoleon', this also being associated with the use of all other singular terms designating individual men. And – to complete the picture – a *sortal* or *substantival* general term will be precisely one which, like 'man', has thus associated with it, as indeed a component of its very sense, some unique *criterion of identity* for the use of singular terms designating objects describable by that general term. By contrast, an *adjectival* general term – to use P. T. Geach's terminology – will be one which, like 'red thing', supplies *no* criterion of identity for instances falling under it.[11]

All of this suggests another general formulation of the notion of a criterion of identity which is at once less limiting than that provided by schema (A) and more specific than the loose and informal characterization quoted earlier from Frege – a formulation which makes quite explicit the *sortal relativity* of identity criteria. This is, moreover, a formulation which has in fact found a certain amount of favour in the literature. According to this school of thought, the general form that a criterion of identity will take is the following:[12]

(B) $\forall x \forall y ((\varphi x \ \& \ \varphi y) \rightarrow (x = y \leftrightarrow Rxy))$

where 'φ' is a general term of the sortal or substantival variety and 'R' again expresses a certain equivalence relation.[13] A paradigm example of a criterion of identity conforming to this schema is provided by the axiom of extensionality of set theory: for the latter may be taken as telling us that if x and y are *sets*, then x is identical with y if and only if x and y *have the same members*. Of course, sets are once again *abstract* objects, like directions, and

---

[11] The expressions 'substantival' and 'adjectival', used in this way, are introduced by P. T. Geach – in emulation of Aquinas – in his *Reference and Generality*, 3rd edn (Ithaca, NY: Cornell University Press, 1980), p. 63. In similar vein, P. F. Strawson distinguishes between what he calls *sortal* and *characterizing* universals: see his *Individuals: An Essay in Descriptive Metaphysics* (London: Methuen, 1959), p. 168.

[12] In Chapter 2, I adopted the convention of subscripting 'R' with the sortal symbol 'φ', to emphasize the fact that different sortals are very often associated with different criterial relations. Here I shall take that point for granted.

[13] In what follows, I shall speak of 'type-(A)' and 'type-(B)' identity criteria. It has, however, now become customary to use the terms 'two-level identity criterion' and 'one-level identity criterion' for this purpose: for further discussion, see my 'One-Level versus Two-Level Identity Criteria', *Analysis* 51 (1991), pp. 192–4. I shall avoid this terminology here because I think that it is potentially misleading in certain ways.

What is a criterion of identity? 75

this may prompt some doubts about the possibility of formulating criteria of identity in the mould of schema (B) that are applicable to *concrete* objects, such as *men*. But that (B) is an advance on (A) is suggested by the fact that, whilst we can apparently recast Frege's criterion of identity for directions along the lines of schema (B) – by saying that if x and y are directions, then x is identical with y if and only if x and y are directions of lines that are parallel[14] – we cannot, it seems, similarly recast the foregoing criterion of identity for sets along the lines of schema (A). (We can of course say, along these lines, such things as that the set of which x is the sole member is identical with the set of which y is the sole member if and only if x is identical with y: but that, obviously, does not take us very far.) Even so, the superiority of schema (B) is perhaps not altogether clear-cut, because when Frege's criterion of identity for directions *is* recast along the lines of schema (B), it is no longer the case that the logically necessary and sufficient condition for the identity of directions is expressed without reference to – or, more accurately, without quantification over – *directions*. This is a point to which I shall return later in more general terms, when we look into the question whether this feature of type-(B) criteria of identity is a fatal defect in them. To anticipate my eventual conclusion, I do not think that it is.

4 TYPE-(B) IDENTITY CRITERIA AND THE PROBLEM OF CIRCULARITY

Now, can we plausibly specify criteria of identity conforming to schema (B) in which the general term 'φ' describes objects of some *concrete*, as opposed to *abstract*, sort or kind – such as men, trees, or ships, as opposed to numbers, sets, or directions? (Precisely how to define the concrete/abstract distinction is not at all easy, but it will suffice here to take concrete objects to be ones which are, at least in principle, perceptible and ostendible.[15]) Many philosophers are quite sanguine about this possibility, myself included – although some seem to think that the task is rather easier than I do. One philosopher who is clearly committed to the possibility is

---

[14] How, precisely, one might express this reformulated criterion in logical notation is a matter for some debate, but one obvious option is the following: $\forall x \forall y ((\text{direction}(x)\ \&\ \text{direction}(y)) \rightarrow (x = y \leftrightarrow \exists w \exists z (\text{line}(w)\ \&\ \text{line}(z)\ \&\ \text{of}(x, w)\ \&\ \text{of}(y, z)\ \&\ \text{parallel}(w, z))))$, where 'of' expresses the relation between a direction and a line that obtains when the former is the direction of the latter – so that the 'of' relation is the converse of the relation between a line and a direction that obtains when the former 'has' the latter.

[15] I say much more about the concrete/abstract distinction in my 'The Metaphysics of Abstract Objects', *Journal of Philosophy* 92 (1995), pp. 509–24.

76   *Identity*

Donald Davidson, whose well-known criterion of identity for *events* is quite clearly formulated along the lines of schema (B). According to Davidson, if *x* and *y* are *events*, then *x* is identical with *y* if and only if *x* and *y have the same causes and effects.*[16] The analogy between this and the criterion of identity for sets stated earlier seems quite obvious. And yet there is in fact an important *dis*analogy between the two which is, in my view, fatal to Davidson's proposal.

Briefly, the problem is this. For Davidson, causes and effects are *themselves* events, so that in making critical for the identity of events the sameness of their causes and effects, Davidson is apparently involved in a vicious circularity.[17] No such circularity is involved in the criterion of identity for sets stated earlier, since that only made the sameness of their *members* critical for the identity of sets – and, while sets may themselves be members of sets, so too may objects which are *not* sets (except, of course, in so-called 'pure' set theory of the Zermelo–Fraenkel (ZF) type, about which I shall say more in a moment). Moreover, where sets *do* have sets as members, it will at least ultimately be possible (by repeated applications of the criterion) to settle a question of set identity by reference to the identity of set-members which are *not* themselves sets – assuming, at least, the truth of the axiom of regularity (otherwise known as the *Axiom der Fundierung*). Even in 'pure' ZF set theory, the criterion will serve the same purpose, because it serves to ensure that there is just *one* empty set at the base of the hierarchy of sets. But observe here that a similar defence of Davidson's criterion of event identity is not available: first, because there is no reason to suppose that there is precisely one uncaused event and, second, because there is no reason to think that anything corresponds in the case of events to the hierarchy of sets. In short, what is lacking is an axiomatic *theory of events* providing for Davidson's criterion the sort of framework that axiomatic set theory provides for our criterion of set identity.[18]

---

[16] See Donald Davidson, 'The Individuation of Events', in his *Essays on Actions and Events* (Oxford: Clarendon Press, 1980), p. 179. Later, Davidson withdrew his support for this criterion in response to some criticisms by W. V. Quine: see his reply to Quine in Ernest LePore and Brian McLaughlin (eds.), *Actions and Events: Perspectives on the Philosophy of Donald Davidson* (Oxford: Blackwell, 1985); and, for further discussion, my *A Survey of Metaphysics* (Oxford University Press, 2002), pp. 224–8.

[17] Davidson denies that there is any *formal* circularity in his proposed criterion. And that is certainly correct if we state the criterion as follows: $\forall x \forall y ((\text{event}(x) \,\&\, \text{event}(y)) \rightarrow (x = y \leftrightarrow (\forall z (\text{cause}(z, x) \leftrightarrow \text{cause}(z, y)) \,\&\, \forall z (\text{effect}(z, x) \leftrightarrow \text{effect}(z, y)))))$. But – as we shall soon see – this is not to the point. A criticism similar to mine is developed by J. E. Tiles in his *Things that Happen* (Aberdeen University Press, 1981), pp. 1 ff.

[18] See further my 'Impredicative Identity Criteria and Davidson's Criterion of Event Identity', *Analysis* 49 (1989), pp. 178–81.

What is a criterion of identity? 77

Perhaps the point against Davidson can be made more graphically by saying that the set-theoretical principle which is more truly analogous to his proposed criterion of event identity is the principle that if x and y are sets, then x is identical with y if and only if x and y *include exactly the same sets* – which is an undoubtedly valid principle, since every set includes itself (that is, has itself as a subset) and mutually inclusive sets are identical. Now, the latter principle will patently *not* serve as a criterion of identity for sets, precisely because it transparently already *presupposes* an account of the identity conditions of sets. The corresponding presupposition in Davidson's proposed criterion is not perhaps quite so transparent as this, but emerges once it is noted that to say that x and y have the same causes and effects is – for Davidson, at least, since the only notion of causation that he admits is that of event causation – just to say that *the same events* are causes of both x and y and that *the same events* are effects of both x and y.

The important lesson to issue from this, then, is that, in formulating a criterion of identity in conformity with schema (B), the greatest care must be taken not to *presuppose* already, in framing the criterial relation R, an account of φ identity, where 'φ' is the general term whose associated criterion of identity is being sought. The problem is that such a presupposition may be buried fairly deeply, so that no *explicit* or *formal* circularity can be discerned in the statement of the proposed criterion. However, the next question that we need to address is whether such a presupposition might somehow be built into the *very nature* of any type-(B) identity criterion, with fatal consequences for all criteria of that type.

5 DO TYPE-(B) IDENTITY CRITERIA NECESSARILY FALL PREY TO A CIRCULARITY PROBLEM?

I raise this question because I anticipate at this stage an objection along the following lines, which picks up a point touched upon earlier. I have urged – or so it might seem – that a criterion of identity for φs formulated on the model of schema (B) should not be such that the condition expressed on the right-hand side of the biconditional, of the form 'Rxy', already presupposes for its interpretation an account of φ identity.[19] But it may be objected against me – and indeed against schema (B) as a model of identity

---

[19] In point of fact – and this is crucial – I have *not* urged precisely this: I have urged only that the criterial *relation*, R, should not presuppose an account of φ identity, not that the criterial *condition*, Rxy, should be (fully) interpretable independently of a grasp of φ identity. The significance of this distinction will emerge shortly.

78   *Identity*

criteria quite generally – that there will *inevitably* be just such a presupposition, precisely insofar that, in order to interpret the expression '*Rxy*', we shall need to be in a position to *identify individual φs as the values of the variables 'x' and 'y'*. We are returning then to the point acknowledged earlier, that type-(B) criteria of identity carry *reference* to φs – or, more accurately, involve quantification over φs – in their expression of the criterial condition for φ identity. And the crucial question is: *does this matter?*

To make the matter more specific, suppose that we are attempting to formulate a criterion of identity for *men* and that, having framed one along the lines of schema (B), we go on to try to apply our criterion in a particular instance involving the use of two singular terms – as it might be, 'Napoleon' and 'Bonaparte'. According to our criterion, we purport to know that if *a* and *b* are *men*, then *a* is identical with *b* if and only if *a* stands to *b* in the criterial relation *R* (whatever that might be). But, it may be objected, unless we already *understand* the use of the singular terms '*a*' and '*b*' – and thereby grasp whatever criterion of identity it is that governs that use, in accordance with the Fregean thesis – we cannot be in a position to assess the truth or falsehood of the proposition that *a* stands to *b* in the relation *R*. Hence our alleged criterion of identity cannot in fact be correct, since our very capacity to understand and apply it already *presupposes* a grasp of whatever criterion of identity it is that governs the use of a singular term to refer to an individual man.

6 WHAT IS THE PRIMARY PURPOSE OF A CRITERION OF IDENTITY?

In order to defend schema (B) against this sort of objection, we need to examine more searchingly just what purpose a criterion of identity should be expected to serve. What kind of semantic information is such a criterion supposed, primarily, to convey? Information about the sense of a singular term belonging to a certain class, or information about the sense of a certain general term? From Frege's remarks in the *Grundlagen*, one might initially suppose the former, though I think that in fact, even by his account, the latter is more properly true. Of course, the two kinds of information are not independent: what is at issue, however, is a question of priority.

Let us return to Frege's example concerning directions. We are told that the identity statement 'The direction of line *a* is identical with the direction of line *b*' is to be understood as being logically equivalent to 'Line *a* is

What is a criterion of identity?   79

parallel to line b – and this is presented, ostensibly, as conveying semantic information about the use of a singular term of the form 'the direction of line x'. Yet it is clear from the context of Frege's remarks that his primary aim is to cast light on the meaning of the *general* term 'direction'. For what he is doing in these sections of the *Grundlagen* is casting about for a way of defining the concept of *number*, and using the concept of *direction* as a heuristic aid in his search. What he is specifically investigating is the possibility of defining 'number' *contextually* by laying down a definitional equivalent to the proposition 'The number which belongs to the concept F is the same as that which belongs to the concept G'. In fact, he subsequently makes it clear that such an approach is inadequate, because it fails to help to determine the truth conditions of various other sorts of propositions whose expression may involve the use of the general term 'number'. But this is not to say that genuine and useful semantic information concerning the concept of *number* or *direction* is not, after all, conveyed by laying down a criterion of identity for numbers or directions: plainly, indeed, *it is*, even if the information falls short of providing a complete explication of the concept in question.

Now, to the extent that a criterion of identity for directions conveys vital semantic information concerning the general term 'direction', it *also* conveys vital semantic information concerning any singular term of the form 'the direction of line x', simply because the sense of the general term is a component of the sense of any such singular term. Could it be, then, that what Frege meant by his key thesis – that 'if we are to use the symbol a to signify an object, we must have a criterion for deciding in all cases whether b is the same as a' – was effectively no more than this: that when a singular term is formed with the aid of a sortal or substantival general term, then simply *because* (as it may be supposed) a component of the sense of the latter is a certain criterion of identity, that criterion must be grasped in order to understand the correct application of the singular term? If so, then it is not *obvious* that the thesis is intended to extend to singular terms not formed in this way, such as proper names strictly so called – although this conclusion can, of course, be reached if it is conceded, as many self-styled 'Fregeans' would doubtless willingly concede, that the sense of any proper name incorporates that of some sortal or substantival general term.

Seen in this light, the Fregean thesis is primarily one concerning the semantics of a certain category of general terms – sortal or substantival general terms – although it has implications also for the semantics of singular terms just to the extent that such terms incorporate as a component of their sense, either explicitly or implicitly, the sense of some sortal

80   *Identity*

term. That *all* singular terms in fact meet this condition is a plausible view. Singular terms such as 'the direction of line *a*', and indeed 'line *a*', do so quite explicitly, as does one such as 'the man standing next to me'. And proper names arguably do so implicitly, since we are standardly introduced to their correct use either with the aid of singular terms of the previous sort – as when one is told 'John Smith is the man standing next to me' – or else with the aid of demonstratives used in conjunction with sortal terms, as when one is told 'That man is John Smith'.[20] In short, it is plausible to claim that reference to individuals is only ever secured through the application of general concepts of the sortal or substantival variety.

7 IN DEFENCE OF TYPE-(B) IDENTITY CRITERIA

Now, what bearing does all of this have on the objection raised earlier to criteria of identity formulated in conformity with schema (B)? The objection turned on the fact that, in a type-(B) criterion of φ identity, reference to individual φs – or, at least, quantification over them – is not excluded from the expression of the criterial condition on the right-hand side of the biconditional. And it was observed that no such complaint could be raised against type-(A) criteria, of which Frege's own criterion of identity for directions is an instance. One question that we must therefore address is this: was it important for Frege's purposes that *no reference be made to directions* in stating the criterial condition for the identity of directions? And if so, why? The answer is that initially it *was* important, because initially Frege was holding out the hope that a *complete definition* of the concept of *direction* might be supplied contextually by the provision of a criterion of identity for directions. Now, obviously, in a definition, the *definiendum* must not be included in the *definiens*, so that it was at least important for *Frege* at this point that the term 'direction' should not appear on the right-hand side of the biconditional. And this term *would* apparently have to appear there if explicit reference to directions were to be

---

[20] This is *not* to imply that a proper name thus introduced acquires for the auditor just the sense of the singular term through whose aid the introduction is made – that, for example, 'John Smith' acquires for the auditor the same sense as 'the man standing next to the speaker'. The most that is being suggested is that the auditor, if he is to grasp the correct use of the proper name thus introduced, must grasp that a *component* of its sense is that of the *general* term which features in the singular term through whose aid the introduction is made – that, for example, 'John Smith' incorporates in its sense the sense of the general term 'man'. We shall see later that provision must also be made for the introduction of proper names by means of simple demonstratives unattached to sortal terms – although, at the same time, we shall see that this does not materially affect the view of proper names being advocated here.

What is a criterion of identity? 81

made on the right-hand side of the biconditional, given that the canonical way to refer to a direction is by means of a singular term of the form 'the direction of line x'. But, furthermore, it should be evident that, even if such explicit use of the term 'direction' were to be avoided, a circularity fatal to Frege's proposed contextual definition would still be present even by virtue of any unavoidable *quantification* over directions on the right-hand side of the biconditional – because an understanding of the definition would then still presuppose a grasp of the very concept supposedly being defined.

However, here we must remember that Frege in fact goes on to *reject* the suggestion that a contextual definition of the concept of direction can be supplied by the provision of a criterion of identity for directions, for reasons mentioned earlier. These reasons make it clear that this approach *cannot* provide for a *complete* definition of 'direction', even though such a criterion will convey *partial* semantic information concerning the concept of direction. But since the hope that a criterion of identity for directions might supply a complete definition of the concept of direction has now been given up, the rationale behind the requirement that such a criterion should make no reference to and involve no quantification over *directions* on the right-hand side of the biconditional has disappeared. Hence the apparent advantage of type-(A) criteria over type-(B) criteria has vanished. Furthermore, it is clear that the unnecessarily stringent requirement satisfied by type-(A) criteria is precisely the source of their limitations observed earlier. Such criteria are available only in the case of sorts of objects, such as directions, to which reference may often be eliminated in favour of reference to objects of *other* sorts, upon which they are ontologically dependent – and hence not in the case of objects of an ontologically independent sort.

But, if all of this is so, what becomes of my earlier criticism of Davidson's criterion of event identity on the grounds of its circularity? That objection still stands, because what was being objected to was not merely the reference to, or quantification over, *events* in the expression of the criterial condition for event identity, but rather the fact that the very criterial relation R invoked in that condition is itself specified *in terms involving event identity*. It may well be that reference to, or quantification over, events is ineliminable in this context, but that is no reason to suppose that the identity conditions of events can only be expressed in terms making appeal to *the identity or diversity of events* related to them in certain ways – any more than the corresponding thing follows in the case of sets. I conclude, then, that type-(B) criteria of identity can be absolved from any

82   *Identity*

general charge of vicious circularity, even though Davidson's particular proposal cannot be thus absolved.

It may be felt, however, that I have still not adequately tackled the challenge to type-(B) identity criteria posed in section 5 above, particularly as illustrated in the second paragraph of that section. There it was urged, on behalf of an objector, that unless we already *understand* the use of certain singular terms, '*a*' and '*b*', and thereby grasp whatever criterion of identity it is that governs that use, we cannot be in a position to assess the truth or falsehood of the proposition that *a* stands to *b* in the alleged criterial relation *R* – and hence that our very capacity to understand and apply a type-(B) principle already presupposes a grasp of the relevant criterion of identity, which cannot therefore be expressed by that principle. To this I would reply that it is a misconception to suppose that a criterion of identity is a principle whose primary purpose is that of being invoked to settle particular questions of identity or diversity concerning individuals. Such a criterion is not – at least as I understand the notion of an identity criterion, and, I believe, as Frege did also – an *epistemic* or *heuristic* principle for the discovery of particular truths of identity. (That Frege thought likewise is suggested by his remark, quoted earlier from §62 of the *Grundlagen*, that it need not always be in our power to *apply* a criterion of identity.) Rather, as I have tried to explain, criteria of identity are primarily *semantic* principles – albeit ones with important metaphysical implications – whose grasp is essential to a proper understanding of general terms of a certain kind, namely sortal or substantival general terms. I can concede that, in view of this, 'criterion' is perhaps not the most apt term for such a principle, but its use has unfortunately become entrenched and indeed partly reflects the prevalence of confusion on this score. The crucial point, then, is that what a type-(B) criterion of identity is intended to convey – namely an aspect of the sense of a certain sortal term – can be sufficiently grasped by a person *not* already equipped to deploy singular terms governed by that criterion, provided at least that this person understands *in general* what it is to make singular reference to or to quantify over individuals. This proviso and its implications will be our next topic for discussion.

8 CAN THE FREGEAN THESIS HOLD WITH COMPLETE
UNIVERSALITY?

A question which now becomes pressing is this: if we are to settle upon schema (B) as providing the canonical form of a criterion of identity, can we simultaneously endorse the Fregean thesis as holding quite universally for *all* singular terms? That is to say – and assuming that all singular terms

What is a criterion of identity? 83

incorporate in their sense the sense of some sortal or substantival general term – can it be the case that *every* such general term has associated with it, as a component of its very sense, some unique criterion of identity that can be formulated in accordance with schema (B)? Of course, we might seek to make this true by definition, by stipulating that only a general term meeting this condition qualifies as a *sortal*. But that would only serve to obscure what is in fact an interesting and difficult question – namely whether there are any general concepts which we apply by individuating and identifying particulars as falling under them and yet which are such that this application is entirely *criterionless*. The question is not the merely superficial one of whether we are always *aware* of employing criteria of identity in our application of certain general terms for these purposes, but rather the deeper one of whether there always *exist* such criteria whose – perhaps only implicit – employment by a subject can always in principle be elicited. We shall see shortly that empirical psychological findings are certainly relevant to this question.

Now, it is at least *arguable* that there are and must be 'criterionless' sortals and hence that the Fregean thesis does not hold with complete universality – not, at least, when a criterion of identity is understood as a principle conforming to schema (B). One line of argument for this would be the following. A criterion of identity conforming to schema (B) can, clearly, only be grasped by someone who at least understands what it is *in general* to make singular reference to particular objects, because such a criterion employs the apparatus of quantification with individual variables. Therefore – it may be urged – a grasp of such a criterion cannot be a requirement of *every* significant use of a singular term to refer to a particular object. For, it may be said, what acquiring a grasp of a criterion of identity for φs does is to help to confer, upon someone who previously lacked it, an ability to make singular reference to particular φs. And this it does by helping to confer upon that person an understanding of that general concept of a φ that is incorporated in the sense of any singular term capable of being used to refer to a particular φ.[21] But, it may be maintained, only someone *already conversant* with the practice of singular reference to objects of *some* sort is in a position to be helped in this way to

---

[21] This is a slight oversimplification because, for instance, someone possessing the general concept of an *animal* but not that of a *dog* is still in a position to make singular reference to *particular dogs* by means of singular terms incorporating in their sense only the general concept of an animal – for example, a singular term such as 'the animal in that cage'. This is because 'dog' shares the same criterion of identity as 'animal'. But, for that very reason, the oversimplification is not inimical to the line of argument that I am developing. See Chapter 2 for further discussion relevant to this point.

84   *Identity*

extend the range of his objects of singular reference – and consequently, it seems, his familiarity with that practice must ultimately be grounded in the application of *criterionless* general concepts. In short, if this line of reasoning is correct, it cannot be through a grasp of type-(B) criteria of identity that a speaker or thinker *first* engages in the practice of singular reference.

9 DUMMETT ON CRITERIA OF IDENTITY

Now, it would appear that Michael Dummett, for one, would agree with this last statement – and yet *not* agree that there are criterionless sortals, nor that the Fregean thesis fails to hold with complete universality.[22] This is because he would not agree that all criteria of identity must be expressible in conformity with schema (B) – nor even, indeed, in conformity with schema (A). And this in turn is because he holds the view that at least *some* criteria of identity must be such that a grasp of them does *not* already presuppose a general capacity to employ singular terms of some sort. For he holds that a capacity to employ the linguistic apparatus of singular reference is one of the things that a child must acquire on the basis of a more primitive level of linguistic achievement which altogether excludes the use of this apparatus[23] – and that the acquisition proceeds precisely through the progressive grasp of certain primitive *criteria of identity* which, obviously, would not require for their articulation the apparatus either of singular reference or of quantification with individual variables.

What would a primitive 'Dummettian' criterion of identity appeal to and how might it be articulated – what would be its *logical form*? I should make it clear that 'primitive', in this context, is my choice of epithet, not Dummett's own. Dummett himself is disconcertingly obscure about these matters, although we may assume that he would ultimately seek to invoke certain spatiotemporal patterns of form, continuity, and persistence amongst non-particularized 'features' of a subject's perceptual environment.[24] However, a central element of his position is that acquiring a grasp of such a criterion at least involves acquiring an ability to make, in appropriate circumstances, statements of the form 'This is the same φ as

[22] My ensuing discussion of Dummett's position is based on my understanding of what he says in his *Frege: Philosophy of Language*, chiefly Chapter 16, and in his *The Interpretation of Frege's Philosophy* (London: Duckworth, 1981), Chapter 11.

[23] See Dummett, *The Interpretation of Frege's Philosophy*, p. 216.

[24] For an elaborate attempt to develop principles of this sort, see Tiles, *Things that Happen*. Compare also Strawson, *Individuals*, pp. 202 ff. and pp. 214 ff. – although Strawson, like Dummett, declines to go into details.

What is a criterion of identity?

that' – accompanied, if need be, by appropriate ostensive gestures – where 'φ' is a sortal term.[25] Thus at one point he mentions the case of a child pointing simultaneously to the head and tail of a cat and saying 'This is the same cat as that'. And, while accepting that it is not by learning to do this correctly that a child *starts* to learn the use of the word 'cat', Dummett nonetheless clearly thinks that acquiring an ability to make such identifications with the aid of simple demonstratives constitutes an important staging post in the progression towards a full competence to make singular reference to objects – objects such as cats. It is enough to know this much about Dummett's doctrine to enter into the following discussion.

It is evidently vital to the viability of any position such as Dummett's that the use of a sentence involving a demonstrative may be significant and unambiguous even though no act of singular reference is effected through its utterance. It is also essential to his position that a sortal term may be significantly employed in a way which does not presuppose a grasp of whatever criterion of identity is associated with it – a thesis which Dummett does in fact also uphold but which I shall not seek to challenge here.[26] Now, Dummett does explicitly maintain that a statement of the form 'That is F' – where 'F' may or may not be a sortal – may be significant and unambiguous even though no identifiable object is singled out by the demonstrative 'that', of which the property F is then predicated.[27] He even finds support for this contention in the opening sections of Wittgenstein's *Philosophical Investigations*, concerning ostensive definition.[28] I find this contention unattractive and the evidence of support for it in those sections of the *Philosophical Investigations* tenuous. Wittgenstein, it seems to me, is saying rather that in certain contexts it is quite unnecessary for a speaker to supplement a demonstrative by a sortal expression in order to effect an unambiguous act of singular reference intelligible to his intended audience because the *context of utterance itself* – including here such things as the activities that the speaker and audience may be co-operatively engaged in, such as playing a game of chess – suffices to eliminate any possible ambiguity.[29]

---

[25] See Dummett, *The Interpretation of Frege's Philosophy*, p. 217.
[26] See Dummett, *Frege: Philosophy of Language*, p. 537, where he says, 'I can understand when it is right to say, "That is a book", before knowing any criterion for the identity of books'.
[27] See Dummett, *Frege: Philosophy of Language*, pp. 572 ff.
[28] See Dummett, *Frege: Philosophy of Language*, pp. 577 ff.
[29] See Ludwig Wittgenstein, *Philosophical Investigations*, trans. G. E. M. Anscombe (Oxford: Blackwell, 1958), § 31.

86   *Identity*

This aside, Dummett's contention concerning statements of the form 'That is F' is clearly thought by him to be related quite intimately to certain suggestions of Strawson's concerning the possibility of a 'feature-placing' language altogether lacking the apparatus of singular reference.[30] The implication here is that there is a use of a statement of the form 'That is F' in which it merely conveys the sort of information that might be conveyed more artificially by saying something like 'It is F over there', where the 'it' is no more referential than the 'it' in 'It is raining'.[31] I submit that this is not a correct observation about the adult use of demonstratives in English, which use is, I believe, directed only at singular reference.[32] Furthermore, the highly speculative thesis that there is a stage in an infant's linguistic development at which its use of demonstratives does and must operate like this – a thesis to which Dummett seems to be committed – is, I believe, neither borne out by empirical evidence nor defensible by a priori philosophical argument. For what work has been done by developmental psychologists such as T. G. Bower on early infant perception and related motor activity strongly suggests in fact that, from their very earliest months – and certainly before any significant level of linguistic ability has been achieved – human infants perceptually individuate discrete objects in their environment and do so in a way which indicates the exercise of an innate cognitive capacity.[33] That being so, however, there is simply no reason to suppose that, in order to teach a child the correct use of the linguistic apparatus of singular reference (including the referential use of demonstratives), one must graft this onto a more primitive level of linguistic achievement which altogether excludes the use of that apparatus. The teacher can simply rely on the child's innate cognitive capacity to

---

[30] See Dummett, *The Interpretation of Frege's Philosophy*, p. 217, and Strawson, *Individuals*, pp. 202 ff. There is indeed in general a close affinity between Dummett's and Strawson's views concerning the conceptual underpinnings of singular reference, although Strawson seems less committed to making any empirically significant claim about actual human language mastery or acquisition. I have chosen to concentrate on Dummett's account partly for this reason, but more because of his explicit espousal of what I have called the (full-blown) Fregean Thesis.

[31] Compare Dummett, *Frege: Philosophy of Language*, p. 577.

[32] It may be felt that certain uses of demonstratives in *questions* clearly falsify this claim – for instance, questions of the type 'What is *that*?' (uttered, perhaps, in conditions of poor visibility), where it seems that, far from a singular reference being *made*, one is being *sought*. I think that various responses are available to me here, such as that reference is being made to a phenomenal appearance assumed by the speaker to be intersubjectively perceptible, and that what is really being requested is a description of the *cause* of the appearance. However, the issue is not crucial to the points that I shall go on to develop in this chapter, so I shall not dwell on it here. I do go into such matters more fully in my 'Sortals and the Individuation of Objects', *Mind and Language* 22 (2007), pp. 514–33.

[33] See T. G. Bower, *Development in Infancy* (San Francisco: Freeman, 1974) and *A Primer of Infant Development* (San Francisco: Freeman, 1977).

individuate perceptually at least some of the very same objects to which the teacher himself may make demonstrative reference for teaching purposes. And this is where Wittgenstein's remarks, cited earlier, *are* very important. For if the teacher, ostending an object and saying 'That is F' or 'That is a', in order to begin to teach the child the correct use of the predicate 'F' or the singular term 'a', *always* needed to supplement the demonstrative – or, in the earliest stages, the bare ostensive gesture – with a sortal term already understood by the child, then clearly his task would be impossible. What renders it achievable, however, is not – as Dummett would have it – that demonstratives and ostensive gestures may be significantly used in certain contexts *without* serving to make singular reference, but rather that the teacher can rely at least sometimes upon the contextual disambiguating factor of an identity between the object that he is ostending and that on which the child's perceptual attention is concurrently fixed – that is, upon the fact that he and the child are simultaneously individuating *the same object*, he ostensively and linguistically and the child perceptually.

The question now arises, if the foregoing account is broadly correct, of whether the innate individuative capacities that I am ascribing to prelinguistic infants are capacities whose exercise necessarily involves, on the part of the infant, the application of *criteria of identity*, grasped in some non-linguistic mode of thought – or, at least, in a mode of thought which does not involve the understanding of any fragment of a *natural* language, such as English. To propose this would be to differ from Dummett not least on the score of whether all humanly employed criteria of identity are language-based and culturally transmitted. It would also be to reject as otiose the notion of what I earlier called a 'primitive Dummettian criterion of identity', supposedly possessing a logical form different from that of either schema (A) or schema (B). But it would not, of course, commit one to a rejection of the Fregean thesis in its full-blown form, since it would merely imply that *some* of our criteria of identity are *innate*, not learned – not that some of our sortal terms and concepts are entirely *criterionless*. However, there are philosophers who would, I am sure, endorse precisely the latter view, where an infant's deployment of certain sortal concepts is concerned. They would propose that an infant's most basic cognitive capacities to individuate certain perceptible objects in its physical environment depend *not* on an implicit intellectual grasp of any principle deserving of the title 'criterion of identity', but simply on certain sorts of *sensory and motor behaviour*, which are evolved features of the human brain and its control mechanisms – in particular, perceptual *tracking* behaviour and correlated motor responses such as *reaching* and *grasping*. On this sort of

88 *Identity*

account, the infant's most primitive acts of object individuation are, thus, not at bottom *mental* acts in any intellective sense, but instead essentially *bodily* ones. And then the claim would be that an infant incapable of such primitive bodily acts of object individuation could not subsequently be trained in the correct use of the referential apparatus of any natural language.

Now, at one time I had considerable sympathy for a view of this sort,[34] partly because I was persuaded by the line of argument sketched in section 8 above for the necessity of there being at least *some* humanly graspable sortal concepts that are *criterionless*, as part of an account of how human subjects can acquire mastery of the linguistic apparatus of singular reference.[35] And it seemed to me then that the sort of view just outlined would very naturally and plausibly serve this apparent theoretical need. However, it has since become evident to me that the 'perceptual tracking' model of infant object individuation is deeply flawed, because it cannot really manage to explain what it *has* to explain – namely how prelinguistic infants can succeed in *unambiguously singling out* certain discrete objects in their physical environment. Since I have discussed these matters extensively in Chapter 2 above, I shall say no more about them now. As for the line of argument that led me into sympathy with the 'perceptual tracking' model, that too now seems to me to be unpersuasive. For, once again, we can plausibly appeal to the *innateness* of certain relevant cognitive capacities. Only if one assumed that the cognitive capacities essential for mastery of the linguistic apparatus of singular reference had to be *acquired* from experience and training would there be pressure to suppose that these must be grafted onto some more basic set of cognitive capacities. But if a capacity for singular thought about discrete environmental objects can be taken to be *innate*, as the work of Bower and others suggests, then, evidently, nothing more cognitively 'basic' need be presumed in order to explain the subsequent mastery of that linguistic apparatus.

Let me now return briefly to Dummett. His position, it seems clear, is founded at least partly on his open espousal of what he himself calls the

---

[34] See the original paper on which much of this chapter (of the same title) is based, my 'What Is a Criterion of Identity?', *Philosophical Quarterly* 39 (1989), pp. 1–21.

[35] I should mention that I do have certain quite different reasons, of a logico-metaphysical kind, for supposing that at least some sortal concepts must be criterionless, notably the concept of a *person*: see my *More Kinds of Being: A Further Study of Individuation, Identity and the Logic of Sortal Terms* (Malden, MA and Oxford: Wiley-Blackwell, 2009), Chapters 2 and 8. I am still persuaded that these reasons are correct, as I shall make clear in Chapter 6 below. But I now think that it is crucial to disentangle these considerations from the ones that – as I now believe – misled me concerning the prerequisites of infant language mastery.

What is a criterion of identity? 89

'amorphous lump' picture of reality, whereby reality is 'carved' into discrete objects *by us*, entirely through our application of ultimately language-based criteria of identity.[36] This prevents him from countenancing – indeed, constrains him to dismiss as naive – the view that human infants are capable of enjoying perceptually based singular thoughts prior to their acquisition of a mastery of the apparatus of singular reference embodied in some culturally transmitted natural language, and hence creates for him a spuriously difficult problem as to *how* that mastery is achieved. But, for reasons that I shall speak more about in Chapter 6, I consider that the 'amorphous lump' picture of reality is not merely empirically unsupported but fundamentally incoherent.

10 THE FREGEAN THESIS UPHELD

I conclude that the search for primitive Dummettian criteria of identity is uncalled for, since there is no empirical or philosophical reason to suppose that they are required in order to account for an infant's mastery of the linguistic apparatus of singular reference or, more generally, to underpin our capacity to individuate objects. Now, admittedly, this is not *quite* the end of the matter, since it might still be hypothesized – and, indeed, conceivably be confirmed empirically – that an infant's exercise of its innate capacity to individuate objects in its perceptual environment is ultimately grounded in certain cerebral information-processing procedures which utilize a computational code whose syntax and semantics are those of a 'feature-placing' language, rather than a subject–predicate one like that of first-order quantificational logic. Hence some of the questions presented by the search for primitive Dummettian criteria of identity, which I have avoided by appeal to innate individuative capacities, might conceivably arise again at the level of what some philosophers have – rather inaptly – called the 'language of thought',[37] in the form of questions concerning the nature of the algorithms supposedly utilized by the brain in its realization of the exercise of those capacities. However, disputes at *this* level will have no direct bearing on the Fregean thesis as both Dummett and I have been interpreting it – namely as a thesis concerning the semantics of the singular terms used by human beings in their communications with each other by means of natural languages or by means of humanly invented artificial languages, such as the formalized languages of logic and mathematics. And, in any case, it seems that empirical

---

[36] See Dummett, *Frege: Philosophy of Language*, p. 577.
[37] See Jerry A. Fodor, *The Language of Thought* (New York: Crowell, 1975).

90   *Identity*

scientists are still a very long way off from possessing the requisite tools and data to be able to address these new questions concerning the 'format' of human cerebral information processing.

Fortunately, then, we do not need to go into the obscure matter of just what primitive Dummettian criteria of identity are supposed to appeal to and how they might be articulated. But having rejected such criteria as otiose and spurious – at least in the context of the semantics of natural and artificial languages – we may, I contend, nonetheless retain the claim that the Fregean thesis holds with complete universality: that there must be a criterion of identity associated with *every* significant singular term.[38] We can also still maintain that these criteria may always be formulated in accordance with schema (B) – although how *precise* such a formulation may be where ordinary language is concerned is a contentious matter, to which I shall return shortly. We can similarly still maintain, of course, that every such singular term incorporates in its sense the sense of some sortal term, which duly determines the criterion of identity associated with that singular term. We need not abandon, then – not, at least, for any reason thus far under consideration – the view that a necessary condition of a general term's being a *sortal* term is that a criterion of identity should be a component of its sense. We need not countenance the thesis that there are and must be *criterionless* sortals, supposedly supplying concepts in terms of which human infants 'primitively' individuate objects in their perceived environment, because even an infant's perceptual individuation of such objects may be – indeed, I think, *must* be – seen as being governed by criteria of identity, even if only by criteria that are merely *implicitly* grasped by the subjects responsive to them. As I remarked in Chapter 2, something like the concept of a relatively cohesive, discrete, and intactly mobile *hunk of matter* seems to figure prominently in a human infant's segmentation of its perceived environment into distinct objects. But, as I also indicated there, it would be wrong to think of this concept as *not* being a sortal, and also wrong to think that its application is not governed by a distinctive criterion of identity – wrong, in particular, to suppose that its application is somehow secured *just* by an infant's perceptual 'tracking' behaviour and

---

[38] I am setting aside here, for present purposes, the considerations mentioned in an earlier footnote that lead me to think that certain sortal terms and concepts, notably the concept of a *person*, are criterionless. In their case, however, my claim is only that a properly *non-circular* criterion of identity is not available, and I am happy to concede – indeed, to insist – that there are important constitutive principles substantively *constraining* the identity conditions of individuals falling under such concepts, so that these identity conditions are not just 'brute', in the sense that nothing informative can be said about them.

What is a criterion of identity? 91

associated motor responses, such as reaching and grasping, without the benefit of any implicit intellective grasp of such an object's distinctive identity conditions.

Now, it is evidently possible that the sortal concepts featuring in an *infant's* most basic individuative practices are not precisely to be identified with any of the sortal concepts still exercised by an adult equipped with a full mastery of a natural language. To that extent, we should not expect to be able to capture any one of these infantile sortal concepts *exactly* in terms of any normal English expression, such as 'hunk of matter', since the latter has for adults connotations which it would be unreasonable or implausible to project upon infant subjects. This acknowledgement, however, does not in principle undermine my earlier stance on the question of how infants might at first be introduced to the use of singular terms in natural language, even if it makes the matter a little more complicated. There is no question of my having to go back on my repudiation of the 'amorphous lump' picture of reality, only a question of a slight degree of mismatch between infantile and adult individuative schemes.

II TYPE-(B) IDENTITY CRITERIA FOR CONCRETE NATURAL-LANGUAGE SORTALS

It only remains now to be shown that some sortal terms in natural language describing kinds of *concrete* objects can indeed be seen as being governed by criteria of identity which can be formulated in accordance with schema (B) – for the only specific proposal to this effect so far investigated has been Davidson's, which was found to be defective. I would suggest that a good many *artefactual* sortals may fairly readily be shown to submit to such a treatment – sortals such as 'ship', 'watch', and 'table'. These are certainly *not* criterionless sortals, supplying concepts of the type allegedly exercised in an infant's primitive acts of perceptual individuation, even if we thought – mistakenly, in my view – that concepts of that type existed. For a child must clearly *learn* to recognize that there are objects such as ships which, to be adequately conceived of, need to be thought of as being capable of persisting through certain kinds of change in their component parts. Of course, spelling out explicitly an appropriate criterion of identity in this case is by no means an easy matter, as the notorious problem of the ship of Theseus makes clear.[39] Nonetheless, at

---

[39] I discuss this problem and some of its implications in my 'On the Identity of Artifacts', *Journal of Philosophy* 80 (1983), pp. 220–32.

least to a first approximation we may suggest as a type-(B) criterion of identity for ships something like the following principle: if x and y are ships, then x is identical with y if and only if the collections of parts of which x and y respectively are composed are such that one of these collections has been generated from the other by a process of gradual replacement of component parts broadly preservative of the structural and functional relationships of those parts – where a *total retention* of parts constitutes, of course, a 'null' replacement. This proposal needs to be filled out, evidently, by a suitable description of the *sorts* of component parts that are properly in question – not, for instance, subatomic particles, but characteristic *ship*-parts, such as masts or propellers – and their requisite structural and functional relationships, which may differ, of course, from one kind of ship to another (for instance, sailing ships and steamships).

Now, the ultimate test of a satisfactory criterion of identity is that its deliverances should nowhere come into conflict with the formal logical laws of identity. But it is unreasonable to suppose that any such precisely satisfactory criterion of identity *actually* governs the ordinary-language use of a sortal such as 'ship'. This, indeed, is why philosophers can concoct puzzle cases which bring our linguistic intuitions into conflict where the identity conditions of objects such as ships are concerned. What does this imply, though? *Not* that the ordinary-language use of 'ship' is not governed by any criterion of identity *at all*, but only that actual usage may reflect the employment of a variety of competing criteria, none of which may quite meet the exacting standards demanded of a satisfactory criterion of identity for abstract mathematical objects such as sets. Nor should we expect ordinary unreflective language users to be able to articulate *explicitly* the criterion governing their use of a sortal such as 'ship': their implicit employment of a specific criterion may, rather, often be revealed only through their ability to respond in principled ways to appropriate questions put to them concerning the identity or persistence of ships subjected to various kinds of change. Finally, it is not to be expected, nor would it be commendable, for philosophers to rest content with having extracted the vague and often conflicting criteria governing sortals in actual everyday use: rather, it is part of their proper task to suggest such *revisions* of that use as may best contribute to the elimination of this vagueness and conflict, to the extent at least that this may be achieved without depriving the reformed concepts of useful application.

12 CONCLUSIONS

The main conclusions that I have arrived at in this chapter may now be summarized as follows.

1 It is no *defect* in type-(B) criteria of identity that they involve quantification over the very sorts of individuals for whose identity they provide a criterion, although in framing such criteria every caution must be taken not to presuppose already an account of the identity conditions of the individuals concerned. On the other hand, type-(A) criteria of identity, while they do – unnecessarily, as it turns out – avoid quantification over the sorts of individuals for whose identity they supply a criterion, are for that very reason severely limited in their scope, in a way in which type-(B) criteria are not: which is why I favour schema (B) over schema (A) as representing the general canonical form of a criterion of identity.

2 Contrary to what Dummett suggests, we need not suppose that a child's initiation into the use of singular terms in natural language must proceed on the basis of its acquired grasp of identity criteria in principle expressible in a language altogether lacking the resources for singular reference or quantification over individuals – a 'feature-placing' language. For we may plausibly contend instead that such initiation merely exploits the child's *innate* capacities for the perceptual individuation of objects – capacities whose exercise plausibly involves, moreover, at least the *implicit* intellectual grasp of certain basic criteria of identity, rather than just purely bodily perceptual 'tracking' behaviour and correlated motor responses. Hence, like Dummett, we may consistently endorse the Fregean thesis as holding with complete universality, but without conceding to him that this requires us to recognize a class of identity criteria which conform *neither* to schema (A) *nor* to schema (B). Nor, of course, need we accede to Dummett's 'amorphous lump' picture of reality.

3 Consequently, we are at liberty to claim – at least so far as any consideration arising in this chapter is concerned – that singular terms in natural language are *always* governed by criteria of identity and that such criteria may *always* be expected to be capable of expression in conformity with schema (B). The only caveat required here is that we should not overestimate the precision of the criteria governing *actual* ordinary-language usage, which may well fall short in many cases of the logical ideal. It remains a legitimate task for *philosophers*, however, to propose revisions to and refinements of those actual-language criteria, in order to bring them into closer proximity with that ideal.

CHAPTER 6

Identity conditions and their grounds

As we saw in Chapter 5, a *criterion of identity* for entities of a kind K is a principle specifying, in an informative and non-circular way, the conditions that are logically necessary and sufficient for an entity x and an entity y of kind K to be numerically the same K. If C is a criterion of identity for Ks, then a full grasp of the concept of a K will include a grasp of the fact that the identity of Ks is governed by C. In this sense, C is built into the concept of a K. Let us call a concept that has a criterion of identity built into it in this way an *individuative* concept. Then we can ask: What is the source or foundation of individuative concepts and how are they related to the reality that they purport to characterize? Can we freely invent such concepts, subject only to the constraint of logical consistency, and then deploy them in 'carving up' reality in any of many different equally legitimate ways? Or are we necessarily constrained by reality itself in the formation of our individuative concepts – in which case, how? If it is a mind-independent fact that reality contains entities governed by some possible identity criteria and does not contain entities governed by others, how are we to determine which of them it does contain? And what is it about the entities that reality does contain that is the source or foundation of their identity conditions? In this chapter, I shall defend robustly realist and essentialist answers to these questions. And in the course of defending these answers, I shall argue that reality must contain some entities whose identity is *primitive*, in the sense that no informative and non-circular principle can capture their identity conditions.

I IDENTITY, IDENTITY CONDITIONS, AND CRITERIA OF IDENTITY

Many philosophers have, for various reasons, expressed scepticism about the very idea of a criterion of identity, conceived as a metaphysical – as opposed to a merely epistemic or heuristic – principle. Some think that

Identity conditions and their grounds 95

any role that such a principle could be supposed to play is already played by Leibniz's law, so that nothing further needs to be said on the matter. Others accuse advocates of the idea of supposing, mistakenly, that there is anything substantive to be said about the relation of identity, whose nature is in fact perfectly simple and straightforward. Yet others accuse them of the even grosser error of imagining that identity must be differently *defined* for different kinds of entities, and thus of failing to understand that all talk of identity is perfectly univocal. However, in my view, all such criticisms are wide of the mark, misconstruing what a criterion of identity is properly conceived to be. As we saw in Chapters 2 and 5, a criterion of identity for entities of kind K is simply a principle which specifies, in an informative and non-circular way, the conditions that are logically necessary and sufficient for an entity x and an entity y of kind K to be numerically the same K. (Leibniz's law, be it noted, is not in this manner a principle restricted in its application to any single *kind* of entities, and so cannot qualify as a criterion of identity in the sense at issue.) It is manifestly the case that there *are* such criteria and that these criteria can differ for different kinds K. For example, if x and y are *sets*, then x and y are the *same* set if and only if x and y possess the same members. By contrast, if x and y are *ordered sets*, then they are the same *ordered set* if and only if they possess the same members *in the same order*. As a consequence, no set can be *identified* with any ordered set. Why not? Well, consider the ordered sets $\langle a, b \rangle$ and $\langle b, a \rangle$, which possess the same members but in a different order. (I assume, for the purposes of the example, that a and b are themselves distinct.) By the criterion of identity for ordered sets, these ordered sets are not identical with each other. However, if each of them were a *set*, they would be the *same* set according to the criterion of identity for sets, because they possess the same members. But then we would have the intolerable consequence that these entities are *both identical and distinct* – a contradiction.

To this objection, a so-called 'relative' identity theorist, of P. T. Geach's persuasion, might respond that these entities are the same *set*, but different *ordered sets* – the supposed lesson being that entities should never be said to be identical or distinct *simpliciter*, or *absolutely*, but only qua entities of this or that kind, and that identical Ks may nonetheless be distinct Js.[1] But of

---

[1] See P. T. Geach, *Reference and Generality*, 3rd edn (Ithaca, NY: Cornell University Press, 1980), pp. 181 and 216. I criticize Geach's view in my *Kinds of Being: A Study of Individuation, Identity and the Logic of Sortal Terms* (Oxford: Blackwell, 1989), Chapter 4, and again in my *More Kinds of Being: A Further Study of Individuation, Identity and the Logic of Sortal Terms* (Oxford and Malden, MA: Wiley-Blackwell, 2009), Chapter 4.

96   *Identity*

what does the relative identity theorist purportedly speak here when he says that *they* are at once the same set but different ordered sets? We must take him to be speaking of the ordered sets $\langle a, b \rangle$ and $\langle b, a \rangle$, for it was these items that were introduced for purposes of illustration. But what then is the *it* with which *they* are purportedly identical, qua sets? Presumably, the set $\{a, b\}$. However, that set – being a *set* – does not possess its members in any *order*, even though we *refer* to its members in a certain order when we designate it by the expression '$\{a, b\}$'. But any *ordered* set, such as the ordered set $\langle a, b \rangle$, *does* possess its members in a certain order – in this case, a comes before b in the order in which they are possessed. Consequently, the set $\{a, b\}$ cannot be the same *ordered set* as the ordered set $\langle a, b \rangle$, for it lacks an essential property of any ordered set, namely that of possessing its members in a certain order.

Someone may worry at this point that I am neglecting the well-known method of 'reducing' ordered sets to sets, proposed independently by Wiener and Kuratowski.[2] According to this proposal, the ordered set $\langle a, b \rangle$ may be 'reduced' to the set $\{a, \{a, b\}\}$, while the ordered set $\langle b, a \rangle$ may similarly be 'reduced' to the set $\{b, \{b, a\}\}$. This proposal preserves, as it should, the non-identity of the ordered sets $\langle a, b \rangle$ and $\langle b, a \rangle$, by reducing them to *different* sets, and so provides no comfort for the relative identity theorist. But 'reduction' is an unfortunate choice of term in this context, for it is clear that all that the proposal really does is to provide, for any ordered set, a set which can be regarded as its unique *representative*. The ordered set $\langle a, b \rangle$ certainly cannot be *identified* with its representative, the set $\{a, \{a, b\}\}$, because the former has only a and b as its members, whereas the latter has as its members a and the pair $\{a, b\}$. If – as we may readily presume for the sake of the example – neither a nor b is a set, then it follows that $\langle a, b \rangle$ and $\{a, \{a, b\}\}$ differ, for instance, in that the latter, but not the former, possesses a *set* amongst its members.

To this it may be replied, perhaps, that 'membership' must be understood in two different senses – the ordinary set-theoretical sense, and another sense which applies only to ordered sets. Let us differentiate between these putative senses of 'membership' by distinguishing between *being a member$_S$* and *being a member$_O$*. Then it may be said that b is a member$_O$ – but not a member$_S$ – of $\{a, \{a, b\}\}$, in virtue of the fact that $\{a, b\}$ is a member$_S$ of $\{a, \{a, b\}\}$. Or, more exactly, that b is the *second* member$_O$ of $\{a, \{a, b\}\}$, in virtue of the fact that a and $\{a, b\}$ are the only

---

[2] See Patrick Suppes, *Axiomatic Set Theory* (New York: Dover, 1972), p. 32. The version that I discuss here is Kuratowski's.

two members$_S$ of $\{a, \{a, b\}\}$. It might then be thought that nothing now stops us from simply *identifying* the ordered set $\langle a, b \rangle$ with the set $\{a, \{a, b\}\}$, because we are no longer entitled to insist that $\langle a, b \rangle$ does *not* have the pair $\{a, b\}$ as a member: true enough, it doesn't have it as a *member$_O$*, but – it may now be said – it does have it as a *member$_S$*. The fact is, however, that nothing in the concept of the ordered set $\langle a, b \rangle$ connects it in any significant way with the pair $\{a, b\}$. The only connection between these entities was forged, entirely arbitrarily, by the Wiener–Kuratowski proposal itself. It is not as though that proposal provides the only tenable way of 'reducing' ordered sets to sets – indefinitely (indeed, infinitely) many other ways would work just as well. In other words, it is no part of the *essence* of the ordered set $\langle a, b \rangle$ that it bears any ontological relationship with the pair $\{a, b\}$. By contrast, it is very much a part of the essence of the set $\{a, \{a, b\}\}$ that it bears such a relationship with that pair, for the very *identity* of that set is determined by its members, one of which is this pair. In short, the Wiener–Kuratowski proposal, construed as providing a genuine reduction of ordered sets to sets, whereby the former may be *identified* with sets of a certain kind, does not respect the essential differences between sets and ordered sets.

2 CONCEPTIONS, CONCEPTS, AND ESSENCES

I have dwelt on the foregoing example because it is simple and yet also illustrates some important general points concerning objects and criteria of identity. One lesson of the example is that the Wiener–Kuratowski proposal does not provide an adequate *conception* of an ordered set. It does not, because it does not accurately reflect the essence of such an entity. By the *concept* of a K, I shall henceforth – in effect, by stipulation – mean a conception of a K that *is* adequate, inasmuch as it accurately reflects the essence of such an entity. Concepts and conceptions are *ways of thinking of entities* but, in the usage that I am now adopting, conceptions may be more or less adequate ways of thinking of the relevant entities, whereas concepts are to be understood precisely as *adequate* conceptions of them – adequacy in a conception of a K consisting in the conception's accurately reflecting the essence of Ks. But what *is* the 'essence' of a kind of entities, K? Here I agree with John Locke, who remarked that in the 'proper original signification' of the word *essence* it denotes 'the very being of any thing, whereby it is, what it is'.[3] However, we

---

[3] See John Locke, *An Essay Concerning Human Understanding*, ed. P. H. Nidditch (Oxford: Clarendon Press, 1975), III, III, 15.

98   *Identity*

need to distinguish here between *general* and *individual* essences. The general essence of a K is 'what it is' *to be a K* – and is therefore *shared* by all particular Ks – whereas the individual essence of a particular K is 'what it is' *to be this particular K*, as opposed to some other particular K. So, for example, it is part of the general essence of an ordered set to possess some entities in a certain order as its members, and it is part of the individual essence of a particular ordered set to have its particular members in a certain specific order – for instance, it is part of the individual essence of the ordered set $\langle a, b \rangle$ to have just the entities a and b, in that order, as its members. To the extent that we grasp such facts about the general and individual essences of ordered sets, we possess the *concept* of that kind of entity and of particular entities of that kind, because we possess *adequate conceptions* of them, or adequate ways of thinking of them. Such a concept I shall call an *individuative* concept, because different *particulars* may be said to fall under it, these being individually distinguished from one another in accordance with a criterion of identity that is built into the concept and is grounded in the general essence of that kind of entity. An *in*adequate conception of an ordered set would, for example, be to think of such a thing merely as *what is represented by (or is 'reducible' to) the corresponding set*, according to the Wiener–Kuratowski proposal. Such a conception might be satisfactory for some purposes, but it would fail to reflect the essence of an ordered set and in that sense fail to be adequate. These observations can be extended to entities of other kinds, although in many cases it will be much harder to determine whether or not a conception of a putative kind of entities can be deemed adequate.

But, it may be asked, how do we know that we *do* in fact possess an adequate conception of entities of some putative kind – even, say, of *ordered sets*? After all, the history of set theory notoriously reveals that early set theorists *mistakenly* thought that they possessed an adequate conception of *sets*. The inadequacy was revealed by Russell's famous paradox, and consisted in the fact that a set was conceived to be, in effect, the extension of any possible predicate that is meaningful – a conception which rested on the false presupposition that every such predicate *has* an extension. (The predicate 'is non-self-membered' is meaningful, but cannot, on pain of contradiction, be supposed to have an extension – the set of sets that are not members of themselves – for there can be no such set.) A minimum condition on the adequacy of a conception of a K is that it should at least be possible – that is, *really*, or 'metaphysically', possible – that Ks, thus conceived, should exist. Or so I suggest. I suppose it might be objected by some philosophers that we can have adequate conceptions of

Identity conditions and their grounds 99

metaphysically *im*possible entities, such as, perhaps, *round square cupolas*. However, this is in effect to abandon all constraints on adequacy of conception, thereby undermining the very notion of such adequacy. An adequate conception of *Ks* must be a *coherent* way of thinking of *Ks* – but there is *no* coherent way of thinking of something whose existence is metaphysically impossible. Yet, it may now be asked, how can we *know* whether *Ks*, conceived in a certain way as entities of a certain kind, *are* metaphysically possible? If what is being asked here is how we can know this *for certain*, without any risk of error, then the answer, I think, is that we cannot *ever* know this. However, I nevertheless think that we are very often entitled to feel confident that we do in fact know that something of this sort is the case, at least in certain instances. To suppose otherwise is to abandon all hope that we can engage in rational thought and discourse – a counsel of despair whose own coherence is dubious in the extreme. What I am saying, in effect, is that a minimum condition of our own rationality is that we can, at least sometimes, grasp the essences of at least some possible kinds of entities. This is consistent with acknowledging that we may be mistaken in thinking that we have grasped the essence of a certain kind of entity, but it is also consistent with acknowledging that such errors may be corrected through further thought and reflection on our own part. We are, for example, entitled to suppose – but not to be absolutely certain – that reflection on Russell's paradox has now provided us with an adequate conception of a *set*, where before our conception was inadequate.

Sets and ordered sets, it would certainly seem, are *abstract* rather than concrete entities. For that very reason, some may be inclined to deny their very existence, even if it is granted that they are entities of a kind whose existence is *possible*. (Others will say that any abstract entity that *could* exist *must* exist – that abstract entities can only be necessary, not contingent, beings – but this seems highly questionable.) In any case, it should surely be agreed that, if one can grasp essences at all, one may grasp the (general) essence of a possible kind of entity without yet knowing whether or not entities of that kind actually exist. In this sense, at least, 'essence precedes existence', for many possible kinds of entities. That seems clearly to be the case with many entities of kinds whose instances, *if* they exist, are necessarily concrete and contingent beings. For example, we seem to have a perfectly clear concept of an entity of the following kind: *a particular quantity or mass of homogeneous and infinitely divisible matter or stuff*. But whether there actually *are* any such entities in existence would appear to be a question that could at best be settled only empirically. As it turns out, the actual world, it would seem, contains no such quantities of matter, but instead – what might be mistaken for them – aggregates of 'fundamental' particles that are either punctiform or else spatially extended but nonetheless non-composite. Such, at any rate, is what modern theoretical physics suggests. Superficial observation of the natural world does not reveal to us which, if either, of these views of physical reality is correct, but the results of controlled experimentation do appear to favour the second hypothesis over the first. The most important point, however, is that scientific experimentation could not be undertaken with a view to supporting *either* hypothesis in the absence of clear concepts, on the part of the scientists concerned, of the kinds of entities whose existence is in dispute. Unless one *already grasps* the essence of entities of a putative kind *K*, one cannot appeal to empirical evidence in support of – or, indeed, against – the claim that entities of that kind actually exist. For we need to know *what it is* whose existence we are affirming or denying before we can appeal to evidence in support of our claim.

3 CONCRETE MATERIAL OBJECTS AND THEIR CRITERIA OF IDENTITY

For purposes of further illustration and discussion, let us focus on some putative concrete entities of less arcane kinds than those postulated by fundamental physics – such as a bronze statue and the lump of bronze of which it is (as we say) 'made'. What, in essence, are entities of these putative kinds supposed to *be*? Well, to a first approximation, a *lump of bronze* is supposed to be a maximal connected aggregate of bronze particles – what Locke called a 'parcel of matter'. By a *connected aggregate* of certain particles I mean a whole consisting of those particles, with each particle in the whole standing to any other in the ancestral of the *adherence* relation, so that between any two such particles there is a chain of particles, adjacent members of which adhere to one another. And by a *maximal* connected aggregate of particles I mean a connected aggregate of particles which is not a proper part of a larger such aggregate. The *criterion of identity* for lumps of bronze is clearly something like this: if x and y are lumps of bronze, then x and y are the *same* lump of bronze if and only if x and y are maximal connected aggregates of exactly the same bronze particles. For present purposes, we need not inquire too closely into the nature of bronze particles: we may treat them as minimal parts of bronze; that is, as parts of bronze which cannot be divided into entities that are themselves parts of bronze. Of course, modern scientific chemistry will give a more informative account, in terms of the atomic theory of matter.

Identity conditions and their grounds

However, I am not persuaded that only someone in possession of such an account can have an adequate conception of what a lump of bronze *is*: to insist upon this would be, it seems to me, to impose too stringent a constraint on adequate conception. It is part of the essence of a lump of bronze that it is composed of bronze particles, and it may well be part of the essence of a bronze particle that it has a certain atomic constitution – but it needn't follow that it is part of the essence of a lump of bronze that it is composed of particles with such a constitution. For *being part of the essence of* need not necessarily be construed as being a transitive relation. In any case, this much seems clear: just because a criterion of identity for entities of a kind K makes reference to, or quantifies over, entities that may be of *other kinds* – as, indeed, our proposed criterion of identity for *lumps of bronze* quantifies over *bronze particles* – it doesn't follow that the criterion in question cannot be adequately stated without mentioning criteria of identity for entities of those other kinds. For example: the criterion of identity for *sets*, as we have seen, is that if x and y are sets, then x is the *same* set as y if and only if x and y have the same members. But entities of *any kind whatever* may be members of sets, many such kinds having different criteria of identity. It doesn't follow that the criterion of identity for sets cannot be adequately stated without mention of those other criteria, whatever they might be. Indeed, if this were a requirement for an adequate statement of the criterion of identity for sets, *no one could ever adequately state such a criterion*, because no one can know all the criteria of identity for all the kinds of entities that do or could exist.

Now, it is evidently a consequence of the criterion of identity for lumps of bronze just proposed that no lump of bronze can survive the loss or replacement of any of the bronze particles composing it, since it cannot be identical with the lump of bronze resulting from any such loss or replacement. For if lump L_1 is composed of particles $p_1, p_2, \ldots, p_n$, and particle p_n is lost or replaced by particle p_m, where p_n is distinct from p_m, then the resulting lump L_2 is composed either of particles $p_1, p_2, \ldots, p_{(n-1)}$ or else of particles $p_1, p_2, \ldots, p_{(n-1)}, p_m$ – and in either case L_1 and L_2 are maximal connected aggregates of *different* bronze particles, and so are distinct lumps of bronze according to the proposed criterion. Indeed, subsequent to such a loss or replacement of particle p_n, there is clearly *no* lump of bronze in existence with which L_1 can any longer be identified – neither L_2 nor any other lump – and so L_1 must have ceased to exist. (A particle may be taken to be *lost* by a lump of bronze when it no longer adheres to any of the particles of which that lump is a maximal connected aggregate, whether because the particle ceases to exist or because it merely becomes separated

102 *Identity*

from the other particles. A particle is replaced when, instead of it, *another* particle adheres to the remaining particles in question. It may be thought worrisome that *adherence* threatens to be a *vague* relation, in the sense that there are, plausibly, *borderline cases* of adherence between particles. I am not persuaded that this really presents any serious problem, but cannot go into the matter in any detail at the moment. At any rate, if it is a problem, it is one that I shall ignore for the time being.)

But what about a *bronze statue*? What kind of entity is *that* supposed to be? Well, clearly, is it is supposed to be a material object made of bronze and possessing a certain specific shape, fit to represent whatever it is supposed to be a statue *of*. (Let us set aside, for present purposes, the sort of 'statues' that might be produced by so-called abstract artists, which need not represent anything.) Of course, a *lump of bronze* is made of bronze and will inevitably possess, at any given time at which it exists, some shape or other. But that in itself doesn't suffice to show that a bronze statue may be identified with a lump of bronze – the lump of bronze of which, at any given time, it is made. And, indeed, reflection reveals that a bronze statue is conceived to be an entity of such a kind that it can, in principle, survive the loss or replacement of some of the bronze parts of which it is made. If, for instance, some bronze particles from the interior of a statue were to be lost or replaced – indeed, even if they were to be replaced by particles of a different kind, such as lead – this would not be regarded as implying that the statue itself had ceased to exist. And yet, as we know, the implication *would* be that the *lump of bronze* of which the statue had formerly been made had ceased to exist. This suffices to show that the criterion of identity for bronze statues differs from that for lumps of bronze, and consequently that no bronze statue can be *identified* with a lump of bronze. There really is no reasonable way to avoid this conclusion, and with it the conclusion that sometimes two distinct material objects – to wit, a bronze statue and the lump of bronze of which, at any given time, it is made – exist in exactly the same place at the same time. At least, there is no reasonable way to avoid the latter conclusion short of denying the very existence of either lumps of bronze or bronze statues. For, thus far, I have not been inquiring into the reasons we may have for thinking that entities of either of these kinds *actually exist*, only into their *natures or essences*.

As for the question of what the criterion of identity for bronze statues *is*, given that it differs from that for lumps of bronze, that is not quite so easy to answer, precisely because the criterion must allow for the possibility of such a statue's surviving a loss or replacement of some of the bronze particles composing it at any given time, but not such a loss as to alter

Identity conditions and their grounds 103

significantly its outward shape. It would be a useful exercise to try to formulate such a criterion in a satisfactory fashion, but that is a task that I shall set aside for present purposes, as the desiderata that need to be met are clear enough. Meanwhile, we can learn something from the fact that such a task is not a trivial one. We learn, first, that we were right to insist that criteria of identity are substantive metaphysical principles, by no means rendered redundant by Leibniz's law. We also learn that we may have a practical grasp of such principles before we are capable of formulating them explicitly – and for many purposes the practical grasp is all that is needed.

4 SOME MISUNDERSTANDINGS OF THE IDENTITY-CRITERIA SCEPTICS EXPOSED

This is a convenient point at which to expose more fully some of the misunderstandings of those who are sceptical about criteria of identity. Consider, in particular, those who object to the foregoing line of argument – based on an appeal to criteria of identity – for the conclusion that two distinct material objects may exist in exactly the same place at the same time, such as a bronze statue and the lump of bronze of which it is made. Typically, they raise an objection of the following sort.[4]

Consider the bronze statue, S, and the lump of bronze, L, at a certain moment of time, t. *Ex hypothesi*, S and L are composed at t of exactly the same bronze particles, arranged in exactly the same way. But, surely – so the objectors urge – all of S's properties at t are *determined by*, or *supervene upon*, the properties and relations of the bronze particles at t, and the same applies to all of L's properties at t. In that case, however, how can those particles simultaneously compose two distinct objects, which *differ* in certain of their properties? After all, we have been supposing that S and L differ in their *identity conditions* and thus in their *persistence* conditions, so that S, for example, has the property of being able to survive a change in its component particles, while L does not. Again, L supposedly has the property of being able to survive a significant change in its shape, but S does not. But, the objector asks, what can possibly be the ontological ground of these supposed differences in their properties at t, given that S and L are, at t, indistinguishable in respect of their material composition? The property of being able to survive a certain sort of change is a *modal*

---

[4] See, for example, Eric T. Olson, 'Material Coincidence and the Indiscernibility Problem', *Philosophical Quarterly* 51 (2001), pp. 337–55.

property, which is akin – it might be thought – to an object's *powers* or *dispositions*. But an object's powers or dispositions are seemingly grounded in properties and relations of its material constituents. For instance, if an object is *soluble*, or *brittle*, or *elastic*, this will be because it is composed of particles possessing certain properties or arranged in a certain way. Hence two objects that were composed of exactly the same particles arranged in exactly the same way couldn't possibly differ in respect of the powers or dispositions that they possessed. How, then, could S and L, which are composed of exactly the same particles arranged in exactly the same way, differ in that L can survive a significant change of shape but S cannot? Isn't this as absurd as supposing that L can *dissolve*, or *break*, or *stretch* – that is, that L is soluble, or brittle, or elastic – but S cannot? What would *make L and S* differ in this supposed way, given their identical material composition?

Here it may be replied that L and S differ in this way precisely because L is a *lump of bronze*, whereas S is instead a *bronze statue* – and consequently they possess different persistence conditions. But the objector will respond that this answer merely pushes back the problem one step. For now he will ask how it is that S and L, despite having an identical material composition, come to differ in respect of what *kind* of thing they are – S having the property of being a bronze statue, but *not* the property of being a lump of bronze, while L has the property of being a lump of bronze, but *not* the property of being a bronze statue. Even granted that such properties exist and are had by objects composed by material particles arranged in a certain way, how can two objects composed by exactly the *same* particles arranged in exactly the *same* way differ in that only *one* of them has one of these properties, while only *the other* has the other property? In virtue of what do the two properties get assigned to different objects? How do we even have *two* objects here, enabling the previous question to be so much as raised?

The first thing to be said about this supposed conundrum is that it is patently mistaken to see any sort of parallel between the fact that a bronze statue cannot survive a significant change of shape and the fact, say, that a brittle object cannot be bent without breaking. Brittleness in an object is indeed grounded in the nature of the object's material constitution, in a way that detailed scientific investigation could reveal. A statue made of glass would be brittle for this reason. But the fact that such a statue could not survive a significant change of shape has nothing, essentially, to do with its brittleness. True enough, if a brittle statue were to break owing to its brittleness, it could well undergo a significant change of shape and thereby cease to exist. But the reason why a statue cannot survive a

Identity conditions and their grounds

significant change of shape and why, hence, a statue that broke in that way would cease to exist, is simply that having (approximately) the shape it does is *part of the essence* of any statue, and thus one of its *essential properties*. *What it is* for something to be a *statue* is, in part, for it to have a certain shape. But the essence of a material object is not *conferred upon it* by its material constitution, in the way that its powers or dispositions may be. On the contrary, it is part of the essence of any material object that it should have a certain sort of material composition. For instance, it is part of the essence of a bronze statue that, at any time at which it exists, it should be composed of bronze particles – or, at least, of bronze and/or suitably similar particles, if it has undergone repair – arranged in a certain overall shape. Similarly, it is part of the essence of a living organism that, at any time at which it exists, it should be composed of organic tissue capable of sustaining the characteristic metabolic processes of life. Thus, far from its being the case that a bronze statue's essential properties are conferred upon it by its material constitution, it is the statue's essence that determines what sort of material composition it can have. To believe that bronze statues exist is to believe that the world includes entities whose (general) essence is that of a bronze statue, and *therefore* that bronze particles sometimes compose such entities, with the persistence conditions that are implied by that essence. Trying to derive the existence of bronze statues and their persistence conditions from facts about how bronze particles are sometimes arranged, without appeal to the essence of entities of that kind, would be putting the cart before the horse. (Nor would it help to include facts about the intentions of sculptors and the like.) The same applies with regard to lumps of bronze and *their* persistence conditions. And yet, providing precisely such derivations is what the envisaged objector is, in effect, insisting that we should be able to do. It is an entirely unreasonable demand to make, and that it cannot be met is indicative of no failing in the position that the objector is trying to oppose.

Nor, of course, is there anything special about bronze statues and lumps of bronze in the foregoing regard. The same applies to the bronze particles whose existence and nature the objector takes to be unproblematic. He must have *some* view as to what *these* essentially are, if he seriously thinks that there is reason to believe in their existence. This view will have to include some account of *their* persistence conditions, if he takes them to be entities in whose nature it is to persist. One cannot seriously be said to believe in the existence of entities of some putative kind K if one simply has *no conception* of what the essence of such entities might be. For one cannot believe that Ks exist if one has no conception of *what it is* to be a K.

106 *Identity*

What it is to be a *K*, however, is the general essence of *K*s, which is determinative of the identity conditions of *K*s – and hence of their persistence conditions, if they are by their nature persisting entities. (I should emphasize that I am speaking here of *individual* persistence conditions, rather than of *sortal* persistence conditions, in the sense of the latter explained in Chapter 2. *Individual* persistence conditions are the conditions necessary and sufficient for the continued existence of a given individual, and are determined by that individual's criterion of identity, whereas *sortal* persistence conditions are the conditions necessary and sufficient for an individual of a given sort's continuing to exist *as an individual of that sort*. In other words, individual persistence conditions are just 'diachronic' *identity* conditions.) Now, in the case of entities like bronze statues and lumps of bronze, the objector demands that we explain how their persistence conditions are determined by, or supervene upon, facts about things of *other* kinds, namely facts about the properties and relations of the bronze particles composing them – and then takes us to task when we find it impossible to meet the demand. But if this sort of demand were made general, it would apply also with regard to these other things – in this case, bronze particles. Clearly, however, the demand cannot be made *perfectly* general, on pain of either circularity or an infinite regress. Indeed, it is a misconceived demand, and should not have been made even in respect of entities like bronze statues and lumps of bronze. The objector is simply labouring under a misapprehension concerning the relationship between facts about essence, persistence conditions, and material constitution. Facts about essence *explain* facts about persistence conditions, and *impose constraints on* facts about material constitution. The objector mistakenly – indeed, incoherently – supposes that the proper direction of explanation and determination is the reverse of this.

5 PROBLEMS WITH 'CONCEPTUALIST' ACCOUNTS OF ESSENCE
AND IDENTITY CONDITIONS

However, seeing off the objector in this fashion does not leave us without difficult questions on our hands. To be sure, it would be misguided to try to explain the essence and persistence conditions of composite material objects like bronze statues and lumps of bronze in terms of facts about their material constitution – facts about the properties and relations of the particles that compose them. Facts of the latter sort are simply not suited to be the ground or source of facts about the essence and persistence conditions of such objects. But what, then, *is* their ground or source? Here

Identity conditions and their grounds

we need to ask what, if anything, essences *are* – what their ontological status is. One very common view would be that, to the extent that talk about essences is legitimate at all, essences are *conceptual* in character. On this view, the essence of a kind of entities *K* is simply *constituted* by 'our' concept of a *K* – or, if not by 'our' concept, then at least by *some* thinking being's concept. But what is a *concept*? As I indicated earlier, I myself regard a concept as a way of thinking of something – but I have also stipulated that a concept is an 'adequate' conception of something, which accurately reflects the nature or *essence* of the entity or entities in question. Clearly, then, it is not open to *me* to say that the essence of *Ks* is constituted by our concept of a *K*, because this would leave no room for the notion that the concept of a *K* is a conception of *Ks* that reflects the essence of *Ks*. Essences, on my account, must be *mind-independent*, if the question can sensibly be put as to whether or not a conception of *Ks* adequately reflects the essence of *Ks*. But before I defend and explicate my own view, what can be said of the rival view, that essences are always *constituted* by concepts? Let us call this view *conceptualism*. First, conceptualism is a strongly anti-realist view. Second, it is a view that is doubtfully coherent. Let us deal with the first point first.

In virtue of what, according to conceptualism, can it be truly said that there exist entities that fall under, or satisfy, our concepts – including, most centrally, our *individuative* concepts? That is to say, what does it take for there to *be Ks*, on this view? This is simple enough, it may be said: there must be entities that possess whatever features they are that we have built into our concept of a *K*. So, for example, if *K* is *lump of bronze*, conceived as a maximal connected aggregate of bronze particles, then there must be just such things. This will be the case if, sometimes, some bronze particles adhere to one another so as to form a maximal connected whole. Well and good: but remember that conceptualism is the doctrine that *all* essences are constituted by concepts. So, in particular, the doctrine must be taken to extend to the essence of *bronze particles* – *what it is* to be a bronze particle. (It must also extend to the essence of the relation of *adherence*, but I won't dwell on that equally important fact for the moment, for the concept of adherence is not an individuative concept.) Bronze particles, on this view, exist just in case there are some things that possess whatever features we have built into our concept of a bronze particle. However, either the concept of a bronze particle is relevantly similar to that of a lump of bronze, in that it characterizes the nature of such an entity in terms of properties and relations of entities of *other* kinds, or it is not. If it is, then the next question is just pushed back one stage. If it is not – and this is the next question – then what *does* it take for the world to contain entities falling under the concept? What, in this case, must *the world* contribute to the fact that entities of this putative kind exist? Since, according to conceptualism, all essences are *constituted* by concepts – where concepts are understood to be 'ways of conceiving' deployed by thinkers – the conceptualist cannot suppose that *how the world is*, in respect of *what kinds of entities it contains*, is something that is the case independently of what concepts thinkers deploy. On this view, *what it is* for the world to contain entities of a kind K just *is* for the concept of a K to have application, or be applicable. Consequently, an adherent of this view cannot cash out what it is for such a concept *to have application* in terms of there being in the world entities answering to the concept. For, as I say, on this view, there *being in the world* such entities just *is* a matter of the concept's 'having application'. So a different understanding of 'having application' must at least implicitly be in play.

What is this alternative understanding? I think that it can only be something like this: the concept of a K 'has application' just in case thinkers find it useful, or convenient, to conceive of the world as containing Ks. This may require the concept in question to be *logically consistent* – thus ruling out, for example, the applicability of such concepts as 'round square cupola' – but otherwise the constraints would seem to be purely pragmatic. This, it seems clear, is a deeply anti-realist view. It is a view according to which, in Hilary Putnam's well-known words, there isn't a 'ready-made world'[5] – or, if you like, there isn't any truth about 'what is there *anyway*', to use Bernard Williams's equally familiar phrase.[6] Or, yet again, it is a view according to which, to employ Michael Dummett's somewhat less felicitous metaphor, reality is an 'amorphous lump' – one that can be 'cut up' in indefinitely many different but equally legitimate ways, depending on what 'conceptual scheme' we or other thinkers happen to deploy.[7] It *may* also be the view to which David Wiggins is committed, willy-nilly, by the doctrine that he calls 'conceptualist realism' – committed in virtue of the fact that the only notion of *individuation* that he admits is a cognitive one, whereby individuation is a *singling out of objects by thinkers*.[8]

---

[5] See Hilary Putnam, 'Why There Isn't a Ready-Made World', in his *Realism and Reason: Philosophical Papers, Volume 3* (Cambridge University Press, 1983).

[6] See Bernard Williams, *Descartes: The Project of Pure Enquiry* (Harmondsworth: Penguin, 1978), p. 64. Williams himself, of course, is *not* a conceptualist anti-realist, holding that what he calls an 'absolute conception' of reality *is* possible.

[7] See Michael Dummett, *Frege: Philosophy of Language*, 2nd edn (London: Duckworth, 1981), p. 563.

[8] See David Wiggins, *Sameness and Substance Renewed* (Cambridge University Press, 2001), p. 6.

Identity conditions and their grounds   109

Not only is this view deeply anti-realist; it is also, as I have said, doubtfully coherent. For those who philosophize in these terms rarely stop to think about how their doctrine is supposed to accommodate *thinkers*, their *thoughts*, and the *concepts* that they deploy. For these, too, are putative kinds of entities, whose essences, according to the conceptualist doctrine, must like all others be constituted by 'our' concepts of them. It is at this point that the conceptualist manifestly paints himself into a corner from which there is no escape. There simply is no coherent position to be adopted according to which *all* essences are constituted by concepts, because concepts themselves are either *something* or else *nothing* – they either exist or they do not. If they don't, then conceptualism is out of business. But if they do, then they themselves have an essence – *what it is* to be a concept. The conceptualist, to be consistent, must say that the essence of *concepts* is constituted by our *concept* of a concept. But what could this *mean*? And what could it mean, according to conceptualism, to say that the concept of a concept 'has application' – that *there are* concepts? I don't believe that conceptualism has any intelligible answer to such questions. The lesson, I take it, is that at least *some* essences must be mind-independent, in a way that conceptualism denies. The next task is to try to understand what this entails and how it can be possible.

6 A REALIST VIEW OF ESSENCE AND IDENTITY CONDITIONS

So what *are* essences, if they are not – or, at least, not always, 'constituted by concepts'? The temptation is to say that they are abstract or 'Platonic' entities that can be grasped only by the intellect. This temptation should be resisted, in my view – though not for the reason that I am hostile to abstract entities quite generally, for I am not. But it would be equally disastrous, I think, to try to locate essences as entities to be found in the world of concrete things existing in space and time. This, in effect, was the error of the objector who challenged us to explain how the essence of a material object of any kind is determined by, or supervenes upon, its material constitution. Or, rather, it was the error of any essentialist who was tempted to try to meet that challenge in the terms in which it was posed. Paradoxical though it might superficially seem to be, the well-advised essentialist will say that essences are not *entities* at all – are not to be included amongst what *there is* in the world, whether abstract or concrete. Rich though the world is in respect of the many kinds of entities that it contains, the *essences* of entities of those kinds are not *further entities* to be included in an inventory of what there is. A fortiori, essences are not

110 *Identity*

'constituted' by anything – neither by concepts nor by entities of other types, such as properties or propositions. Part of the point here is that *all* entities have essences, so that if we took essences themselves just to be entities of a certain kind, then they too would have to have essences, and so on ad infinitum. The essence of an entity of kind K can certainly *involve* other entities of various kinds – as, for example, the essence of a bronze statue involves *bronze particles* and a certain characteristic *shape*. But the essence is not *itself* an entity, nor is it somehow 'composed' or 'constituted' by the entities, or kinds of entity, which it 'involves'. Indeed, we cannot really do much better than to repeat that the essence of a K is *what it is* to be a K – without, of course, any implication that 'what it is to be a K' is itself *something*, an entity of another kind. If there are, or even merely *could be*, Ks, then there is a *fact of the matter* as to *what it is to be a K*, which obtains – at least in many cases – quite independently of thinkers and their concepts. (Some kinds of entities are genuinely mind-dependent in some fashion, which is why I qualify the foregoing statement in the way that I do.) It is such a fact that a thinker must grasp in order to be able to possess, and evaluate, the belief that Ks exist. For, as I have said before, one is in no position to be able to judge whether or not there is evidence in favour of the existence of Ks unless one knows what Ks are supposed to *be* – what their *essence* is. But facts about essence are not made true by the existence of anything whatever. Essential truths are, in that sense, *truths without truthmakers*. And any rational thinker must be able to grasp at least some essential truths, simply in order to be able to know *what it is* that he or she is thinking and reasoning *about*. Moreover, essences are the ultimate grounds of all *modal* truths – at least, where the kind of modality that we are concerned with is so-called *metaphysical* possibility and necessity. If something is possibly or necessarily the case in this sense, it is so in virtue of the essences or natures of the entities, or kinds of entities, that are implicated in the modal fact in question. For example, that it is metaphysically impossible for a statue to survive the loss of its shape is a fact that obtains in virtue of the essence of a statue – in virtue of *what it is* to be a statue. Similarly, that it is metaphysically possible for a bronze statue and a lump of bronze to exist in exactly the same place at the same time is a fact that obtains in virtue of the essences of a bronze statue and a lump of bronze.

And so it is with *all* facts about what is metaphysically possible or necessary. These facts are *not* grounded in truths about so-called 'possible worlds', however we choose to conceive of the latter. But *are* there, in fact, possible worlds? Before we can answer that existential question, we must

Identity conditions and their grounds III

first determine what it is that we are supposed to be talking about – what kind of entity a possible world putatively *is*, and so what its *essence* is. We may be told, for instance, that a possible world is a maximal consistent set of propositions, or that a possible world is a maximal spatiotemporally connected sum of concrete objects. But are such entities *possible? Could* entities of these kinds exist – in the metaphysical sense of 'could'? Perhaps so – although careful reflection on the matter may reveal that the case is otherwise. For, in each case, the putative essence of possible worlds is specified in terms of entities of other kinds – sets, propositions, sums, and concrete objects. And it may turn out that, in virtue of the essences of entities of these kinds, there *could be no such thing* as a 'possible world' in either of the senses canvassed. Be that as it may. It doesn't really matter for our purposes, for it is already apparent that facts about possible worlds *could not* be the ultimate ground of all metaphysical possibility and necessity. For they can only constitute that ground if they themselves exist and hence are *possible*, and whether this is so will depend upon the essences of other entities of the kinds just mentioned. But then, even if possible worlds *do* exist, they cannot constitute the ground of all metaphysical possibility, because they cannot constitute the ground of the possibilities on which *their own* existence depends. The lesson is that no deep insight into modal metaphysics can be gained by reflection on possible worlds. Essences alone are the ground of all modal truth. Possible worlds are, at best, just *one* kind of entity amongst very many that do or could exist. And if they do or could exist, *some* modal truths will obtain in virtue of their essences, both general and individual. For example, such a modal truth might be that nothing can exist in more than one possible world. But, even so, many other modal truths will obtain in virtue of the essences of *other* kinds of entity. Possible-worlds metaphysics is an attempt to get the metaphysics of modality on the cheap. It is a snare and a delusion for the unwary metaphysician. But this is a subject to which I shall return in much more detail in Chapter 8, since it certainly deserves fuller examination.

7 REPLIES TO SOME ANTICIPATED OBJECTIONS

I imagine that essentialism of the sort that I am recommending will be attacked for a number of predictable reasons, one of which will be this. It will be complained that such essentialism implies excessive liberality about the *kinds* of entity that could possibly exist. For instance, it may not seem to exclude the possibility of such (allegedly) *entia non grata* as something of the following supposed kind: a material object consisting of a lump of bronze and a live cat situated ten metres away from that lump. The thought is that such an object would supposedly be one which, in virtue of its essence, would come into existence whenever a live cat moved to a position ten metres away from a lump of bronze and would go out of existence whenever the cat moved to a different distance from the lump – and that it is absurd to suppose that anything can come into or go out of existence for this sort of reason. However, it would be rash to suppose, *quite generally*, that no entity of any genuine kind can be such that it is part of its essence that it comes into existence when two entities of other kinds move to a certain distance from each other and goes out of existence when they move further apart. After all, a *hydrogen atom* is just such an entity: it comes into existence when a proton and an electron are close enough to each other for the latter to be captured by the former and goes out of existence when the electron is subsequently ejected from its orbital.

Why, however, do we say that a *new entity* – a hydrogen atom – is first created and later destroyed in these circumstances? Because *new causal powers* are brought into being when a proton and an electron stand in the specified relation to one another – causal powers that are not possessed by either free protons or free electrons individually. These powers must be attributed to *something* as their bearer, and this thing is a hydrogen atom. It is – or so I am strongly inclined to urge – part of the essence of any material object to have certain causal powers that are not possessed by any of its material constituents (if it has any) individually. That, indeed, is why I am very doubtful whether a mere 'mereological sum' of material objects should be considered to be a further material object in its own right. For all that is supposedly required for the existence of a certain mereological sum is the *coexistence* of the various objects of which it is said to be the sum. I cannot, however, see how such a sum differs from the *bare plurality* of those objects. In short, I don't see how it can be supposed that *they* together compose *it* – and hence that *it* exists – merely in virtue of their coexistence. A genuine principle of composition for material objects of any kind must, I believe, be one in virtue of which an object composed according to that principle acquires causal powers additional to any that are possessed by its material components individually.

Returning, then, to our example of the putative object composed by a lump of bronze and a live cat situated ten metres away from it: if I could be persuaded that new causal powers *were* brought into being by this quite specific arrangement, analogous to those acquired by a hydrogen atom upon its formation from a proton and an electron, then I would be happy

Identity conditions and their grounds 113

to recognize this as an object of a genuine kind. But I shall need a lot of persuasion! Note, in this connection, that *lumps of bronze* do not fare badly by this criterion, for in virtue of the mutual *adherence* of their constituent particles, they *do* acquire causal powers that are not possessed by the particles individually – powers such as a certain *moment of inertia* that is different from any possessed by any of those particles individually. Note, too, that what I have just said about 'mereological sums' of material objects does not carry over to *sets* of material objects, because sets are abstract objects and are not, in any case, *composed* by their members – the members of a set are not *parts* of it (even if, following David Lewis's proposal, we could say that *subsets* of a set were parts of it).[9] Finally, note that the requirement that material objects should have causal powers over and above those individually possessed by their component parts (if they have any) does not present problems for such objects as bronze statues, which are 'made' of, but not identical with, lumps of matter. For even if a bronze statue has the same causal powers as the lump of bronze of which it is made, it still has, therefore, causal powers over and above those individually possessed by the bronze particles composing both it and the lump – for the lump itself, as I have just remarked, has such additional causal powers. Moreover, it is at least arguable that the statue has *some* causal powers not even possessed by the lump, such as the power to evoke an aesthetic response in someone viewing it.

8 SOME ADDITIONAL OBSERVATIONS AND A SUMMARY CONCLUSION

As I have already indicated, it is one thing to establish that entities of a putative kind *K* genuinely *could* exist, but another to establish that they actually *do* exist. The former task is at least partially an a priori one, which is completed once we succeed in grasping the *essence* of entities of kind *K*. Consider again the putative kind *lump of bronze*. A lump of bronze, if there can be such a thing, is in essence a maximal connected aggregate of bronze particles and, supposedly, a material object. Provided that there is such a species of matter as *bronze*, and provided that it is *particulate* in nature – rather than, say, homogeneous and infinitely divisible – then, provided also that bronze particles can *adhere* together in the way necessary for them to compose such an aggregate, such an aggregate can exist. But there is a further requirement to be met if such an aggregate is to qualify as a

---

[9] See David Lewis, *Parts of Classes* (Oxford: Blackwell, 1991).

Identity

material object, namely that in virtue of its component bronze particles' adhering together in the specified way, additional causal powers are generated which can be attributed to the aggregate as a whole but not individually to its component particles. Only empirical inquiry, it seems, can ultimately reveal to us whether bronze is a distinctive species of matter that is particulate in nature; whether its particles can adhere together; and whether, in virtue of their adhering together, new causal powers are generated. Then, however, the further empirical discovery that sometimes bronze particles *do* adhere together in the required way will suffice to establish that some lumps of bronze do actually exist. What is clear is that, inasmuch as a grasp of essences is necessary in order to establish empirically that entities of any putative kind actually exist, the task of establishing such existential truths cannot be a wholly a posteriori one, but includes, rather, ineliminable a priori elements.

We have also seen that, in the case of many kinds of entity, their essence involves entities of *other* kinds – as, for example, the essence of entities of the kind *lump of bronze* involves *bronze particles*, and the essence of entities of the kind *hydrogen atom* involves *protons* and *electrons*. When the essence of entities of a kind K involves entities of other kinds, Ks stand in a relationship of *essential dependence* with entities of those other kinds. Thus, for instance, *hydrogen atoms* are essentially dependent on the protons and electrons that compose them. Again, *sets* are essentially dependent on their members. However, it would seem that essential dependence is necessarily an *asymmetrical* relationship.[10] Thus protons and electrons are not essentially dependent on hydrogen atoms, as is demonstrable by the fact that they can exist without them. More importantly, the *identity* of a hydrogen atom plausibly depends on the identities of its constituent proton and electron, just as the identity of a set depends on the identities of its members. (We may speak loosely of hydrogen atoms *exchanging* electrons, but I think it would be preferable to say that hydrogen nuclei capture and lose electrons.) By contrast, the identity of a proton or an electron does not depend on the identity of any hydrogen atom of which it may happen to be a component, nor does the identity of any entity depend on the identity of the sets of which it is a member. But because essential dependence is an asymmetrical relationship, it would seem that – barring an infinite regress of an apparently unacceptable sort – there must be some *fundamental* kinds of entities, whose essences do not involve entities of any other kind

---

[10] See further my *The Possibility of Metaphysics: Substance, Identity, and Time* (Oxford: Clarendon Press, 1998), Chapter 6.

Identity conditions and their grounds

and whose *identities*, therefore, do not depend on the identities of entities of any other kind. Entities of such kinds will have *primitive* identity and, accordingly, no informative and non-circular statement of their identity conditions – no *criterion* of identity – will be forthcoming in their case. This does not mean, however, that it will be impossible to determine whether – and if so, when – persisting entities of such kinds come into being and go out of existence. For if, as it seems they must, such entities have distinctive *causal powers*, we may be able to tell, with some degree of confidence, whether or not such an entity continues to exist by seeing whether or not its distinctive causal powers continue to be exercised. This, in effect, is how in practice we tell whether or not something like an *electron* continues to exist or has been destroyed. The distinctive causal powers of an electron are grounded in its essential properties, such as its distinctive rest mass, unit negative charge and spin of one-half. When, for example, an electron is 'annihilated' by interacting with a positron, their opposing charges cancel each other and their combined mass is converted into a burst of energy. From these effects we can judge that nothing remains that possesses the distinctive rest mass and charge of an electron and that, therefore, the original electron has ceased to exist. This is despite the fact that an electron, being a simple or non-composite entity, is not essentially dependent for its existence or identity on any other particular entity of any kind.

I am now in a position to give a summary answer to the most pressing question that has arisen in this chapter: *How are identity conditions grounded?* The answer, I propose, is that the identity conditions of entities of any kind *K* are grounded in the essence of *K*s – *what it is* to be a *K*. The essence of a kind *K* is not, however, a further *entity* of any kind, neither abstract nor concrete. As rational beings, we must be able to grasp the essences of at least some kinds of entities. Indeed, it is part of the essence of a *rational being* that it has such a grasp. In grasping the essence of entities of a kind *K*, we come to grasp their *identity conditions* and may – albeit, very often, only with some effort – be able to formulate an explicit *criterion of identity* for *K*s, which specifies their identity conditions in an informative and non-circular way. Such a criterion will make reference to, or quantify over, entities of *other* kinds involved in the essence of *K*s, unless *K* is a *fundamental* kind of entity – in which case, its essence will *not* involve entities of any other kinds and no informative and non-circular criterion of identity for *K*s will be forthcoming. It is knowledge of essences that grounds all of our *modal* knowledge of what is metaphysically *possible* or *necessary*, including our knowledge of what sorts of changes an entity

116 *Identity*

can or cannot *survive* or *persist* through, if indeed it is an entity in whose nature it is to persist. The persistence conditions of such an entity are *not* grounded in its material constitution, if it is a material object, but in its general *essence*. This is why it is a mistake to find it at all puzzling that two distinct material objects, of different kinds and possessing different identity conditions, may simultaneously be composed by the same material constituents, as in the case of the bronze statue and the lump of bronze of which it is 'made'. Our *individuative concepts* – our concepts of those kinds that have *individual objects* as their instances, distinguishable in principle from one another – are *ways of thinking* of entities of those kinds that accurately reflect their general *essences*, thus involving a grasp of their identity conditions and thereby an understanding of what makes one particular instance of such a kind distinct from another. The essences of such kinds are not *constituted* by our individuative concepts, but are in general entirely mind-independent. *Conceptualism* – the doctrine that all such essences are constituted by our individuative concepts – leads inexorably to an incoherent global anti-realism and must be rejected. However, it is not enough, in general, to grasp the essence of entities of a kind K in order to know whether or not entities of that kind *actually exist*. For that purpose, we must appeal to *empirical* evidence – at least in the case of *concrete*, as opposed to *abstract*, entities. At the same time, to the extent that such empirical inquiry always depends upon a grasp of essences, there is an unavoidable a priori element in our knowledge of the existence of entities of any kind whatever.

PART III
Modality

CHAPTER 7

Identity, vagueness, and modality

I have said a great deal about identity in previous chapters and now want to develop in more depth the transition, already begun in Chapter 6, to an explicit focus on *modality* – that is, the important family of notions that includes those of necessity, possibility, and contingency. However, before going into the heart of such notions, there are some important issues in philosophical logic that I want to discuss concerning the relationship between identity and modality. More specifically, I want to examine certain controversial modal claims concerning identity that have been much debated in the philosophical literature of the past forty years or so, particularly the alleged *necessity* of identity – that is, the claim that truths of identity are *necessarily* true. Paralleling this claim, as we shall shortly see, is another often-made claim about identity: that truths of identity can never be *vague* or *indeterminate*, other than merely as a consequence of imprecision in our language or thought about the world. *The world itself*, it is often maintained, cannot be vague or contain 'vague objects'. Both of these claims about identity – that it can never be contingent and never be vague – are ones whose alleged proofs, I shall argue, are open to question and indeed open to question for very similar reasons. The alleged proofs, I shall try to show, are subtly question-begging and try to make logic deliver answers to metaphysical questions that logic is inherently incapable of answering. I shall start with the issue of vagueness and identity and, along the way, show how this parallels the issue of necessity and identity.

I VAGUE OBJECTS AND VAGUE IDENTITY: EVANS'S ARGUMENT

A good place to begin a discussion of vagueness and identity is with Gareth Evans's classic one-page article 'Can There Be Vague Objects?',[1] whose brevity belies its subtlety and importance. Despite the paper's title, Evans's

---

[1] Gareth Evans, 'Can There Be Vague Objects?', *Analysis* 38 (1978), p. 208.

119

120 *Modality*

purpose was to demonstrate, by means of a *reductio ad absurdum* argument, that there cannot fail to be a fact of the matter as to whether an object *a* is identical with an object *b* – so that his direct concern seems really to be with vague *identity* rather than with vague *objects*.[2] It will prove instructive in due course to compare Evans's argument with another notorious 'proof' of a metaphysically contentious doctrine, the Barcan–Kripke proof of the necessity of identity. More precisely, Evans's argument may fruitfully be compared with a closely related proof of the *non-contingency* of identity. It seems not implausible, indeed, that Evans had the Barcan–Kripke proof partly in mind as a model for his own argument, given the obvious similarities between them and the notoriety of the Barcan–Kripke proof at the time at which he was writing.

As has just been said, what is at stake in Evans's paper is the possibility of there *failing to be a fact of the matter* as to whether an object *a* is identical with an object *b*. That this is so seems clear from his opening remark – 'It is sometimes said that the world might itself *be* vague' – for he contrasts vagueness of this supposed kind with 'vagueness being a deficiency in our mode of describing the world', with which he clearly has no quarrel. In other words, his target is what may be called *ontic* rather than *semantic* vagueness – although whether 'vagueness' is really an apt word in the ontic case is a moot point. As we have already observed, it is also a moot point whether, in the light of its contents, the title of Evans's paper is apt in representing it as concerning the question whether there can be vague *objects*. It seems that the real question is, rather, whether there can be objects whose *identities* are ontically indeterminate: that is, once again, whether there can ever fail to be a fact of the matter as to whether an object *a* is identical with an object *b*.

Here, however, another preliminary observation is in order before we turn to Evans's argument itself. This concerns Evans's curious remark that the idea whose coherence he seeks to call into question is 'the idea that the world might contain certain objects about which it is a *fact* that they have fuzzy boundaries'. This remark confirms that Evans's concern is with *ontic* rather than with semantic vagueness, but it is puzzling in its suggestion that the idea of ontic indeterminacy of identity is necessarily connected with the idea of the possession of 'fuzzy boundaries' – by which one assumes is meant 'fuzzy' *spatial or temporal* boundaries. It is true that cases

---

[2] A closely related argument was independently developed by Nathan Salmon – see his *Reference and Essence* (Oxford: Blackwell, 1982), pp. 243–6. See also David Wiggins, *Sameness and Substance Renewed* (Cambridge University Press, 2001), pp. 162–3. But I shall concentrate on Evans's version.

of *semantic* vagueness frequently concern the drawing of such boundaries. For instance, it may be said that our use of the name 'Mount Everest' does not determine a precise spatial boundary between terrain that is part of the mountain so named and terrain that is not. In this case, there are many different ways of drawing a precise spatial boundary, all of which are equally consistent with our use of the name: the 'fuzziness' lies not in any boundary that may be drawn, for each boundary that may be drawn is a precise one – rather, it lies in our language, which does not determine that any given one of these precise boundaries must be drawn in preference to any other. But it is far from obvious that ontic indeterminacy of identity would have to be grounded in a genuine 'fuzziness' in boundaries themselves, quite independent of language – as though boundaries could somehow *really* be 'smeared out'. It isn't even clear what could be meant by saying this. Fortunately for the advocate of ontic indeterminacy of identity, however, making sense of such a notion is not crucial to the position that he seeks to defend. As we shall see in section 5 below, the most plausible cases of ontically indeterminate identity do not turn on the issue of boundaries at all. However, Evans's assumption – that ontic indeterminacy of identity would have to have something to do with 'really' fuzzy boundaries – is widely shared and has done much to perpetuate scepticism about the possibility of such indeterminacy.[3]

Now let us turn to Evans's remarkably simple argument. His 'proof' contains just five lines. It begins with the following proposition, assumed for *reductio*:

(1) $\nabla(a = b)$

Evans indicates that (1) is to be understood as expressing the assumption that the sentence '$a = b$' is of indeterminate truth-value, with the idea of indeterminacy being expressed by the sentential operator '∇'. So, it seems, (1) may read as 'It is indeterminate whether it is true that $a = b$', or, more concisely, 'It is indeterminate whether $a = b$'. And as was implied earlier, we may take this to be another way of saying 'There is no fact of the matter as to whether $a = b$'. For the purposes of *reductio*, (1) is being assumed to be *true*, so it is being assumed that there *is* a fact of the matter as to whether there is no fact of the matter as to whether $a = b$. We shall return to this point later, since it bears on something that Evans says at the very end of his paper.

---

[3] See Rosanna Keefe, *Theories of Vagueness* (Cambridge University Press, 2000), p. 15.

122   *Modality*

To explain and justify the next step of his proof, Evans says that '(1) reports a fact about *b* which we may express by ascribing to it the property "$\lambda x[\nabla(x = a)]$"'(I use here, for clarity, the more familiar lambda symbol in place of Evans's circumflex). Because Evans takes (1) to report this (purported) fact and expresses the (purported) fact by

(2) $\lambda x[\nabla(x = a)]b$

he takes it that (2) follows from (1). I shall assume that (2) may be read as '*b* has the property of being such that it is indeterminate whether it is identical with *a*', or equivalently as '*b* has the property of being such that there is no fact of the matter as to whether it is identical with *a*'.

Next, Evans asserts as a premise this:

(3) $\sim\nabla(a = a)$

which we may read as asserting 'It is *not* indeterminate whether *a* is identical with *a*', or equivalently as 'There *is* a fact of the matter as to whether *a* is identical with *a*'. Presumably, what justifies this premise is that it is *true*, and so a *fact*, that *a* is identical with *a*, whatever object *a* might be. For, surely, if it is indeed a fact that *a* is identical with *a*, then there is a fact of the matter as to whether *a* is identical with *a* – the fact in question being the fact that *a* is identical with *a*.

Evans then supposes that, just as (2) follows from (1), so the following follows from (3):

(4) $\sim\lambda x[\nabla(x = a)]a$

Modelling our reading of (4) on that of (2) above, (4) may be read as 'It is not the case that *a* has the property of being such that it is indeterminate whether it is identical with *a*', or equivalently as 'It is not the case that *a* has the property of being such that there is no fact of the matter as to whether it is identical with *a*'.

Finally, Evans says that 'by Leibniz's law, we may derive from (2) and (4)' the conclusion of his proof:

(5) $\sim(a = b)$

Evans clearly has in mind here the version of Leibniz's law which asserts that if an object *a* is identical with an object *b*, then *a* has any property that *b* has and vice versa. Contraposing, if *a* does *not* have some property that *b* has, then *a* is *not* identical with *b*. Now, in lines (4) and (2) respectively it is stated that *a* does *not* have a certain property – the property of being such that it is indeterminate whether it is identical with *a* – and that *b* *does* have

Identity, vagueness, and modality 123

this property. Consequently, it may be inferred from (2) and (4) by the contrapositive of Leibniz's law – as above interpreted – that *a* is not identical with *b*, which is what (5) states.

(5) itself does not directly contradict (1), so we do not yet formally have a *reductio ad absurdum* proof of the falsehood of (1). To make good this seeming deficiency, Evans makes the following final remark, which has given rise to some puzzlement and a great deal of discussion:

If 'Indefinitely' and its dual, 'Definitely' ('$\triangle$') generate a modal logic as strong as S5, (1)–(4) and, presumably, Leibniz's law, may each be strengthened with a 'Definitely' prefix, enabling us to derive

(5*) $\triangle\sim(a = b)$

which is straightforwardly inconsistent with (1).

The first oddity about this remark is that we were initially prompted to read the sentential operator '∇' *not* as 'indefinitely', but as something like 'it is indeterminate whether'. In fact, the nearest that Evans comes to spelling out exactly how we are to read a formula like (1) is when he says, by way of introducing (1) as an assumption for *reductio*, 'Let "*a*" and "*b*" be singular terms such that the sentence "*a* = *b*" is of indeterminate truth-value'. This actually suggests a reading of (1) as 'The sentence "*a* = *b*" is of indeterminate truth-value'. However, this is a metalinguistic statement, whereas Evans quite explicitly intended his symbol '∇' to be a *sentential operator*; that is to say, an expression that forms a sentence of a given language when it is prefixed to another sentence of the same language. This is why it seems natural to read (1) as was proposed earlier, namely as 'It is indeterminate whether (it is true that) *a* is identical with *b*'.

However, another possible reading would be something like 'It is indeterminately true that *a* is identical with *b*', where this is seen as being analogous to the modal statement 'It is contingently true that *a* is identical with *b*'.[4] And, indeed, this analogy might superficially seem advantageous if one wants, as was suggested earlier, to draw certain parallels between Evans's proof and the Barcan–Kripke proof of the necessity of identity. But this reading requires us to understand (1) as expressing, so to speak, a *way* in which it is (supposedly) *true* that *a* is identical with *b* – to wit, 'indeterminately', as opposed to 'determinately'. It is not inconceivable that Evans himself did have something like this in mind.[5] And, indeed, a

---

[4] Compare Terence Parsons, *Indeterminate Identity: Metaphysics and Semantics* (Oxford: Clarendon Press, 2000), pp. 45 and 204 ff.

[5] Compare again Parsons, *Indeterminate Identity*, pp. 204 ff.

124   *Modality*

reading like this might well be appropriate if *semantic* vagueness were at issue, because a 'supervaluational' treatment of such vagueness would supply a reading of 'It is indeterminately true that *a* is identical with *b*' as saying that the sentence '*a* is identical with *b*' *is true on some but not all precisifications* of the references of the names '*a*' and '*b*'.[6] After all, it may be said, being true *on some precisifications* is, at least in some sense, a way of being true. However, we are now taking it that semantic vagueness is *not* what is at stake – and it is not easy to make clear sense of an 'ontic' analogue of such 'indeterminate truth'. We are taking the interest of Evans's proof to lie in its apparent demonstration that there cannot fail to be a fact of the matter as to whether or not an object *a* is identical with an object *b*. And this is undoubtedly how most other philosophers have viewed it too. So we shall carry on viewing it in this way.

But now the question is whether, if we view the proof in this way, we can make sense of Evans's final remark, quoted above. At first sight, at least, it doesn't look as though we can. For if '∇' is read as 'it is indeterminate whether (it is true that)', or 'there is no fact of the matter as to whether', how could this sentential operator be understood to have a *dual*, '$\triangle$', in the sense familiar in modal logic? The modal operators '$\Diamond$' and '$\square$' are 'duals' in this familiar sense, with each being definable in terms of the other together with negation – so that '$\Diamond p$' is equivalent to '$\sim\square\sim p$' and '$\square p$' is equivalent to '$\sim\Diamond\sim p$'. Obviously, Evans's remark, quoted above, that (5*) is 'straightforwardly inconsistent with (1)' presumes an analogous equivalence between '∇p' and '$\sim\triangle\sim p$', because only if (1) is thus equivalent to '$\sim\triangle\sim(a = b)$' does it contradict (5*). But if we read Evans's other operator, '$\triangle$', as 'it is not indeterminate whether (it is true that)', or 'there is a fact of the matter as to whether', *do* '∇' and '$\triangle$' turn out to be suitably interdefinable with the help of negation? *Is* it the case that '∇p' is equivalent to '$\sim\triangle\sim p$' on this reading? That is to say, is 'It is indeterminate whether *p*' equivalent to 'It is not not indeterminate whether not *p*'? (The double negation here is required, of course, since we have elected to read '$\triangle$' as 'it is *not* indeterminate whether'.)

Now, 'It is not not indeterminate whether not *p*' is obviously equivalent, by double negation elimination, to 'It is indeterminate whether not *p*', so our question reduces to one of whether this is in turn equivalent to 'It is indeterminate whether *p*'. But then, surprising though this might have seemed prior to investigation, it turns out that our question does in fact have a positive answer. For it seems clear that 'It is indeterminate

---

[6] Compare David Lewis, 'Vague Identity: Evans Misunderstood', *Analysis* 48 (1988), pp. 128–30.

Identity, vagueness, and modality

whether *p'* is true if and only if 'It is indeterminate whether not *p'* is true. That is to say, it seems clear that, as we have proposed otherwise to express it, 'There is no fact of the matter as to whether *p'* is true just in case 'There is no fact of the matter as to whether not *p'* is true. For if there *was* a fact of the matter as to whether not *p*, this would either be because it was a fact that not *p* or because it was a fact that *p* – and, either way, it would follow that there was likewise a fact of the matter as to whether *p*. We see, then, that even if Evans's operators '∇' and '$\triangle$' are interpreted in the fashion that we have proposed, they do turn out to be interdefinable with the help of negation in a manner that exactly parallels the interdefinability of the dual modal operators '$\Diamond$' and '$\square$'.

However, this is by no means enough to confirm Evans's speculation, in his final remarks, that his two operators 'generate a modal logic as strong as S5'. So we are not in a position to endorse his attempt to turn his derivation of (5) from (1) and (3) into an argument with a conclusion that is 'straightforwardly inconsistent with (1)', namely (5*), by 'strengthening' (1) to (4) and Leibniz's law with the prefix '$\triangle$'. At the same time, it also appears that nothing so ambitious as this is needed in order to turn Evans's derivation of (5) from (1) and (3) into a formal *reductio ad absurdum* proof, given the interpretation of the operators '∇' and '$\triangle$' now being proposed. For it appears that on this interpretation we can simply *extend* the existing derivation of (5) from (1) and (3) by going on to derive (5*) directly from (5). Recall once more that, as we are now proposing to interpret it, '$\triangle$' may be read as 'it is not indeterminate whether (it is true that)', or equivalently as 'there is a fact of the matter as to whether'. Now, for the purposes of *reductio*, (1) is assumed be *true*. As Evans himself says, it supposedly 'reports a fact'. And we may agree with Evans that premise (3) is *true* – indeed, that it is logically true. But if the derivation of (5) from these is valid, then it is *truth-preserving*, so that if (1) and (3) are true, so too is (5). But if (5) is true, then it is *true*, and so a *fact*, that *a* is not identical with *b*, in which case there *is* a fact of the matter as to whether *a* is not identical with *b*: which is what (5*) says. So we may extend Evans's original argument by deriving (5*) directly from (5). To be sure, to call (5*) a *strengthening* of (5), given our proposed reading of Evans's sentential operator '$\triangle$', would be highly misleading. For on this interpretation it is not the case that (5*) entails but is not entailed by (5) and so (5*) is not in this sense 'stronger than' (5). The question at issue now, however, is whether the original derivation of (5) from (1) and (3) may legitimately be turned into a derivation of (5*) from (1) and (3), given the proposed interpretation of the operator '$\triangle$' – and it seems clear enough that it can.

126   *Modality*

And then all that is further needed in order to turn Evans's original argument into a formal *reductio* of (1), on this interpretation, is the interdefinability of '∇' and '$\triangle$' that we established earlier, for this allows us to derive the negation of (1) from (5*).

Let us now briefly sum up our findings so far. It seems that Evans's sentential operator '∇' can and should be interpreted as meaning 'it is indeterminate whether (it is true that)', or equivalently as 'there is no fact of the matter as to whether', and that on this interpretation it is, with the help of negation, interdefinable with his other sentential operator, '$\triangle$', so that '∇p' is logically equivalent to '$\sim\triangle\sim p$'. It also appears that, with '∇' and '$\triangle$' thus interpreted, Evans has no problem in turning his original argument from (1) and (3) to (5) into a formal *reductio ad absurdum* proof of the impossibility of ontic indeterminacy of identity, subject only to the following condition: that his *original* argument – which we shall henceforth refer to simply as 'Evans's argument' – is itself valid. We shall shortly see, however, that there is reason to suppose that Evans's argument is *not* in fact valid.

2 IS EVANS'S ARGUMENT QUESTION-BEGGING?

There is reason to suspect, on closer inspection of Evans's argument, that it is subtly *question-begging*. By a 'question-begging' argument is meant, roughly speaking, one which in some manner already assumes or presupposes something that it is supposed to establish. Now, of course, by no means every question-begging argument can be convicted of containing an invalid step. An argument for a conclusion p that had p as its only premise would be blatantly question-begging, but it does not contain an invalid step: for p certainly entails p. However, an argument can be more subtly question-begging than this. It may be, for example, that the validity of a step in the argument depends in some way upon something that the argument is supposed to establish – and in this sort of case, its being question-begging may well be indicative of its being invalid. Such may be the case with Evans's argument.

Why, then, might we consider that Evans's argument is subtly question-begging? For the following reason.[7] The crux of Evans's argument is his

---

[7] See my 'Vague Identity and Quantum Indeterminacy', *Analysis* 54 (1994), pp. 110–14; and my *The Possibility of Metaphysics: Substance, Identity, and Time* (Oxford: Clarendon Press, 1998), pp. 63 ff. For further discussion, see Harold Noonan, 'E. J. Lowe on Vague Identity and Quantum Indeterminacy', *Analysis* 55 (1995), pp. 14–19; and my 'Reply to Noonan on Vague Identity', *Analysis* 57 (1997), pp. 88–91.

Identity, vagueness, and modality 127

use of Leibniz's law in an attempt to show that, on the supposition that (1) is true, a and b differ in their properties and hence that a is *not* identical with b. The property that b is supposed to possess but a to lack is symbolized by Evans as '$\lambda x[\nabla(x = a)]$'. That b possesses this property is asserted in (2), which is taken to follow from (1). But notice that if it is valid to derive (2) from (1), then it is equally valid, by parity of reasoning, to derive the following from (1):

(2*) $\lambda x[\nabla(x = b)]a$

(2*) asserts that a possesses the property of being such that it is indeterminate whether it is identical with b. But now we may ask the following question: is this property, $\lambda x[\nabla(x = b)]$, which has just been attributed to a, the same as or different from the property that was previously attributed to b, $\lambda x[\nabla(x = a)]$? These 'two' properties 'differ' only by permutation of a and b. So it would appear that, on the assumption that it is indeed indeterminate whether a is identical with b, it is by the same token indeterminate whether these properties themselves are identical – and thereby equally indeterminate whether they are different. (Recall that 'It is indeterminate whether p' is equivalent to 'It is indeterminate whether not p'.) But in that case it seems that the most that can be concluded is that it is *indeterminate* whether a and b differ in their properties and hence not that a is *not* identical with b, but only that it is *indeterminate* whether a is identical with b – which is just what was originally assumed.

If this diagnosis is correct, Evans's argument is question-begging in the following way. The argument attempts to establish, through an application of Leibniz's law, the non-identity of a and b, by showing that b possesses a property that a lacks. And it attempts to derive this conclusion from the assumption that it is indeterminate whether a is identical with b. However, given that assumption, the very property in respect of which b is supposed to differ from a is one such that it is in fact *indeterminate* whether it is different from a property that a must equally be supposed to possess. Hence the alleged difference in the properties of a and b, required to establish their non-identity, already presupposes their non-identity and hence cannot be used to establish it. The problem arises, of course, from a special feature of the properties concerned, namely their *identity-involving* character. The properties in question are $\lambda x[\nabla(x = a)]$ and $\lambda x[\nabla(x = b)]$, which are 'identity-involving' in that each of them involves the identity of an object – a in the one case and b in the other. But since the properties 'differ' only by permutation of a and b, their own identity or distinctness turns entirely on the identity or distinctness of a and b themselves. Hence, if the

128   *Modality*

latter is indeterminate, as has been assumed, so too is the identity or distinctness of these properties indeterminate – the consequence being that Leibniz's law is powerless to distinguish the objects by means of such properties.

However, although this diagnosis calls into question the ability of Evans's argument to establish its intended conclusion, it does not yet show where exactly the argument can be supposed to go wrong. But it will be noticed that in offering this diagnosis we have said nothing about a crucial step in the argument, namely the derivation of (4) from (3). (3) seems to be a perfectly uncontentious logical truth, but (4) is the line in which a is asserted *not* to possess the property attributed to b in line (2). Now, as we have seen, given that the inference from (1) to (2*) is valid – which it must be if the parallel inference from (1) to (2) is valid – (1) entails that a possesses a property that is *not determinately distinct from* the property that a is denied to possess in (4). The two claims (2*) and (4) are clearly in tension with each other, because the first attributes to an object a property that is not determinately distinct from a property that the second denies that object to possess. But that a possesses the property attributed to it in (2*) is not an inconsistent claim in itself and cannot be inconsistent with the trivial logical truth (3). Hence the inference from (3) to (4) must *generate* a tension between (2*) and (4) that did not exist between (2*) and (3). And this implies that the claim made in (4) goes beyond anything entailed by (3). We may conclude that if Evans's argument is invalid, the most plausible place to locate its invalidity lies in the inference from (3) to (4). This suggestion is one that we shall return to shortly.

3 LESSONS FROM THE PARALLEL BETWEEN EVANS'S ARGUMENT AND THE BARCAN–KRIPKE PROOF OF THE NECESSITY OF IDENTITY

As was remarked earlier, there is a seeming parallel between Evans's argument and the Barcan–Kripke proof of the necessity of identity[8] – or, more exactly, between Evans's argument and a closely related modal proof of the *non-contingency* of identity.[9] To say that objects a and b are

---

[8] For this see Saul A. Kripke, 'Identity and Necessity', in M. K. Munitz (ed.), *Identity and Individuation* (New York University Press, 1971). Of course, one important formal difference is that Kripke's proof does not involve property abstraction. However, in section 4 below we shall be looking at a 'stripped-down' version of Evans's argument which likewise avoids property abstraction, so this difference is not as important as might at first be imagined.

[9] On these parallels, compare David Wiggins, *Sameness and Substance Renewed*, p. 163, and Rosanna Keefe, 'Contingent Identity and Vague Identity', *Analysis* 55 (1995), pp. 183–90.

Identity, vagueness, and modality 129

contingently identical is to say that they are identical but might have been non-identical. This is a supposition that one might attempt to reduce to absurdity by means of an argument formally paralleling Evans's, simply by reading his operator '∇' as meaning 'it is contingent that', on the understanding that 'It is contingent that p' is equivalent to 'p and possibly not p'. Thus reinterpreted, Evans's argument may be paraphrased as follows. Suppose that (1) it is contingent that a is identical with b. Then it follows that (2) b possesses the property of being such that it is contingently identical with a. However, (3) it is not contingent that a is identical with a. And from this it follows that (4) a does not possess the property of being such that it is contingently identical with a. But from (2) and (4) it follows by Leibniz's law that a is *not* identical with b, which contradicts our initial assumption that a is contingently identical with b (recalling here, once more, that 'a is contingently identical with b' means 'a is identical with b but a might not have been identical with b').

One thing to notice about this argument for the non-contingency of identity (hereafter 'NCI') is that it does not need to be supplemented in the way that Evans's argument had to be in order to turn the latter into a formal *reductio ad absurdum* proof, because when Evans's operator '∇' is read as 'it is contingent that' the conclusion (5) directly contradicts the assumption (1). Although the arguments are formally indistinguishable, then, their status as formal proofs is not the same.

Notwithstanding this difference between Evans's argument and the argument for NCI, both may be charged with committing the same error of formal inference. The error, if error it is, lies in the inference of (4) from (3). And, indeed, the Barcan–Kripke proof of the necessity of identity may also be charged with committing an exactly similar logical error.[10] In the latter case, the erroneous step, according to this line of objection, is the inference of 'a possesses the property of being such that it is necessarily identical with a' from 'It is necessary that a is identical with a'. Since this step – the Barcan–Kripke step, as I shall call it – is much more familiar than, although formally exactly like, the step from (3) to (4) in Evans's proof and the argument for NCI, let us focus on it for the time being. Now, of course, a general complaint may be raised against the Barcan–Kripke step that it moves from a proposition ontologically committed merely to the existence of a certain *object*, a, to one ontologically committed in addition to the existence of a certain *property* – and, indeed, to what

---

[10] Compare my 'On the Alleged Necessity of True Identity Statements', *Mind* 91 (1982), pp. 579–84.

130 *Modality*

may appear to be a very strange kind of property. However, general complaints of this sort, for what they are worth, need not at present concern us, either with regard to the Barcan–Kripke proof or with regard to Evans's argument and the argument for NCI. We need have no hostility towards properties in general and – while it must be acknowledged that we cannot, on pain of paradox, suppose every meaningful predicate to express a property – it would be tendentious to respond to the arguments now under consideration by contending that the properties that they invoke simply do not exist. Certainly, if one can find fault with the arguments without needing to deny the existence of the properties, this will be a more satisfactory method of rebuttal.

So what, exactly, might be thought to be wrong with the Barcan–Kripke step? Just the following. Even if it is conceded that 'It is necessary that a is identical with a' entails that a possesses some corresponding property, it may be disputed what property this is – and, of course, there might be more than one such property. One property that a might be thought to possess in virtue of the necessary identity of a with a is the property of being necessarily identical with itself or, more simply put, *the property of necessary self-identity*. This, clearly, is a property that a could share with many other things – plausibly, indeed, it is one which it does and must share with every other thing. Obviously, this is a quite different property from the property of being necessarily identical with a which, it seems evident, a alone can possess. The question then is whether a may be said to possess the latter property simply in virtue of the fact that it is necessary that a is identical with a.

To answer this question, we need to think about the grounds of necessary truths. Some necessary truths are grounded purely in the laws of logic, which are themselves necessary truths.[11] An instance of a logical law need not itself qualify as a logical law, but it will inherit the necessity of the law of which it is an instance. The law of the reflexivity of identity – that everything is identical with itself – is a necessary truth. And an instance of the law, such as the singular proposition that a is identical with a, inherits that necessity. Hence it is necessary that a is identical with a. Against this it may be objected that if a is a contingent being, then a does not exist in every possible world, whence it cannot be true in every possible world that a is identical with a. There are various ways to reply to this objection – for instance, by championing a kind of 'free' logic that allows a singular proposition to be true even if its singular terms are

---

[11] Compare my *The Possibility of Metaphysics*, pp. 13 ff.

Identity, vagueness, and modality 131

'empty', thus denying that it entails the corresponding existential proposition. According to such an approach, that *a* is identical with *a* may be true even in a possible world in which *a* does not exist, so that even if *a* is a contingent being, it may nonetheless be affirmed that it is necessary that *a* is identical with *a*. Another strategy is to say that, where *a* is a contingent being, the proposition that *a* is identical with *a* is necessary in a restricted sense, namely in the sense that it is true in every possible world in which *a* exists. But whatever we say, it seems clear that we should say that some sort of necessity attaches to the fact that *a* is identical with *a* and that the ground of this necessity lies in the laws of logic.

What is by no means clear, however, is that the fact that *a* possesses the property of being necessarily identical with *a* – supposing there to be such a fact – is one whose ground could be held to lie solely in the laws of logic. The problem is that it would, it seems, be a substantive *metaphysical* fact of an essentialist character, whereas the laws of logic are properly conceived as being metaphysically neutral. No similar concern attaches to the thought that the laws of logic can ground the fact that *a*, like anything else, possesses the property of being necessarily self-identical. The laws of logic can ground facts about the properties of individuals, but only, it would seem, facts involving properties that are perfectly general in this way. The putative property of being necessarily identical with *a* is not, however, a perfectly general property. On the contrary, it is a property which, if it exists, *a* alone can possess. And the existence of such properties and their attribution to individual objects are matters for metaphysics, not logic. The problem with the Barcan–Kripke step, then, is that it purports to extract a metaphysical fact from a purely logical one. Our proposed objection to Evans's argument and the argument for NCI is just the same: that each of them tries to pull a metaphysical 'rabbit' out of a purely logical 'hat'. This, then, is what seems objectionable about the inference from (3) to (4) in each case.

Here it may be protested that there can be nothing logically suspect about that inference because it simply exploits the formal device of so-called *property abstraction*, which is equally at work in the inference from (1) to (2). However, here we may pose a dilemma for the defendants of the arguments. Either property abstraction is simply a notational reformulation, so that '$\lambda x[Fx]a$' is just an elaborate way of rewriting 'Fa', or else the property abstract '$\lambda x[Fx]$' is seriously intended to denote a *property*, in a way in which the predicate in 'Fa' need not be supposed to do. It should be borne in mind here, as always, that not every predicate can automatically be taken to denote a property, on pain of contradiction. If so-called

132   *Modality*

property abstraction is *not* understood necessarily to involve the denotation of a property, then it may indeed be no more than an elaborate rewriting device with a highly misleading name. But in that case lines (2) and (4) of Evans's argument and the argument for NCI are simply superfluous and we should evaluate the arguments in the form in which they would be left without them. This we shall do in a moment. On the other hand, if property abstraction *is* understood necessarily to involve the denotation of a property, then neither the inference from (1) to (2) nor the inference from (3) to (4) can be construed as a perfectly innocent logical step that cannot be subject to the sort of objection that was raised earlier.

4 A STRIPPED-DOWN VERSION OF EVANS'S ARGUMENT

Now we need to explore the possibility, just mentioned, of simply *stripping down* Evans's argument and the argument for NCI by removing lines (2) and (4). The problem now, of course, is that the arguments are supposed to involve an application of *Leibniz's law*, construed as the principle that if an object a is identical with an object b, then a has any property that b has and vice versa. And this principle cannot be applied unless properties are invoked in the arguments. The best that one could do instead is to invoke the principle of the substitutivity of identity. But how could that possibly work in the case of Evans's argument? How are we supposed to derive (5) directly from (1) and (3) by means of this principle? It might be supposed that we could assert the following as an instance of the principle of the substitutivity of identity:

(6) $a = b \rightarrow (\sim\!\nabla(a = a) \rightarrow \sim\!\nabla(a = b))$

and contrapose this to give

(7) $(\sim\!\nabla(a = a) \ \& \ \nabla(a = b)) \rightarrow \sim\!(a = b)$

Then, conjoining (1) and (3) and applying *modus ponens* to their conjunction and (7), we might suppose that we could detach the consequent of (7), which is (5).

One apparent problem with this strategy is that we seem to be using classical truth-functional operators and classical bivalent logic, when the presence of the indeterminacy operator precludes us from doing that.[12] Thus, for example, the contraposition of (6) to give (7) might be called into question. However, interesting though this line of objection may be,

---

[12] Compare Parsons, *Indeterminate Identity*, p. 47.

Identity, vagueness, and modality 133

it has the drawback that it will appear question-begging to someone who has yet to be persuaded that the notion of ontic indeterminacy of identity is really intelligible. In any case, such an objection would obviously not be appropriate when the operator '∇' is interpreted as expressing *contingency*, as in the argument for NCI, so let us consider whether it would be legitimate to reformulate *that* argument in this stripped-down fashion. And here we may again note that, in fact, the Barcan–Kripke argument in its original Kripkean formulation did not make use of property abstraction and proceeded along lines just like those now under consideration.[13]

The answer that we may give to this query recapitulates one that may be given regarding Kripke's original argument for the necessity of identity.[14] In essence, it is this. The principle of the substitutivity of identity is in fact a schema, of the form

(*) $x = y \rightarrow (Fx \rightarrow Fy)$

where the predicate letter 'F' may be uniformly replaced throughout by any predicate and the variables be bound by universal quantifiers or replaced by constants to give a logically true formula. In the case of the argument for NCI, the predicate that would need to be substituted for 'F' in (*) to deliver (6) as an instance of the principle is '$\sim\nabla(a = \xi)$', where 'ξ' marks an argument-place to be completed by the name of an object. (6) is obtained when 'x' and 'y' are replaced by 'a' and 'b' respectively. However, in order to derive (5) from (6), (1) and (3), we must discern this same predicate as present in (3), on pain of falling foul of a fallacy of equivocation. Now, of course, it is an article of faith of Fregean semantics that a proposition like (3), '$\sim\nabla(a = a)$', may be 'carved up' in different ways without this implying that it involves any kind of ambiguity. Thus it is assumed that (3) may equally well be characterized as saying of *a* that it is not contingent that *a* is identical with it and as saying of *a* that it is not contingent that it is identical with itself. However, that these really are just two ways of saying exactly the same thing is not, perhaps, as uncontentious as the Fregean orthodoxy assumes it to be.

Even if we set aside the question whether the predicates now at issue denote properties, it is clear that these predicates have different *meanings* – 'is not contingently self-identical' and 'is not contingently identical with *a*' certainly do not mean the same and so it is at least questionable whether, when they are predicates of the same subject term, 'a', the sentences thus

---

[13] See Kripke, 'Identity and Necessity', p. 136.
[14] See my 'On the Alleged Necessity of True Identity Statements'.

134 *Modality*

formed have exactly the same meaning. When two expressions with *different* meanings are each combined with another univocal expression, to form in each case a meaningful sentence, it would seem surprising that this could result in their forming sentences with exactly the *same* meaning. It is certainly not obvious that '*a* is not contingently self-identical' and '*a* is not contingently identical with *a*' are synonymous, but both of these English sentences are supposed to be representable by the same symbolic formula, '$\sim\nabla(a = a)$', which is assumed to be univocal. And the closest English equivalent to this formula, 'It is not contingent that *a* is identical with *a*', is assumed just to be another way of saying exactly the same thing. But all of this is certainly open to debate. Indeed, returning to the business about 'property abstraction', it seems that one way of construing this technical device is precisely as a means of *predicate disambiguation*, rather than a means of denoting properties. The idea would be that a formula like '$\nabla(a = a)$' is ambiguous, because it can be parsed as resulting from the combination of the name '*a*' with either of two different predicates, with one parsing being read as '$\lambda x[\nabla(x = x)]a$' and the other as '$\lambda x[\nabla(a = x)]a$'. The whole point of avoiding ambiguity in formal logic is that in such logic there should be a one-to-one correspondence between meaning and form, so that valid inferences can be identified as such purely in virtue of their form. The upshot of all this is that the 'stripped-down' version of the argument for NCI, invoking the principle of the substitutivity of identity in place of Leibniz's law, may be accused of involving a fallacy of equivocation which arises from an insufficiently perspicuous logical syntax.

We need to make it clear exactly what, according to this construal, is objectionable about the 'stripped-down' versions of the arguments for NCI and against the indeterminacy of identity. The objection to the argument for NCI is that in order for the conclusion (5) to be derived from (1) and (3) by means of the principle of the substitutivity of identity, the monadic predicate chosen to replace the schematic letter 'F' in that principle will have to be '$\sim\nabla(a = \xi)$', rather than '$\sim\nabla(\xi = \xi)$'. However, (3)'s status as a purely logical truth is plausible only if it is parsed as the result of filling both argument-places of the *second* of these predicates with the name '*a*'; that is, as saying of *a* that it is not contingent that it is self-identical. Indeed, if (3) is instead parsed as saying of *a* that it is not contingent that it is identical with *a* – which it needs to be if the argument for NCI is not to involve a fallacy of equivocation – then it appears that the argument turns out to be question-begging in a perfectly straightforward way, because (3) so parsed is effectively nothing less than an assertion of the non-contingency of identity. Recall that *a* here is an arbitrarily chosen object.

Identity, vagueness, and modality 135

And what (3) so parsed says of this object – and so, in effect, of any object – is that it is not contingent that it is the very object that it is: in other words, that it could not have been any other object. But this is precisely what the doctrine of the non-contingency of identity amounts to. The alternative parsing of (3) is quite different in its metaphysical import, for on that parsing (3) merely says of any arbitrarily chosen object that it could not have failed to be self-identical. And an exactly parallel objection can be levelled at Evans's argument, namely that his premise (3), depending on how it is parsed, is either too weak to sustain his conclusion that identity is never indeterminate or else implicitly presupposes it. On the innocuous parsing, (3) says of an arbitrarily chosen object that it is not indeterminate whether it is self-identical, whereas on the question-begging parsing it says of an arbitrarily chosen object that it is not indeterminate whether it is just *that* object. But precisely what it *means* to assert that an object may have indeterminate identity is that an object may be such that it is indeterminate whether it is just *that* object, as opposed to another.

5 A PLAUSIBLE EXAMPLE OF ONTICALLY INDETERMINATE IDENTITY

It is one thing to query Evans's argument and quite another to say that there are genuine counterexamples to his conclusion. But there do seem to be some,[15] which are worth describing here, partly in order to illustrate the point made earlier that ontic indeterminacy of identity need have nothing to do with 'fuzzy' spatial or temporal boundaries and partly to provide material for some remarks about the notion of 'singular reference'. One example involves the capture of a free electron by a helium ion, which thus comes to have two orbital electrons, one of which is subsequently emitted. Throughout this episode there exist two electrons, neither of which begins or ceases to exist during the period of time involved. But, it may plausibly be maintained, there is no fact of the matter as to whether the electron that is emitted is identical with the electron that was captured. This is because, during the period in which both electrons are orbiting the helium nucleus, they are in a state of so-called quantum 'superposition' or 'entanglement'. During this time, there are certainly two electrons orbiting the nucleus, each with a spin in a direction opposite to that of the other: but there is, it seems, no fact of the matter as to *which* electron has the spin in one of the

---

[15] Compare my 'Vague Identity and Quantum Indeterminacy'; and my *The Possibility of Metaphysics*, pp. 62 ff.

136 *Modality*

directions and *which* has the spin in the other direction. In fact, nothing whatever differentiates one of the electrons from the other during this time. Suppose, now, that we call the captured electron '*a*' and the emitted electron '*b*'. Then the claim is that there is no fact of the matter as to whether *a* is identical with *b*.

One might imagine that there are in fact two alternative possible courses of events in this scenario. The first is that the captured electron continues to orbit the nucleus and the electron that was previously orbiting it is later emitted. The second is that the captured electron is later emitted and the electron that was previously orbiting the nucleus continues to do so. But our claim is that no fact of the matter can distinguish between these supposedly different courses of events. By this is meant not just that we cannot possibly *tell* which course of events actually occurred, but that it is a misconception to think that there really are these two distinct possibilities. The facts of the matter just amount to this and not more than this: that one electron was captured, two electrons orbited the nucleus for a while, and then one electron was emitted. There is simply no further fact of the matter as to the identity or distinctness of the captured electron and the emitted electron. That this is the proper way to characterize the situation seems to be not only perfectly intelligible but also almost certainly correct. If Evans's argument were correct, this could not be so. But now we have good reason not only to reject Evans's argument as fallacious, but also to reject the thesis that it is supposed to prove – that ontic indeterminacy of identity is impossible. It is not only possible, but also very plausibly exemplified in the domain of sub-atomic particles.[16]

Here, however, the following complaint may be raised. It may be urged that if one is to offer a genuine example of ontically indeterminate identity, then it is important that the singular terms employed – in this case, the names '*a*' and '*b*' – are not terms whose references are vague. They must be 'precise' designators, for if they are not, then it would appear that we are merely dealing with a case of *semantic* vagueness, not genuine ontic indeterminacy of identity. But is it not the case, in the foregoing example, that the names '*a*' and '*b*', introduced as names of the captured electron and the emitted electron respectively, are vague rather than precise designators? For isn't it the case that the manner in which these terms have been introduced leaves it indeterminate whether '*a*' applies to the emitted electron and '*b*' applies to the captured electron? So isn't it just this

---

[16] See further Stephen French and Decio Krause, *Identity in Physics: A Historical, Philosophical, and Formal Analysis* (Oxford: Clarendon Press, 2006).

Identity, vagueness, and modality

indeterminacy of *reference* that leaves it indeterminate whether the sentence '*a* is identical with *b*' is true?

This line of objection would appear to be misplaced. Of course, it would not be misplaced if it were *correct* to suppose that there really are two distinct possible courses of events in the scenario, as outlined earlier. For in that case we could quite properly say that the name '*a*' has been introduced in such a fashion that it is left undetermined whether it refers (1) to an electron that is captured and thereafter continues to orbit the nucleus, or (2) to an electron that is captured and is thereafter emitted, or indeed (3) to an electron that is captured and to *another* electron that is later emitted – and similarly with regard to the name '*b*'. But our claim is that *there simply are no distinct possibilities* of the sort now being suggested. To suppose that there are is precisely to suppose that the example under discussion does *not* involve genuine ontic indeterminacy of identity – and as such entirely begs the question at issue. In other words, only if it is already *assumed* that the example does not really involve ontic indeterminacy of identity can it be classified as a case of semantic vagueness arising from our failure to fix precisely the references of the names involved. If this is right, we simply *couldn't* fix the references of these names any more 'precisely', because the facts themselves don't admit the distinctions that would be required for this.

The lesson is that some singular terms may *necessarily* fail to make determinately identifying reference. In our example, the name '*a*' and the definite description 'the captured electron' are such terms. But this is not to say that they are 'vague designators' in the sense required by the preceding line of objection, for a vague designator in that sense is a singular term whose reference *could be* made determinate in principle, or which, in other words, is capable of 'precisification'. We might, of course, still call them 'vague designators' in *another* sense – implying thereby simply that statements containing them may be of indeterminate truth-value, without any presumption that their references could be precisified so as to eliminate such indeterminacy.[17] It would be improper to complain, then, that our proposed counterexample to Evans's thesis defeats itself by turning into a harmless case of semantic vagueness, because it can only be seen in that light if it is already presumed that ontic indeterminacy of identity is not involved in the case. And it would be

---

[17] On these contrasting conceptions of a vague singular term, compare Keefe, *Theories of Vagueness*, pp. 159–60.

138 *Modality*

similarly question-begging, of course, to raise a similar complaint in defence of the argument for NCI, by invoking the distinction between 'rigid' and 'non-rigid' designators. Both complaints attempt to rebut a metaphysical thesis by semantic sleight of hand. As such, they repeat the original error of Evans's argument and the parallel argument for NCI: the error of trying to establish substantive metaphysical claims by means of purely logical argument.

CHAPTER 8

Necessity, essence, and possible worlds

The claim that I want to argue for in this chapter is one which, I acknowledge, many analytic metaphysicians will consider to be at best highly provocative and at worst extremely repugnant. It is that talk of possible worlds can contribute nothing whatever of substance to our understanding of the nature and ground of metaphysical modality – that is, metaphysical necessity and possibility. If I am right, then a great many philosophers and logicians have been wasting a good deal of their time in elaborating accounts of the putative nature of possible worlds and their supposed relationships to one another. I readily concede that their time has not been *completely* wasted, to the extent that what they have been doing is engaging in a purely technical exercise of modelling various different systems of modal logic set-theoretically, using 'possible worlds' as elements in the set-theoretical structures constructed for these purposes. For these purposes, however, it really doesn't matter what 'possible worlds' are supposed to *be*, much less whether or not they really exist. My criticisms will be directed primarily at those amongst these theorists whose attitude towards talk of possible worlds is ontologically serious, although it will extend also to those who, while not being ontologically serious about possible worlds, still think that the 'fiction' of possible worlds can reveal something about the nature and ground of metaphysical modality – if indeed there really are any theorists of the latter kind. In this chapter, then, I shall be trying to complete the task, begun in Chapter 6, of showing that possible-worlds metaphysics is an irretrievably flawed attempt to get the metaphysics of modality 'on the cheap'.

I THE LANGUAGE AND ONTOLOGY OF POSSIBLE WORLDS

Why did philosophers ever start talking about possible worlds? For something like the following reason, it seems, even if what I am about to say is, in virtue of its brevity, somewhat of a caricature of a complicated story. First of all, philosophers wanted to understand the nature of necessity and

140 *Modality*

possibility, as reflected in our modal vocabulary and patterns of modal reasoning. We say things of the form 'It is necessarily the case that p' and 'It is possibly the case that q', and we reason, for example, from the former as a premise to 'It is actually the case that p' as a conclusion, and from this in turn to 'It is possibly the case that p'. Again, we reason from 'It is possibly the case that p and q' as a premise to 'It is possibly the case that p and it is possibly the case that q' as a conclusion, but not vice versa. How are we to codify this kind of reasoning? One way is to try to formulate some axiomatic system of modal logic containing certain distinctively modal axioms and rules of inference, in the hope that it will reflect the patterns of modal reasoning that we are, intuitively, most strongly inclined to regard as valid. But it turns out that many different systems of modal logic can be constructed, no one of which indisputably satisfies this goal better than any other. We want to decide which of these systems to endorse. For that purpose, it seems, we need to inquire more closely into what we *mean* when we make modal claims. What does it mean to say 'It is possibly the case that p', for instance? It is also observed that modal logic is non-truth-functional and, more generally, non-extensional. The truth or falsehood of 'It is possibly the case that p' is not determined solely by the truth or falsehood of p – for, although it is true if p is true, it need not be false if p is false. So what does determine its truth or falsehood?

Then, however, the following felicitous observation is made: the relation between 'necessary' and 'possible' is rather similar to that between 'all' and 'some', which is one that we already understand very well. If we introduce quantification over a putative class of entities, 'worlds', by constructing statements of the form 'In some world, w, it is the case that p' and 'In every world, w, it is the case that p', and interpret 'It is possibly the case that p' as meaning the former and 'It is necessarily the case that p' as meaning the latter, then – lo and behold! – we find that we can account for many of the putative entailment relations between modal statements that we find intuitively compelling. Indeed, if we go further and postulate 'accessibility relations' between 'worlds', and impose different conditions on the character of these relations – reflexivity, symmetry, transitivity, and the like – we find that we can reconstruct, in these terms, various of the different rival axiomatic systems of modal logic that we started with. We seem now to be making genuine headway with our attempt to understand modal claims and modal reasoning, because we have found a language in which to recast them – the language of possible worlds – whose logical characteristics are entirely familiar to us, since it is extensional and simply makes use of the familiar logical notions of truth-functions and quantifiers.

Necessity, essence, and possible worlds

Is this really an advance in our understanding, though, or only the semblance of that? Well, if understanding something is reducing it to, or recasting it in terms of, something else that is already more familiar to us, then, indeed, this is an advance in our understanding. But one is bound to wonder whether it wasn't just an accident of our intellectual history that the more familiar thing was, in any given case, in fact more familiar to us. One may certainly wonder about that in the present case. Just because classical first-order predicate logic was already very familiar to us when the attempt began to be made to codify systems of modal logic, it doesn't follow, of course, that things *had* to be that way around – difficult though it may be, from our current perspective, to think of our intellectual history as proceeding in a contrary direction. Be that as it may, let us grant that for us, at least, with the intellectual history that we actually have, interpreting modal statements and reasoning in terms of possible worlds constituted an advance – at least of some sort – in our understanding of the former. Still, the process could hardly have been left at the stage that I have so far brought it to in my thumb-nail sketch. Someone was bound to ask: Well, if 'It is possible that p' means, or is semantically equivalent to, 'In some (accessible) world, w, it is the case that p', don't we have to know what 'worlds' *are* – what sort of entities we are putatively quantifying over here – if we are really to understand what we mean by making such a modal claim? In point of fact, I think it might have been much better if this question *hadn't* been asked, although that can only be said with the benefit of hindsight. At the time at which the question was raised, there was pretty widespread endorsement of Quine's notorious criterion of ontological commitment – 'to be is to be the value of a variable'.[1] In that climate, not to have been prepared to venture a view as to what sort of things 'worlds' might be would have smacked of intellectual dishonesty, if not downright cheating. If we are going to take quantification over 'worlds' seriously, it would have been said, then we must venture to say what worlds are supposed to be – and, indeed, offer an account of their identity conditions, in view of Quine's other famous dictum, 'No entity without identity'.[2] But if we are not going to take it seriously, how can we suppose that it really throws any light at all upon the meaning of modal claims?

What happened, thus, was that a good many philosophers set themselves to carry out this task: to construct theories of possible worlds, telling

---

[1] See W. V. Quine, 'Existence and Quantification', in his *Ontological Relativity and Other Essays* (New York: Columbia University Press, 1969).
[2] See W. V. Quine, 'Speaking of Objects', in his *Ontological Relativity and Other Essays*.

142   *Modality*

us about the nature of these putative entities and explaining their supposed identity conditions. What would count as a *good* theory of this kind? Well, first of all, of course, the theory would have to represent 'worlds' as being things of a kind such that the various quantified sentences whose variables supposedly range over these things make sense to us, as putative translations of ordinary modal statements. For example, it obviously wouldn't do to suppose that 'worlds' are things like planets or galaxies, not least because one of the worlds is supposed to be *the actual world* and that cannot with any plausibility be identified with, say, the Earth or the Milky Way. We *might* perhaps suppose, however, that the actual world is *the entire universe*, in the cosmologist's sense – the very big thing that supposedly originated with the Big Bang and is now some 13 billion or so years old. David Lewis, of course, took that sort of route in his theory of possible worlds.[3] Accordingly, he took other possible worlds to be other very big things of a similar sort: in effect, *parallel universes*. Other theorists – fearing, perhaps, the charge that they were crudely intruding into the domain of empirical science – took a more Platonic line, proposing that worlds, including the actual world, are abstract entities of an extremely complicated sort, such as maximal consistent sets of propositions.[4] Thus the actual world, on this view, turns out to be the set of all actually true propositions – assuming, of course, that there is such a set. Let us call these two broad schools of thought the *concretists* and the *abstractionists* respectively. The concretists complain, inter alia, that the abstractionists rely upon modal notions in their account of what worlds are because, for instance, the notion of *consistency* is a modal notion – two propositions being mutually consistent just in case they could both be true together. The abstractionists reply, perhaps, that their aim is not to *reduce* modal notions to non-modal ones, but just to 'explicate' them in terms of possible worlds as they conceive of the latter. Perhaps, too, they attempt a *tu quoque* response, contending that the concretists also must, at least implicitly, assume their worlds to be *possible* universes – not, for instance, ones in which some contradictions are true. A vigorous debate thus proceeds between the abstractionists and the concretists, each denying that the other has postulated the right kind of thing to be the value of a 'world' variable in the various possible-worlds translations of modal statements. This debate, understandably, develops into something of a stalemate, so a tie-breaker is needed. Appeal is perhaps

---

[3] See David Lewis, *On the Plurality of Worlds* (Oxford: Blackwell, 1986).
[4] See, for example, Alvin Plantinga, *The Nature of Necessity* (Oxford: Clarendon Press, 1974), though he invokes (what he calls) *states of affairs* rather than propositions.

Necessity, essence, and possible worlds 143

made, at this point, to familiar principles of theoretical economy and simplicity and a cost-benefit sheet is drawn up for each theory – rather differently, of course, by its advocates and by its opponents. The method of *inference to the best explanation* is perhaps invoked, as though the rival theorists are somewhat in the position of theoretical scientists with contrary hypotheses concerning the underlying nature of some empirically observable phenomenon, such as the motion of the planets or the spectra of chemical substances.

Other theorists then emerge upon the scene, seeing themselves as standing to the concretists and abstractionists rather as instrumentalists stand to theoretical scientists who advocate different 'realist' hypotheses in explanation of certain observable phenomena. These – the modal 'fictionalists' – are the philosophers who, in Russell's memorable phrase, hope to reap all the advantages of theft over honest toil.[5] Granted, they say, that concretism can be seen to be more economical and comprehensive than abstractionism, once the cost-benefit analysis has been done properly, it is surely even more economical to repudiate its ontological commitments and interpret modal claims as involving no more than a *pretence* that concrete worlds – parallel universes – exist. That way, we can still appeal to concretism to explain what we mean in making modal claims and how modal logic works, without having to commit ourselves seriously to the claim that the concretist's putative worlds are real. But matters are not quite so straightforward, their realist opponents protest. It proves more difficult than might have been supposed to throw away the bathwater of concrete possible worlds without also throwing away the baby that the fictionalist wanted to save. And so the debate goes on – and on, and on! But should we, in all seriousness, be engaged in this seemingly endless and irresolvable three-way debate between concretism, abstractionism, and fictionalism? Standing back from it all, won't a level-headed and unprejudiced philosopher want to say at this point: a plague on all your houses? It is not as though there are no other options on the table. There is, for instance, so-called *combinatorialism* – though what, exactly, that really amounts to is far from perfectly clear, and its adequacy as a theory of modality may certainly be called into question.[6] And, of course, there are always plain old-fashioned anti-realism, eliminativism, and conventionalism, for those whose taste in matters of modality is even more deflationary than the fictionalist's – deflationary to

---

[5] See, especially, Gideon Rosen, 'Modal Fictionalism', *Mind* 99 (1990), pp. 327–54.
[6] See, especially, D. M. Armstrong, *A Combinatorial Theory of Possibility* (Cambridge University Press, 1989).

144 *Modality*

the point of rejecting the notion of modal truth altogether, or representing it as being a matter of semantic stipulation. However, these other options are apt to seem worse than the ones they seek to replace, at least for any philosopher who has sympathy for the thought that there are mind-independent modal truths. What to do, then? Such a philosopher seems left with two equally unappealing alternatives: either to re-enter the debate about possible worlds and try to work out a clearly superior theory concerning them, or else to resort to *modal primitivism* – the view that nothing illuminating can be said about the meaning and ground of modal claims, which must accordingly be accepted as 'brutely' either true or false, or as corresponding or failing to correspond to irreducible modal facts.

2 SERIOUS ESSENTIALISM: ITS CLAIMS AND MERITS

Fortunately, this is a false dilemma. There is another option and this is *essentialism*, suitably understood. I say 'suitably understood' because, of course, many possible-worlds theorists will happily describe themselves as essentialists and propose and defend what they call essentialist claims, formulated in terms of the language of possible worlds. They will say, for instance, that an essential property of an object is one that that object possesses in every possible world in which it exists, or, alternatively, that is possessed by the 'counterpart(s)' of that object in every possible world in which that object has a 'counterpart'. And they will claim that some, but not all, of an object's actual properties are essential to it in this sense. But this is not serious essentialism, as I understand the latter. It is at best *ersatz* essentialism. So what is *serious* essentialism? To begin to answer this, we need to ask what essences are. But this question is potentially misleading, for it invites the reply that essences are entities of some special sort. As we shall see, however, it is incoherent to suppose that essences are entities. According to serious essentialism, as I understand it, all entities *have* essences, but their essences are not further entities related to them in some special way. So, what do we, or rather what *should* we, mean by the 'essence' of a thing – where by 'thing', in this context, I mean any sort of entity whatever? As I remarked in Chapter 6, we can, I think, do no better than to begin with John Locke's words on the matter, which go right to its heart. To recall: essence, Locke said, in the 'proper original signification' of the word, is 'the very being of any thing, whereby it is, what it is'.[7] In short,

---

[7] See John Locke, *An Essay Concerning Human Understanding*, ed. P. H. Nidditch (Oxford: Clarendon Press, 1975), III, III, 15.

Necessity, essence, and possible worlds 145

the essence of something, *X*, is *what X is*, or *what it is to be X*. In another locution, *X*'s essence is the very *identity* of *X*. But here it is appropriate and important to draw a distinction between *general* and *individual* essences. Any individual thing, *X*, must be a thing of some general kind – because, not least, it must belong to some *ontological category*. Remember that by 'thing' here I just mean 'entity'. So, for example, *X* might be a material object, or a person, or a property, or a set, or a number, or a proposition, or ... the list goes on, in a manner that depends on what ontological categories one thinks should be included in it.[8] If *X* is something of kind *K*, then, *X*'s *general* essence is *what it is to be a K*, while *X*'s *individual* essence is *what it is to be the individual of kind K that X is*, as opposed to any other individual of that kind. So suppose, for example, that *X* is a particular cat. Then *X*'s general essence is what it is to be *a cat* and *X*'s individual essence is what it is to be *this particular cat, X*.

But why suppose that things must have 'essences' in this sense? First of all, because otherwise it surely makes no sense to suppose that we can really talk or think comprehendingly about things at all. If we do not know *what a thing is*, how can we talk or think comprehendingly about it? How, for instance, can I talk or think comprehendingly about *Tom*, a particular cat, if I don't know what cats are and which cat, in particular, Tom is? Of course, I am not saying that I must know *everything* about Tom in order to be able to talk or think comprehendingly about him. But I must surely know enough to distinguish the kind of thing that Tom is from other kinds of things, and enough to distinguish Tom in particular from other individual things of Tom's kind. Otherwise, it would seem that my talk and thought – assuming it to be comprehending, rather than a mere parroting of other people's opinions – cannot really fasten upon *Tom*, as opposed to something else.[9] However, denying the reality of essences doesn't only create an epistemological or semantic problem, it also creates an ontological problem. Unless Tom has an 'identity' – whether or not anyone is acquainted with it – there is nothing to make Tom the particular thing that he is, as opposed to any other thing. Anti-essentialism commits

---

[8] For my own account of ontological categories, see my *The Four-Category Ontology: A Metaphysical Foundation for Natural Science* (Oxford: Clarendon Press, 2006).

[9] I say much more about this in Chapter 2, to which I refer the reader for a fuller and in some ways more nuanced account. It may perhaps be allowed that, by parroting another person's opinion, I vicariously manage to 'talk' and 'think' about what they talk and think about, but there must evidently be a terminus to a regress of this kind if there is to be comprehending talk or thought about anything at all. Someone, somewhere, must know what they are thinking about if anyone, anywhere, is to do so.

146 *Modality*

us to anti-realism, and indeed to an anti-realism so global that it is surely incoherent. It will not do, for instance, to try to restrict one's anti-essentialism to 'the external world', somehow privileging us and our language and thought. How could it be that there is a fact of the matter as to *our* identities, and the identities of *our words and thoughts*, but not as to the identities of the mind-independent entities that we try to represent in language and thought? On the other hand, how could there *not* be any fact of the matter as to our identities and the identities of our words and thoughts? Everything is, in Joseph Butler's memorable phrase, *what it is and not another thing*. That has sounded to many people like a mere truism without significant content, as though it were just an affirmation of the reflexivity of the identity relation. But, in fact, Butler's dictum does not merely concern the identity relation but also identity in the sense of *essence*. It implies that there is a fact of the matter as to what any particular thing is, its 'very being', in Locke's phrase. Its very being – its identity – is what makes it the thing that it is and thereby distinct from any other thing.

Essences are apt to seem very elusive and mysterious, especially if talked about in a highly generalized fashion, as I have been doing so far. Really, I suggest, they are quite familiar to us. First, we need to appreciate that in very many cases a thing's essence involves *other things*, to which it stands in relations of essential dependence. Consider the following thing, for instance: the set of planets whose orbits lie within that of Jupiter. What kind of thing is that? Well, of course, it is a *set*, and as such an abstract entity that depends essentially for its existence and identity on the things that are its members – namely, Mercury, Venus, Earth, and Mars. Part of *what it is to be a set* is to be something that depends in these ways upon certain other things – the things that are its members. Someone who did not grasp that fact would not understand *what a set is*. Furthermore, someone who did not know *which things* are this set's members, or at least what determined which things are its members, would not know *which particular set* this set is. So, someone who knew that its members are the planets just mentioned would know which set it is, as would someone who knew what it is to be a planet whose orbit lies within that of Jupiter. This is a simple example, but it serves to illustrate a general point. In many cases, we know what a thing is – both what kind of thing it is and which particular thing of that kind it is – only by knowing that it is related in certain ways to other things. In such cases, the thing in question depends essentially on these other things for its existence and/or its identity. To say that X depends essentially on Y for its existence and identity is just to say that it is *part of the essence* of X that X exists only if Y exists and *part of the essence* of X that X stands in some unique relation to Y.[10] Knowing a thing's essence, in many cases, is accordingly simply a matter of understanding the relations of essential dependence in which it stands to other things whose essences we in turn know.

I said earlier that it is wrong to think of essences as themselves being *entities* of any kind to which the things having them stand in some special kind of relation. Locke himself unfortunately made this mistake, holding as he did that the 'real essence' of a material substance just *is* its 'particular internal constitution' – or, as we would now describe it, its atomic or molecular structure.[11] This is a mistake that has been perpetuated in the modern doctrine, made popular by the work of Saul Kripke and Hilary Putnam, that the essence of water *consists* in its molecular make-up, H_2O, and that the essence of a living organism *consists* in its DNA – the suggestion being that we *discover* these 'essences' simply by careful scientific investigation of the things in question.[12] Now, as we saw earlier, it may well be part of the essence of a thing *that it stands in a certain relation to some other thing*, or kind of things. But *the essence itself* – the very being of the thing, whereby it is, what it is – is not and could not be some further entity. So, for instance, it might perhaps be acceptable to say that it is part of the essence of water *that it is composed of H_2O molecules* (an issue that I shall return to shortly). But the essence of water could not simply *be* H_2O – *molecules* of that very kind. For one thing, if the essence of an entity *were* just some further entity, then *it in turn* would have to have an essence of its own and we would be faced with an infinite regress that, at worst, would be vicious and, at best, would make all knowledge of essence impossible for finite minds like ours. To know something's essence is not to be acquainted with some *further thing* of a special kind, but simply to understand *what exactly that thing is*. This, indeed, is why knowledge of essence is possible, for it is a product simply of *understanding*, not of some mysterious kind of quasi-perceptual acquaintance with esoteric entities of any sort. And, on pain of incoherence, we cannot deny that we understand what at least some things are, and thereby know their essences.

---

[10] See further my *The Possibility of Metaphysics: Substance, Identity, and Time* (Oxford: Clarendon Press, 1998), Chapter 6.

[11] Thus at one point Locke remarks: 'we come to have the *Ideas of particular sorts of Substances*, by collecting such Combinations of simple *Ideas*, as are by Experience ... taken notice of to exist together, and are therefore supposed to flow from the particular internal Constitution, or unknown Essence of that Substance' (*Essay*, II, XXIII, 3).

[12] See, especially, Saul Kripke, *Naming and Necessity* (Oxford: Blackwell, 1980); and Hilary Putnam, 'The Meaning of "Meaning"', in his *Mind, Language and Reality: Philosophical Papers Volume 2* (Cambridge University Press, 1975).

148   *Modality*

Here it may be objected that it is inconsistent of me to deny that essences are entities and yet go on, as I apparently do, to *refer to* and even *quantify over* essences. Someone who voices this objection probably has in mind, once more, Quine's infamous criterion of ontological commitment, encapsulated in his slogan 'to be is to be the value of a variable'. I reply, in the first place, that I could probably say all that I want to about my version of essentialism while avoiding all locutions involving the appearance of reference to and quantification over essences, by paraphrasing them in terms of locutions involving only sentential operators of the form 'it is part of the essence of X that' (where 'the essence of X is not taken to make an independent contribution to the meaning of the operator, which might be represented symbolically by, say, 'E_X' in a sentential formula of the form '$E_X(p)$'). The latter is a kind of locution that I certainly do want to use and find very useful. However, I think that effort spent on working out such paraphrases in all cases would be effort wasted. If a paraphrase is *logically equivalent* to what it is supposed to paraphrase – as it had better be, if it is to be any good – then it surely carries the same 'ontological commitments' as whatever it is supposed to paraphrase, so that constructing paraphrases cannot be a way of relieving ourselves of ontological commitments. We cannot discover those commitments simply by examining the syntax and semantics of our language, for syntax and semantics are very uncertain guides to ontology. In other words, I see no reason to place any confidence in Quine's notorious criterion.

Another crucial point about essence is this: in general, *essence precedes existence*. That is to say, we can in general know the essence of something X prior to knowing whether or not X exists. Otherwise, we could never find out *that* something exists. For how could we find out that something, X, exists before knowing *what X is* – before knowing, that is, what it is whose existence we have supposedly discovered? Consequently, we know the essences of many things which, as it turns out, *do not* exist. For we know what these things *would be*, if they existed, and we retain this knowledge when we discover that, in fact, they do not exist. Conceivably, there are exceptions. Perhaps it really is true in the case of God, for instance, that essence does not precede existence. But this could not quite generally be the case. However, saying this is perfectly consistent with acknowledging that, sometimes, we may only come to know the essence of something after we have discovered the existence of certain *other* kinds of things. This is what goes on in many fields of theoretical science. Scientists trying to discover the transuranic elements knew before they found them *what it was* that they were trying to find, but only because they knew that

Necessity, essence, and possible worlds

what they were trying to find were elements whose atomic nuclei were composed of protons and neutrons in certain hitherto undiscovered combinations. They could hardly have known what they were trying to find, however, prior to the discovery of the existence of protons and neutrons – for only after these sub-atomic particles were discovered and investigated did the structure of atomic nuclei become sufficiently well understood for scientists to be able to anticipate which combinations of nucleons would give rise to reasonably stable nuclei.

Here it may be objected that Kripke and Putnam have taught us that the essences of many familiar natural kinds – such as the kind *cat* and the kind *water* – have been revealed to us only a posteriori and consequently that in cases such as these, at least, it cannot be true to say that 'essence precedes existence', whatever may be said in the case of the transuranic elements. The presupposition here, of course, is that Kripke and Putnam are *correct* in identifying the essence of water, for example, with its molecular make-up, H_2O. Now, I have already explained why I think that such identifications are mistaken, to the extent that they involve the illicit *reification* of essences. But it may still be urged against me that even if, more cautiously, we say only that it is part of the essence of water *that it is composed of H_2O molecules*, it still follows that the essence of water has only been revealed to us – or, at least, has only been *fully* revealed to us – a posteriori. In point of fact, however, the Kripke–Putnam doctrine is even more obscure and questionable than I have so far represented it as being. Very often, it is characterized in terms of the supposed modal and epistemic status of identity-statements involving natural kind terms, such as 'Water is H_2O', which are said to express truths that are at once necessary and a posteriori. In such a statement, however, the term 'H_2O' is not functioning in exactly the same way as it does in the expression 'H_2O molecule'. The latter expression, it seems clear, means 'molecule composed of two hydrogen atoms and one oxygen atom'. But in 'Water is H_2O', understood as an identity-statement concerning kinds, we must take 'H_2O' either to be elliptical for the *definite description* 'the stuff composed of H_2O molecules' or else simply as being a *proper name*, in which case we cannot read into it any significant semantic structure. On the latter interpretation, 'Water is H_2O' is exactly analogous to 'Hesperus is Phosphorus' and its necessary truth reveals nothing of substance to us concerning the composition of water. If we are inclined to think otherwise, this is because we slide illicitly from construing 'H_2O' as a proper name to construing it as elliptical for the definite description 'the stuff composed of H_2O molecules'. Now, when 'Water is H_2O' is understood on the model of 'Hesperus is Phosphorus', its necessary a posteriori truth may in principle be established in a like manner – namely by appeal to the familiar logical proof of the necessity of identity,[13] together with the a posteriori discovery of the co-reference of the proper names involved – but not so when it is construed as meaning 'Water is the stuff composed of H_2O molecules', for the latter involves a definite description. Thus far, then, we have been given no reason to suppose that 'Water is H_2O' expresses an a posteriori necessary truth that reveals to us something concerning the essence of water. The appearance that we have been given such a reason is the result of mere sleight of hand. It might be thought that 'Water is the stuff composed of H_2O molecules' follows unproblematically from the supposed empirical truth 'Water is H_2O' (construed as an identity-statement involving two proper names) and the seemingly trivial, because analytic, truth 'H_2O is the stuff composed of H_2O molecules'. But the latter, when the first occurrence of 'H_2O' in it is interpreted as a proper name, is no more trivial than '*Water* is the stuff composed of H_2O molecules' – and this is how it must be interpreted for the inference to go through.

There is another important consideration that we should bear in mind when reflecting on the frequently invoked analogy between 'Water is H_2O' and 'Hesperus is Phosphorus'. It is all very well to point out that the discovery that Hesperus is Phosphorus was an empirical one. But it was not *purely* empirical, for the following reason. The identity was established because astronomers discovered that Hesperus and Phosphorus *coincide in their orbits*: wherever Hesperus is located at any given time, there too is Phosphorus located. However, spatiotemporal coincidence only implies identity for things of appropriate kinds. It is only because Hesperus and Phosphorus are taken to be *planets* and thereby *material objects of the same kind* that their spatiotemporal coincidence can be taken to imply their identity. (I shall return to this sort of issue in a little more detail shortly.) But the principle that distinct material objects of the same kind cannot coincide spatiotemporally is not an empirical one: it is an a priori one implied by *what it is* to be a material object of any kind – in other words, it is a truth grounded in *essence*. It is only because we know that it is *part of the essence* of a planet not to coincide spatiotemporally with another planet that we can infer the identity of Hesperus with Phosphorus from the fact that they coincide in their orbits. Thus one must already know *what a planet is* – know its essence – in order to be able to establish by a posteriori means that one planet is identical with another. By the same token, then, one must already know *what a kind of stuff is* – know its

---

[13] Of course, I challenge this proof in Chapter 7, but let us set aside those doubts now, for the sake of argument.

Necessity, essence, and possible worlds 151

essence – in order to be able to establish by a posteriori means that one kind of stuff is identical with another. It can hardly be the case, then, that we can *discover* the essence of a kind of stuff simply by establishing a posteriori the truth of an identity-statement concerning kinds of stuff – any more than we can be supposed to have discovered the essence of a particular planet by establishing a posteriori the truth of an identity-statement concerning that planet. So, even granting that 'Water is H_2O' is a true identity-statement that is both necessarily true and known a posteriori, it does not at all follow that it can be taken to reveal to us the essence of the kind of stuff that we call 'water'.

Be all this as it may, however, we still have to address the question whether, in fact, we ought to say that it is part of the essence of water that it is composed of H_2O molecules. So far, we have seen only that the Kripke–Putnam semantics for natural kind terms have given us no reason to suppose that we ought to. I am inclined to answer as follows. If we are using the term 'water' to talk about a certain chemical compound whose nature is understood by theoretical chemists, then indeed we should say that it is part of the essence of this compound that it consists of H_2O molecules. But, at the same time, it should be acknowledged that the existence of this compound is a relatively recent discovery, which could not have been made before the nature of hydrogen and oxygen atoms and their ability to form molecules were understood. Consequently, when we use the term 'water' in everyday conversation and when our forebears used it before the advent of modern chemistry, we are and they were *not* using it to talk about a chemical compound whose nature is now understood by theoretical chemists. We are and they were using it to talk about a certain *kind of liquid*, distinguishable from other kinds of liquid by certain easily detectable features, such as its transparency, colourlessness, and tastelessness. We are right, I assume, in thinking that a liquid of this kind actually exists, but *not* that it is part of its essence that it is composed of H_2O molecules. At the same time, however, we should certainly acknowledge that empirical scientific inquiry reveals that, indeed, the chemical compound H_2O is very largely what bodies of this liquid are made up of. In fact, the natural laws governing this and other chemical compounds make it overwhelmingly unlikely that this kind of liquid could have a different chemical composition in different parts of our universe. But the 'could' here is expressive of mere physical or natural possibility, not *metaphysical* possibility.[14] Only an illicit

---

[14] For extended discussion of the need to distinguish between these two species of possibility, see my *The Four-Category Ontology*, Chapter 9 and Chapter 10.

152 *Modality*

conflation of these two species of possibility could reinstate the claim that water is *essentially* composed of H_2O molecules.[15]

So far, I have urged that the following two principles must be endorsed by the serious essentialist: that *essences are not entities* and that, in general, *essence precedes existence.* But by far the most important principle to recognize concerning essences, for the purposes of the present chapter, is that *essences are the ground of all metaphysical necessity and possibility.*[16] One reason, thus, why it can be the case that X is *necessarily* F is that it is part of the essence of X that X is F. For example, any material object is necessarily spatially extended because it is part of the essence of any material object that it is spatially extended – in other words, part of *what it is to be a material object* is to be something that is spatially extended. But this is not the only possible reason why something may be necessarily F. X may be necessarily F on account of the essence of *something else* to which X is suitably related. For example, Socrates is necessarily the subject of the following event: *the death of Socrates.* This is because it is part of the essence of that event that Socrates is its subject, even though it is not part of Socrates's essence that he is the subject of that event. It is not on account of *what Socrates is* that he is necessarily the subject of that event but, rather, on account of *what that event is.* This is not to say that Socrates could not have died a different death, only that no one but Socrates could have died the death that he in fact died. And what goes for necessity goes likewise, *mutatis mutandis*, for possibility. I venture to affirm that all facts about what is necessary or possible, in the metaphysical sense, are grounded in facts concerning the essences of things – not only of existing things, but also of non-existing things. But, I repeat, facts concerning the essences of things are not facts concerning *entities* of a special kind, they are just facts concerning *what things are* – their very beings or identities. And these are facts that we can therefore grasp simply in virtue of understanding what things are, which we must in at least some cases be able to do, on pain of being incapable of thought altogether. Consequently, all knowledge of metaphysical necessity and possibility is ultimately a product of the understanding, not of any sort of quasi-perceptual acquaintance, much less of ordinary empirical observation.

---

[15] I say much more about the case of water in my 'Locke on Real Essence and Water as a Natural Kind: A Qualified Defence', *Proceedings of the Aristotelian Society*, Supplementary Volume 85 (2011), pp. 1–19. There I discuss, inter alia, the notorious 'Twin Earth' thought experiments.

[16] Compare Kit Fine, 'Essence and Modality', in James E. Tomberlin (ed.), *Philosophical Perspectives, 8: Logic and Language* (Atascadero, CA: Ridgeview, 1994).

Necessity, essence, and possible worlds

How, for example, do we know that two distinct things, such as a bronze statue and the lump of bronze composing it at any given time, can – unlike two *planets* – exist in the same place at the same time? Certainly not by *looking very hard* at what there is in that place at that time. Just by looking, we shall not see that two distinct things occupy that place. We know this, rather, because we know *what a bronze statue is* and *what a lump of bronze is*. We thereby know that these are *different* things and that a thing of the first sort must, at any given time, be composed by a thing of the second sort, since it is part of the essence of a bronze statue to be composed of bronze. We know that they are different things because, in knowing what they are, we know their *identity conditions*, and thereby know that one of them can persist through changes through which the other cannot persist – that, for instance, a lump of bronze can persist through a radical change in its shape whereas a bronze statue cannot. These facts about their identity conditions are not matters that we can discover purely empirically, by examining bronze statues and lumps of bronze very closely, as we might in order to discover whether, say, they conduct electricity or dissolve in sulphuric acid. Rather, they are facts about them that we must grasp *prior* to being able to embark upon any such empirical inquiry concerning them, for we can only inquire empirically into something's properties if we already know *what it is* that we are examining.

3 THE ERRORS OF CONCEPTUALISM

At this point I need to counter a rival view of essence that is attractive to many philosophers but is, I think, ultimately incoherent. I call this view *conceptualism*. It is the view that what I have been calling facts about essences are really, in the end, just facts about certain of *our concepts* – for example, *our concept* of a bronze statue and *our concept* of a lump of bronze. This would reduce all modal truths to conceptual truths or, if the term is preferred, *analytic* truths. Now, I have no objection to the notion of conceptual truth as such. Perhaps, as is often alleged, 'Bachelors are unmarried' indeed expresses such a truth. Let us concede that it is true in virtue of our concept of a bachelor, or in virtue of what we take the word 'bachelor' to mean. But notice that 'Bachelors are unmarried' has a quite different modal status from an *essential* truth such as 'Statues are composed of matter'. In calling the former a 'necessary' truth, we cannot mean to imply that bachelors *cannot marry*, only that they cannot marry *and go on rightly being called 'bachelors'*. The impossibility in question is

154 *Modality*

only one concerning the proper application of a word. But in calling 'Statues are composed of matter' a necessary truth, we certainly can't be taken to mean merely that statues cannot fail to be composed of matter *and go on rightly being called 'statues'* – as though *the very same thing* which, when composed of matter, was properly called a 'statue' might exist as something immaterial. No, we must be taken to mean that statues cannot fail to be composed of matter *full stop*. Statues are things such that, *if they exist at all*, they must be composed of matter. That is because it is part of the essence of a statue to be so composed. In contrast, it is not part of the essence of any bachelor to be unmarried, for a bachelor is just an adult male human being who happens to be unmarried, and any such human being undoubtedly *can* marry. So, 'Statues are composed of matter' is certainly not a mere conceptual truth, and the same goes for other truths that are genuinely essential truths – truths concerning the essences of things. They have, in general, nothing to do with our concepts or our words, but with the natures of the things in question. Of course, since concepts and words are themselves things of certain sorts, there can be truths concerning *their* essences. Indeed, what we could say about 'Bachelors are unmarried' is that it is, or is grounded in, a truth concerning the essence of the concept bachelor, or of the word 'bachelor'. We could say, thus, that it is part of the essence of the concept *bachelor* that only unmarried males fall under it, and part of the essence of the word 'bachelor' that it applies only to unmarried males.

But I said that conceptualism is ultimately *incoherent*. Indeed, I think it is. For one thing, as we have just seen, the proper thing to say about 'conceptual' truths is, very plausibly, that *they are grounded in the essences of concepts*. That being so, the conceptualist cannot maintain, as he or she does, that *all* putative facts about essence are really just facts concerning concepts. For this is to imply that putative facts about *the essences of concepts* are really just facts concerning *concepts of concepts* – and we have set out on a vicious infinite regress. The conceptualist will object, no doubt, that this complaint is question-begging. However, even setting the complaint aside, we can see that conceptualism is untenable. For the conceptualist is at least committed to affirming that *concepts* – or, in another version, *words* – exist and indeed that concept-users do, to wit, *ourselves*. *These*, at least, are things that the conceptualist must acknowledge to have *identities*, independently of how we conceive of them, on pain of incoherence in his or her position. The conceptualist must at least purport to understand *what a concept or a word is*, and indeed *what he or she is*, and thus grasp the essences of at least some things: and if of *these*

Necessity, essence, and possible worlds   155

things, why not of *other* kinds of things? Once knowledge of essences is conceded, the game is up for the conceptualist. And it must be conceded, even by the conceptualist, on pain of denying that he or she knows what *anything* is, including the very concepts that lie at the heart of his or her account. For recall, all that I mean by the 'essence' of something is *what it is.*

So, why is anyone ever tempted by conceptualism? I am afraid that it is the legacy of scepticism, particularly scepticism concerning 'the external world'. The sceptic feels at home with himself and with his words and concepts, but expresses doubt that we can ever really know whether those words and concepts properly or adequately characterize things in the external world. He thinks that we can know nothing about how or what those things are 'in themselves', or indeed even whether they are *many* or *one.* According to the sceptic, all that we can really know is how we *conceive* of the world, or *describe* it in language, not how *it is.* But by what special dispensation does the sceptic exclude *our concepts* and *our words* from the scope of his doubt? For are they not, too, things that exist? There is, in truth, no intelligible division that can be drawn between *the external world,* on the one hand, and *ourselves and our concepts or our language* on the other. Here it may be protested: but how, then, *can* we advance to knowledge of what and how things are 'in themselves', even granted that the sceptic is mistaken in claiming a special dispensation with regard to the epistemic status of our concepts and our words? However, the fundamental mistake is to suppose, with the sceptic, that such an 'advance' would have to proceed *from* a basis in our knowledge of our concepts and words – that is, *from* a knowledge of how we conceive of and describe the world *to* a knowledge of that world 'as it is in itself', independently of our conceptual schemes and languages. This 'inside-out' account of how knowledge of mind-independent reality is to be acquired already makes such knowledge impossible and must therefore be rejected as incoherent.

But what alternative is there? Again, *knowledge of essence* comes to the rescue. Because, in general, essence precedes existence, we can at least sometimes know *what it is* to be a K – for example, *what it is* to be a material object of a certain kind – and thereby know, at least in part, what is or is not *possible* with regard to Ks, in advance of knowing whether, or even having good reason to believe that, any such thing as a K actually *exists.* Knowing already, however, *what it is* whose existence is in question and that its existence is at least *possible,* we can intelligibly and justifiably appeal to empirical evidence to confirm or cast doubt upon existence claims concerning such things. By 'empirical evidence' here, be it noted,

I emphatically do *not* mean evidence constituted purely by the contents of our own perceptual states at any given time, as though all that we have to go on is how the world in our vicinity *looks* or otherwise *appears* to be. That, certainly, is not the conception of 'empirical evidence' that is operative in scientific practice, which appeals rather to the results of controlled experiments and observations, all of which are reported in terms of properties and relations of mind-independent objects, such as scientific instruments and laboratory specimens. The growth of objective knowledge consists, then, in a constant interplay between an a priori element – knowledge of essence – and an a posteriori element, the empirical testing of existential hypotheses whose possibility has already been anticipated a priori. This process does not have a foundational 'starting point' and it is constantly subject to critical reappraisal, both with regard to its a priori ingredients and with regard to its empirical contributions. Here we do not have a hopeless 'inside-out' account of objective knowledge, since our own subjective states as objective inquirers – our perceptions and our conceptions – are accorded no special role in the genesis of such knowledge. Those subjective states are merely some amongst the many possible objects of knowledge, rather than objects of a special kind of knowledge which supposedly grounds the knowledge of all other things. But, to repeat, it is crucial to this account that knowledge of *essences* is not itself knowledge of *objects or entities* of any kind, nor grounded in any such knowledge – such as knowledge of our own concepts.

4 THE REDUNDANCY OF POSSIBLE WORLDS

It is now high time that I returned to my original theme: the language of possible worlds and its bearing upon the nature and ground of metaphysical modality. I have already made it clear that, in my opinion, all modal facts concerning what is metaphysically necessary or possible are ultimately grounded in the essences of things – and hence *not* in facts concerning entities of any sort, since *essences are not entities*. But – it may perhaps be urged – this in itself does not necessarily prevent the language of possible worlds from casting at least some light on the nature and ground of metaphysical modality. Well, let us see. First, let us consider non-fictionalist construals of the language of possible worlds, according to which possible-worlds variables in that language range over a domain of *existing entities* of some kind, such as Lewisian parallel universes or maximal consistent sets of propositions. According to possible-worlds theorists adopting this approach, any modal statement in which the modal

Necessity, essence, and possible worlds   157

terminology involved is expressive of metaphysical modality is *semantically equivalent* to one quantifying over existing entities of the favoured kind – as it might be, parallel universes or maximal consistent sets of propositions. Moreover, according to such an approach, the truth or falsehood of the modal statement in question is grounded in facts concerning those entities. For example, the truth or falsehood of the statement 'Possibly, there are talking donkeys' is, supposedly, grounded in facts concerning the inhabitants of certain parallel universes or facts concerning the membership of certain maximal consistent sets of propositions. But, I suggest, it should strike one as being obviously problematic to suppose that – where the metaphysical modalities are concerned – modal facts are grounded in facts concerning existing entities of *any* kind. The salient point, once again, is that *essence precedes existence*. An *existing* entity must at the very least be a *possible* entity – that is to say, something whose essence does not preclude its existence. And what is *true of* an entity will likewise depend at least in part on *what it is* – its essence. It can only be the case, for example, that some parallel universe *does* in fact contain amongst its inhabitants such a thing as a talking donkey if there *could be* such things as parallel universes and such things as talking donkeys inhabiting them. The very facts that are being proposed as the grounds of modal truths already *presuppose* modal truths, simply because they are, supposedly, facts concerning *existing entities* of certain putative kinds.

The upshot is this. Suppose we grant that there could be such things as Lewisian parallel universes or maximal consistent sets of propositions because, understanding *what these entities are* – knowing their essences – we know that their essences do not preclude their existence. Let us go further and suppose that such things *do in fact exist. Even so*, non-modal facts concerning such entities could not constitute *the ground of all modal truths*. Why not? Because, first and foremost, such facts could not constitute the ground of modal truths concerning *those entities themselves*. If these entities exist, then there must indeed be modal truths concerning them, since there are modal truths concerning *any* existing entity. So, for example, if parallel universes exist, it must either be true, concerning them, that infinitely many of them could exist, or else be true, concerning them, that only finitely many of them could exist. Similarly, it must either be true, concerning them, that two or more of them could be qualitatively indiscernible, or else be true, concerning them, that any two of them must be qualitatively distinct. And so on. Quite evidently, however, the *concretist* – as we have elected to call him – cannot contend that, for example, 'Possibly, there are infinitely many possible worlds' is true or false for the

Modality

same sort of reason that he contends that 'Possibly, there are infinitely many electrons' is true or false. For the latter is true, he maintains, just in case there is a possible world – a parallel universe – in which there are infinitely many electrons (or electron 'counterparts'). But he cannot maintain that the former is true just in case there is a possible world in which there are infinitely many possible worlds. For, knowing what a 'possible world' is supposed to *be* according to the concretist – to wit, a 'parallel universe', akin to our cosmos – we know already that it is not the sort of thing that could have *another* such thing amongst its inhabitants, let alone infinitely many other such things. The implication is that, far from its being the case that non-modal facts concerning possible worlds – *whatever* the latter are conceived to be – are the ground of all modal facts, there must be modal facts which are not grounded in the existence of entities of *any* kind, including possible worlds. And if this must be so for *some* modal facts, why not for *all*, as serious essentialism contends?

In reply, some concretists will no doubt urge, as Lewis himself did, that there are some modal facts which cannot even be *expressed* without using the language of possible worlds, because its expressive power is demonstrably greater than that of a language which utilizes only modal operators, such as 'possibly' and 'necessarily'. However, this cannot be represented as a non-question-begging reason to endorse the language of possible worlds and its ontological implications, because opponents are certainly entitled to challenge the assumption that the additional expressive power of such a language serves to convey *genuine* modal truths which are not otherwise expressible. Since the alleged additional modal truths are, on the concretist's own insistence, only expressible in the language of possible worlds, the credentials of that language must be established *before* the alleged truths can be accepted as genuine, so they cannot be advanced as evidence in favour of it.

Now the *abstractionist* may protest at this point that he, at least – unlike the concretist – never intended to suggest that modal truths could be reduced, without remainder, to *non-modal* truths concerning possible worlds and that this exempts him from the foregoing strictures. The abstractionist openly acknowledges, for example, that he appeals to an unreduced notion of *consistency* in explaining what he takes a 'possible world' to *be* – to wit, a maximal consistent set of propositions, or something like that. This might be an acceptable response if the *only* modal notion being relied upon by the abstractionist were that of consistency – the notion, that is, of the *possible joint truth* of two or more propositions. But my complaint does not focus on this well-known feature of

Necessity, essence, and possible worlds   159

abstractionism and its consequent repudiation of any aspiration to offer a reductive account of modality. Rather, my complaint focuses on the fact that abstractionism, just like concretism, appeals to *existing entities* of certain putative kinds in presenting its account of the semantics of modal statements. In this case, the entities in question are abstract objects such as *propositions* and *sets* thereof. But propositions and sets, if they exist, are just *further entities*, concerning which various modal truths must hold. For example, it must either be true, concerning sets, that they could have contained different members, or else it must be true, concerning sets, that they could not have contained different members. Suppose it is true. Suppose, that is, that the following modal statement is true, where S is any given set whose actual members are certain objects: 'Possibly, S has members that are different from its actual members'. What is *this* supposed to mean, according to the abstractionist? Clearly, something like this: 'Some maximal consistent set of propositions contains the proposition that S has members that are different from its actual members'. But S was supposed to be *any set we like*. So what happens if we try to let S be the maximal consistent set of propositions whose actual members are all and only the propositions that are *actually* true – in other words, if we try to let S be the maximal consistent set of propositions that the abstractionist identifies as *the actual world*, W_a? In that case, the abstractionist translates the putative modal truth 'Possibly, W_a has members that are different from its actual members' as meaning 'Some maximal consistent set of propositions contains the proposition that W_a has members that are different from its actual members' – or, in the language of possible worlds, 'In some possible world, the actual world is different from how it actually is'. But it is very hard to see how the abstractionist could allow *this* to be true. The implication is that his semantics for modal statements compels him to deny, after all, that any set whatever could have contained different members. Now, I am not quarrelling with that verdict as such, since I consider that it is part of the essence of any set that it has the members that it does – that *their* identities determine *its* identity. However, it is plainly not a verdict that should be forced upon one merely by the machinery that one invokes to articulate the semantics of modal statements: rather, it is one that should emerge from an adequate understanding of what sets *are* – an understanding that carries modal implications and one which the abstractionist himself must possess *prior* to constructing his preferred machinery for modal semantics. That abstractionism runs into this and similar problems is just a symptom of the fact that abstractionism, like other possible-worlds accounts of metaphysical modality, has simply

160   *Modality*

mislocated the meaning and grounds of modal truths, by trying to find them in facts concerning a special class of entities of an esoteric kind – in this case, maximal consistent sets of propositions.

What, finally, of *fictionalism*? Well, that approach can be dismissed without more ado, I think, because in seeking to reap the advantages of theft over honest toil, it relies on the toil in question at least being *effective*. If the toil was wasted effort, no advantages can be got from it. But we have seen that both concretism and abstractionism fail on their own terms, whence there is no profit to be had in a theory which rests on a *pretence* that either of them is true. This would be like stealing the harvest of a farmer whose crops had failed. I conclude that the language of possible worlds, whether or not it is interpreted in an ontologically serious manner and *whatever* possible worlds are taken to be, can throw no real light at all on the nature and ground of metaphysical modality. If possible worlds, whatever they are taken to be, exist at all, that is a fact which may hold some interest for the ontologist – who is, after all, concerned to provide as full and accurate an inventory of what there is as is humanly possible – but it is not one that can usefully be recruited for the purposes of modal metaphysics. For that, I suggest, we have no viable option but to turn to *serious essentialism*.

PART IV

Conditionality

CHAPTER 9

The truth about counterfactuals

Do counterfactual conditionals have truth-values? If so, what are the truth-conditions of counterfactuals? Do such conditionals constitute a logically distinct sub-class of conditionals in general and, if so, how do they differ logically from other conditionals? That is to say, how, if at all, does the logic of counterfactuals differ from the logic of other conditionals, in respect of the patterns of valid inference that counterfactuals sustain? Is it correct to think of counterfactuals as belonging to a wider class of 'subjunctive' conditionals, whose truth-conditions and logic differ fundamentally from those of so-called 'indicative' conditionals – or is this grammatical distinction of mood either inapplicable to conditionals or, at best, something of merely pragmatic significance? Is the conditional connective 'if ..., then –' really *ambiguous*? All of these questions need to be answered if we are to arrive at the truth about counterfactuals.

Let me begin by laying my cards on the table. First, I do not think that 'if' is ambiguous. Nor do I think that the subjunctive/indicative distinction, as applied to conditionals, is really semantically or logically very important. I believe that there is a single, unified logic of conditionals. And I believe that conditionals do, in general, have truth-values (although there may be truth-value gaps where conditionals are concerned). At the same time, I do believe that we can distinguish between certain classes of conditionals on semantic grounds, in a way which does not impugn the underlying univocality of 'if'. Also, I believe that many conditionals, and especially many counterfactuals, are highly context-sensitive – in the sense that what proposition is expressed by a counterfactual conditional sentence typically depends upon the context of utterance. All of this I hope to explain and justify in due course.

I SUBJUNCTIVE AND INDICATIVE CONDITIONALS

Consider first the supposed subjunctive/indicative distinction, as applied to conditionals. Counterfactuals are commonly said to be a sub-class of subjunctive conditionals. Of course, this cannot strictly be correct, if we

164   *Conditionality*

define a counterfactual conditional simply as a conditional whose antecedent is false, or presumed to be false by the speaker. For an 'indicative' conditional might have either of these properties. Even so, it may be urged that where an indicative conditional is known or believed to have a false antecedent, there can be little or no point in asserting it, so that in practice the only assertible counterfactual conditionals are subjunctive ones. (I shall discuss later the apparent exception of 'Dutchman' conditionals, such as 'If that's a Ming vase, then I'm a Dutchman'.) And then it may be pointed out that, even so, there are other subjunctive conditionals which are asserted without any presumption on the part of the speaker that the antecedent is false – so that counterfactuals (or all assertible ones) form a proper subset of subjunctive conditionals. Opponents (such as Vic Dudman) object that the grammatical distinction between subjunctive and indicative mood is not in fact one that has genuine application in English – however it may be with languages such as Latin and Italian – so that those who classify counterfactuals as 'subjunctive' conditionals are labouring under the illusion of a false grammatical theory – the 'Latin prose theory'.[1]

I am not as hostile as this to the subjunctive/indicative distinction. I think that it does have application in English, even if it is not marked so prominently by distinct verbal forms in English as in some other languages. But I do not believe that the distinction reflects any underlying distinction of logic or truth-conditions.[2] That such an underlying distinction is indeed involved is often argued for by appeal to the notorious Oswald/Kennedy examples. 'If Oswald did not kill Kennedy, then someone else did' is indicative and plausibly true, but 'If Oswald had not killed Kennedy, then someone else would have' is subjunctive and plausibly false. Yet these two conditionals differ only in respect of mood, it is said, whence it follows that their difference in mood reflects a difference in truth-conditions.[3] My answer to this is that it is easy to find another indicative conditional which differs only in mood from the subjunctive conditional in question, and yet which plausibly does not differ from it in truth-conditions – namely, 'If Oswald hasn't killed Kennedy, then someone else

---

[1] See V. H. Dudman, 'Conditional Interpretations of "If"-Sentences', *Australian Journal of Linguistics* 4 (1984), pp. 143–204; 'Indicative and Subjunctive', *Analysis* 48 (1988), pp. 113–22; and 'On Conditionals', *Journal of Philosophy* 91 (1994), pp. 113–28. See also Jonathan Bennett, 'Farewell to the Phlogiston Theory of Conditionals', *Mind* 97 (1988), pp. 509–27.

[2] See my 'Jackson on Classifying Conditionals', *Analysis* 51 (1991), pp. 126–30, for criticisms of one important attempt to justify such a logical distinction.

[3] See Ernest Adams, 'Subjunctive and Indicative Conditionals', *Foundations of Language* 6 (1970), pp. 89–94.

The truth about counterfactuals

will have'.[4] This is what might be asserted, prior to confirmation of the assassination's occurrence, by a speaker who would subsequently be prepared to assert the counterfactual, 'If Oswald hadn't killed Kennedy, then someone else would have'. So what the examples show is that we can have two different indicative conditionals, one of which coincides in its truth-conditions with a certain counterfactual and the other of which does not. Hence, although we must indeed acknowledge that there are two distinct classes of conditionals involved, we should not conclude that this distinction is one which corresponds to any distinction in grammatical mood. My own view, to be explained more fully later, is that the real difference turns on a difference between the modal notions in terms of which the truth-conditions of the two classes of conditionals are to be stated. As I shall put it, we have a distinction here between 'epistemic' and 'alethic' conditionals, corresponding to a distinction between 'epistemic' and 'alethic' modality. But underlying that distinction we can still recognize a commonality of logical form, which permits us to deny that there is any ambiguity in the sense of 'if'.

2 RIVAL THEORIES OF THE INDICATIVE CONDITIONAL

If there is no distinction of logical importance marked by the difference between subjunctive and indicative conditionals, several currently popular theories of the indicative conditional are doomed to failure. One such theory is the Grice–Jackson theory that indicative conditionals have the truth-conditions of the so-called material conditional, and are further distinguished only in respect of their assertibility-conditions.[5] Since Jackson concedes, of course, that counterfactuals cannot have these truth-conditions (on pain of rendering all counterfactuals vacuously true), it is crucial to his position that counterfactuals differ in their truth-conditions from indicative conditionals. But I have just argued that this is not, in general, so. One can find, for any given counterfactual, an indicative conditional which plausibly has the same truth-conditions, differing from it only in what it suggests with respect to the speaker's presumptions concerning the truth-value of the antecedent.[6] But since the counterfactual in question cannot be supposed to have the

---

[4] See my 'Indicative and Counterfactual Conditionals', *Analysis* 39 (1979), pp. 139–41; and Christopher Bryant, 'Conditional Murderers', *Analysis* 41 (1981), pp. 209–15.
[5] See H. P. Grice, 'Indicative Conditionals', in his *Studies in the Way of Words* (Cambridge, MA: Harvard University Press, 1989); and Frank Jackson, *Conditionals* (Oxford: Blackwell, 1987).
[6] See also Bryant, 'Conditional Murderers'.

166   *Conditionality*

truth-conditions of the material conditional, neither can the corresponding indicative conditional – whence it follows that the Grice–Jackson theory cannot be regarded as an adequate theory of the truth-conditions of indicative conditionals quite generally. This still leaves open the possibility that the Grice–Jackson theory adequately explicates a certain sub-class of indicative conditionals – although only on pain of conceding that indicative conditionals are systematically ambiguous in respect of the meaning of the connective 'if ..., then –' that features in them. It is preferable, I believe, to follow my own route and hold on to the univocality of 'if', while accounting for the distinctions between such indicative conditionals in terms of differences between the types of modality to be invoked in their analysis.

Another popular theory which must go by the board, if I am right to dismiss the subjunctive/indicative distinction as being of no logical importance, is the theory that indicative conditionals lack truth-values altogether and merely have assertibility-conditions – such a conditional being held to be highly assertible to the extent that there is deemed to be a high conditional probability of the consequent relative to, or given, the antecedent.[7] On this view, an indicative conditional does not express a proposition, and consequently does not have a probability of truth (that is, of being true). The argument for this is that if such a conditional did have a probability of truth, its probability would have to be equal to the conditional probability of its consequent given its antecedent, and this can be shown to lead to absurdity (the proof of which is due to David Lewis).[8] Now, once again, the people who support this theory may concede that subjunctive conditionals are different, and do indeed have truth-values.[9] But then, as before, if I am right to reject the subjunctive/indicative distinction as being of no logical significance, it follows that the theory in question will not do, at least for many indicative conditionals (and if not for these, then why for any?).

---

[7] See, for example, Dorothy Edgington, 'Do Conditionals Have Truth-Conditions?', *Critica* 18 (1986), pp. 3–30, reprinted in Frank Jackson (ed.), *Conditionals* (Oxford University Press, 1991). I shall discuss this view much more fully in Chapter 10 below, but some preliminary discussion of it here is appropriate.

[8] See David Lewis, 'Probabilities of Conditionals and Conditional Probabilities', *Philosophical Review* 85 (1976), pp. 297–315, reprinted in Jackson (ed.), *Conditionals*. Lewis himself does not accept the conclusion of this argument, because he rejects the premise. Like Jackson, Lewis proposes that the indicative conditional has the truth-conditions of the material conditional, and that while the assertibility of the indicative conditional is measured by the conditional probability of its consequent given its antecedent, the probability of the conditional differs from this.

[9] Dorothy Edgington does not concede this: see her 'Do Conditionals Have Truth-Conditions?', p. 178. But I suspect that few other theorists would be prepared to go to this extreme.

Even so, it is perhaps incumbent on me to explain how I think that indicative conditionals can have truth-values, given the argument alluded to above. The answer is that I do not accept that the assertibility of an indicative conditional is measured by the conditional probability of its consequent given its antecedent, and accordingly do not consider that the probability of such a conditional's truth must be equal to that conditional probability, with the absurd consequences that follow. Suppose I have a fair die, and am about to throw it. Should I regard as highly assertible the conditional 'If I throw this die, it will not land with the six uppermost', simply because the conditional probability of its landing not-six given that I throw it is high? I don't think so – and I still don't think so even if we make the die a thousand-faced one. On considering whether to buy one lottery ticket out of a thousand on sale, I don't assert 'If I buy this ticket, then I won't win the prize', even though I fully realize that the conditional probability of my not winning, given that I buy the ticket, is very high. Indeed, I'm pretty sure that that conditional is *false* – for if I didn't think so, I would be foolish to enter the lottery. This isn't to say that I am pretty sure that the following conditional is true: 'If I buy this ticket, then I *shall* win the prize'. For the negation of the first conditional is not equivalent to this second conditional. Rather, the negation of the first is equivalent to the much weaker conditional 'If I buy this ticket, then I *may* win the prize'. That this is so will emerge more clearly when I come to state the general form of the truth-conditions of conditionals, which will be seen to involve the explicit employment of modal notions.

3 SOME METHODOLOGICAL CONSIDERATIONS

At this point, let us step back a little to consider some methodological issues. How should we set about devising and defending a theory of conditionals – a theory which at once gives an account of their meaning and systematizes their logic? First, what is such a theory supposed to be a theory *of*? Presumably, it is supposed at least to be a theory of 'If ..., then –' sentences as they feature in ordinary natural language. But this way of stating the aims of such a theory makes it sound a rather parochial affair. Conditional statements do not have to be made using the word 'if', even if we restrict ourselves to English. And why, in any case, should we suppose that 'ordinary usage' reflects any very determinate underlying meaning or principles of inference, as regards 'if'-sentences and related constructions? As philosophers, we are surely not merely in the business of lexicography. Nor should we be engaged in some sort of psychological inquiry into the

168 *Conditionality*

mental processes generating people's utterances of 'if'-sentences. Psychologists – such as those working on the notorious Wason selection task – tend to take a rather dim view of the capacities of ordinary folk to reason correctly with conditionals, and if they are right we ought not to feel too concerned to respect the 'intuitions' of ordinary speakers in framing a semantic theory of conditionals.[10] Our task is more properly conceived of as a normative one, of trying to explain what we *should* mean by uttering conditional statements – and while it would be unsatisfactory to end up with a theory which conflicted with all of our pre-theoretical intuitions about the use of 'if'-sentences, we should be prepared to correct some of those intuitions in the light of theoretical insight. Certain fundamental principles we must undoubtly hold on to – such as that *modus ponens* is without exception a valid rule of inference for the conditional (*modus tollens*, on the other hand, might be something that we should be prepared to compromise over).[11] In framing a general theory of conditionals, including counterfactuals, we should, other things being equal, prefer to represent 'if' as being univocal rather than as being systematically ambiguous, and prefer to represent conditional logic as being reducible to something more basic rather than as being *sui generis*. These are general constraints of simplicity and economy which govern all systematic theory construction. The theory with which we end up should be capable of explaining ordinary usage where that can be deemed not to be confused, but should also be able to explain why deviance should arise in cases in which, according to the theory, ordinary usage is confused. In explaining these features of usage, the theory should respect the distinction between semantics and pragmatics, but not invoke it in an ad hoc way to save the theory from possible embarrassments.

In implementing these general methodological considerations, we should, I think, approach the question of the meaning of conditionals from two ends, hoping to meet in the middle. At one end, we can provisionally lay down what we take to be certain patterns of inference involving conditionals which the theory ought to endorse as valid (for example, patterns invoking the rule of *modus ponens*). At the other end, we can tentatively propose an account of the truth-conditions of conditionals which seems to capture our core understanding of what we intend in

---

[10] I myself am rather sceptical about some of the psychologists' claims in this regard: see my 'Rationality, Deduction and Mental Models', in K. Manktelow and D. E. Over (eds.), *Rationality* (London: Routledge, 1993).

[11] The validity of *modus ponens* has been challenged by some theorists, though I find such challenges unconvincing: see my 'Not a Counterexample to Modus Ponens', *Analysis* 47 (1987), pp. 44–7.

The truth about counterfactuals   169

asserting 'if'-sentences.[12] In order to make these ends meet, we may have to make further adjustments to them, though we should try to keep these to a minimum. The final result should be an account of the truth-conditions of conditionals which generates a reasonably comprehensive system of conditional logic and meets the methodological constraints mentioned earlier. (In effect, what we are aiming at is a state of 'reflective equilibrium' in respect of our intuitions and principles concerning conditionals.) Thus we cannot dogmatically declare in advance that certain contentious patterns of inference involving conditionals are 'fallacious', even if we can find apparent counter-examples to them. That our account of the truth-conditions of conditionals does not sanction such patterns cannot be taken as clear evidence in support of that account without reference to wider methodological considerations. If another theory does sanction those inference-patterns but can explain why they should *appear* deviant, and at the same time offers a simpler and more economical overall account of conditionals and their logic, then this other theory may be more deserving of our allegiance.

4 A SKETCH OF A GENERAL THEORY OF CONDITIONALS

Let us represent the conditional connective (hoping it to be univocal) by the *box-arrow*, '$\Box\!\!\rightarrow$'.[13] (I use the ordinary arrow, '$\rightarrow$', for material implication.) Then I take the following inference-patterns to be at least highly plausible:

(P1) $p \Box\!\!\rightarrow q \vdash p \rightarrow q$
(P2) $p \Box\!\!\rightarrow q \vdash \sim(p \Box\!\!\rightarrow \sim q)$
(P3) $p \Box\!\!\rightarrow q, p \Box\!\!\rightarrow r \vdash p \Box\!\!\rightarrow (q \,\&\, r)$
(P4) $p \Box\!\!\rightarrow q, q \Box\!\!\rightarrow r \vdash p \Box\!\!\rightarrow r$

In connection with (P2), recall my earlier contention (in section 2) that the negation of 'If I buy this ticket, then I won't win the prize' is equivalent to

---

[12] Geoffrey Hunter, in 'The Meaning of "If" in Conditional Propositions', *Philosophical Quarterly* 43 (1993), pp. 279–97, appears to think that only the first of these strategies is available to us, on the grounds that there is 'nothing more to "if" than its logical powers' (p. 290) and consequently that 'there is no semantics for conditionals other than the logical powers as expressed in [an appropriate] axiom-system' (p. 292). But this claim is very much open to question, for few would dispute that the logic of truth-functions, say, or modal logics, can be studied both from a syntactic (or proof-theoretic) and from a semantic (or model-theoretic) point of view – so why should matters be any different as regards the logic of conditionals?

[13] Formal properties of the theory presented in this section are discussed in more detail in my 'A Simplification of the Logic of Conditionals', *Notre Dame Journal of Formal Logic* 24 (1983), pp. 357–66.

170   *Conditionality*

'If I buy this ticket, then I may win the prize'.[14] (P2) thus licences the inference from 'If I buy this ticket, then I shall win the prize' to 'If I buy this ticket, then I may win the prize'. (It might be imagined that 'If I buy this ticket, then I may win the prize' has the logical form '$p \ \square\!\!\rightarrow \Diamond q$', where the diamond, '$\Diamond$', expresses possibility. However, '$p \ \square\!\!\rightarrow \Diamond q$' clearly does not contradict '$p \ \square\!\!\rightarrow \sim q$', whereas 'If I buy this ticket, then I may win the prize' clearly *does* contradict 'If I buy this ticket, then I won't win the prize'. What '$p \ \square\!\!\rightarrow \Diamond q$' symbolizes in these circumstances is, rather, something like 'If I buy this ticket, then it will be possible for me to win the prize'.[15] Definition (D1), stated at the end of this section, has the implication that '$\sim(p \ \square\!\!\rightarrow \sim q)$' entails, but is not entailed by, '$p \ \square\!\!\rightarrow \Diamond q$', at least in a modal logic as strong as S5.)

Note that (P1), taken in conjunction with the fact that *modus ponens* is valid for material implication, implies that *modus ponens* is likewise valid for the box-arrow:

(P5) $p \ \square\!\!\rightarrow q, p \vdash q$

Clearly, however, '$p \ \square\!\!\rightarrow q$' must be *stronger than* (entail but not be entailed by) '$p \rightarrow q$' if not only (P1) but also (P2) is correct, because when the box-arrows in (P2) are replaced by arrows an invalid principle results.[16] (P3) seems uncontentious, but (P4) is more controversial, implying as it does that the box-arrow is a transitive connective. I shall discuss this matter more fully later.

Having proposed some intuitively plausible principles of inference for conditionals (which we should be ready to revise if need be), let us now look at our task from the other end, and try to formulate a plausible account of the truth-conditions of conditionals, designed to reflect what we intuitively intend to convey by making a conditional statement. One plausible idea is

---

[14] See further my 'A Simplification of the Logic of Conditionals'.

[15] The use of a future-tense construction here – 'will be possible' – should not seem mysterious, because all of the conditionals considered in this paragraph are future-tense ones, in the sense that their antecedents and consequents all concern events or states of affairs lying in the speaker's future. It is a peculiarity of English grammar that it does not use a future-tense verb, 'will buy', in the antecedent of such a conditional.

[16] Hunter does not accept (P2), contending, 'It is perfectly possible, even with A contingent, for A $\square\!\!\rightarrow$ B and A $\square\!\!\rightarrow$ ~B both to be true' (Hunter, 'The Meaning of "If" in Conditional Propositions', p. 284, with my notation substituted for his). As an example, he invites us to consider the contrapositives of the two if-sentences 'If he did not catch the 2.15, he did not catch the boat' and 'If he did catch the 2.15, he did not catch the boat', both of which could be true. But, first, I do not accept the validity of contraposition (see section 6 below); and, second, it seems that the second of Hunter's two if-sentences should be understood as one in which 'if really means 'even if – and Hunter himself excludes such if-sentences from his purview (p. 280).

that to affirm something of the form 'If p, then q' is to imply that there is some sort of 'necessary connection' between p and q, in the sense that we deem it to be no accident that p and the negation of q are not jointly true. This suggests that we treat the box-arrow as expressing so-called 'strict' implication, so that '$p \,\square\!\!\rightarrow q$' is equivalent to something of the form '$\square(p \rightarrow q)$', with the box '$\square$' suitably interpreted according to context. However, against this it can be pointed out that, on this interpretation, '$p \,\square\!\!\rightarrow q$' comes out as vacuously true whenever the antecedent p is impossible (invoking the appropriate notion of possibility). This would imply, for instance, that if it was impossible for me to buy a lottery ticket, I should have to affirm as true the statement 'If I had bought a ticket, then I would have won'. It is more plausible to urge that the truth of the latter presupposes that it was indeed possible for me to buy a ticket. However, it would apparently be unsatisfactory to conclude that '$p \,\square\!\!\rightarrow q$' is simply equivalent to the conjunction of '$\square(p \rightarrow q)$' and '$\lozenge p$', for this would have the opposite defect of making all conditionals with impossible antecedents automatically false, thus defeating the purpose of a conditional such as 'If N were the greatest natural number, then there would be a natural number greater than N'. Of course, in the case of a conditional such as the latter, the consequent expresses a necessary truth. So perhaps what we need to say is that when '$p \,\square\!\!\rightarrow q$' is true, then either p is possible or else q is necessary. In the case of 'If I had bought a ticket, then I would have won' – assuming this to be true – the first disjunct holds (it was possible for me to buy a ticket), whereas in the case of 'If N were the greatest natural number, then there would be a natural number greater than N' the second disjunct holds (it is necessary that there is a natural number greater than N, for any natural number N). But if it is neither the case that p is possible nor the case that q is necessary, then I think we should judge '$p \,\square\!\!\rightarrow q$' to be false. The proposal, then, is to define '$p \,\square\!\!\rightarrow q$' as follows:

$$(\text{D\textsc{i}}) \quad p \,\square\!\!\rightarrow q =_{\text{df}} \square(p \rightarrow q) \;\&\; (\lozenge p \vee \square q)$$

5 SOME APPLICATIONS OF THE THEORY

I should stress that (D\textsc{i}) is only intended to define the *logical form* of the conditional: it still leaves ample scope for variation in interpretation through various interpretations of the modal operators '$\square$' and '$\lozenge$'. For instance, the very weakest interpretation of these operators is one on which they are simply redundant, making '$p \,\square\!\!\rightarrow q$' come out as equivalent to '$(p \rightarrow q) \;\&\; (p \vee q)$', which is in turn equivalent simply to 'q'. And, interestingly enough, there is a class of conditionals for which this does

172   *Conditionality*

indeed seem to be the right interpretation, namely 'Austinian' conditionals such as 'There are biscuits on the sideboard, if you want some'.[17] The latter plausibly both entails and is entailed by 'There are biscuits on the sideboard'. Alternatively, the modal operators can be interpreted as expressing some more substantive type of modality, whether epistemic, causal, logical, or deontic, and as incorporating in many cases a sensitivity to contextual parameters.

We can illustrate this flexibility of interpretation by returning again to the example of the Oswald/Kennedy conditionals. I urged earlier that the counterfactual conditional 'If Oswald had not killed Kennedy, then someone else would have' and the indicative conditional 'If Oswald has not killed Kennedy, then someone else will have' should be seen as equivalent, differing only in what they pragmatically imply as regards the speaker's knowledge of the truth-value of the antecedent. And I also urged that the other, more familiar indicative conditional, 'If Oswald did not kill Kennedy, then someone else did', should be seen as differing from the first indicative conditional in respect of the modality involved in its interpretation. Specifically, I suggest that the 'did'-indicative involves an *epistemic* modality, whereas the 'will have'-indicative and the counterfactual both involve an *alethic* modality. (An alethic modality is one which, like causal or logical necessity and possibility, concerns how things are as opposed to what we know of them.) Thus the 'will have'-indicative and the counterfactual both convey the thought that the possible state of affairs of Oswald's failing to kill Kennedy is one which is somehow bound to lead to an alternative assassin's taking over Oswald's role, whether by design or by fate. By contrast, the 'did'-indicative is used to convey the thought that, given what the speaker purports to know, he knows for sure that someone – perhaps Oswald and perhaps someone else – did indeed kill Kennedy. In both cases we can represent the conditional as having the logical form '$\Box(p \to q)$ & $(\Diamond p \lor \Box q)$', but take '$\Box A$' to mean, in the one case, something like 'it is inevitable that A', and in the other case something like 'it is certain that A' (with correspondingly different interpretations for '$\Diamond A$'). Thus the 'did'-indicative is plausibly true, on this analysis, because it is certain (known for sure) that it is not both the case that Oswald did not kill Kennedy and that no one else did either – that is, it is certain that *someone* killed Kennedy – and at the same time it is *not* certain that Oswald

---

[17] See J. L. Austin, 'Ifs and Cans', reprinted in his *Philosophical Papers*, 2nd edn (Oxford University Press, 1970), p. 210. I concede, however, that there may be something to be said for following Hunter and denying that if-sentences like this are really 'conditionals' at all: see his 'The Meaning of "If" in Conditional Propositions', pp. 279–80.

The truth about counterfactuals 173

killed Kennedy. And the other two conditionals plausibly come out as false, because although it was not inevitable for Oswald to kill Kennedy, neither was it inevitable for his failure to be attended by the success of another attempt (that is, it was quite possible for his failure not to be attended by the success of another attempt).

A problem for my approach may seem to be posed by the case of 'Dutchman' conditionals, such as 'If that's a Ming vase, then I'm a Dutchman'. It has been suggested that such a conditional is simply a so-called 'material' conditional, asserted as true only because its antecedent and consequent are both assumed to be false.[18] But no interpretation of the modal operators in definition (D1) will permit '$p \,\square\!\!\rightarrow q$' to reduce in any instance to '$p \rightarrow q$' (in contrast with the way in which it was earlier shown to reduce to 'q' for 'Austinian' conditionals). However, it may be questioned whether the 'Dutchman' conditional can really be taken at its face value, as a conditional with the antecedent and consequent that it appears to have. As I urged previously, a minimal requirement upon conditionals is that they be subject to the rule of *modus ponens* – that someone affirming something of the form 'If p, then q' should be prepared to infer 'q', given the additional information that 'p' is true. But, clearly, someone who affirms 'If that's a Ming vase, then I'm a Dutchman' would *not* be prepared to infer 'I'm a Dutchman' upon discovering – to his surprise – that it *is* a Ming vase. Quite why the idiom takes the form that it does is somewhat perplexing, but I can see no good reason for treating it purely at its face value. (A possible explanation is that the idiom exploits the fact that no conditional with a false consequent can be true if its antecedent is true, so that to assert what appears to be a conditional with a blatantly false consequent serves to emphasize the speaker's rejection of the antecedent. On the other hand, the idiom is clearly related to another rhetorical device which does not exploit the conditional form: if someone asserts 'That's a Ming vase', another speaker may express his contempt for that judgement by asserting, sarcastically, 'Oh, yes, and I'm a Dutchman!')

6 COUNTERFACTUAL 'FALLACIES'

At this point it is appropriate for me to reveal – perhaps to no one's great surprise – that definition (D1), taken in conjunction with standard principles of modal logic, makes all of the principles of conditional logic floated

---

[18] See, for example, J. L. Mackie, *Truth, Probability and Paradox* (Oxford: Clarendon Press, 1973), pp. 71–2.

174   *Conditionality*

earlier – (P1) to (P5) – turn out to be valid. We have, it seems, managed to 'make ends meet'. But not all of those principles will be happily accepted by all theorists of conditionals – least of all, perhaps, principle (P4), which represents conditionals as being transitive. Writers on counterfactuals are apt to say that the 'fallacy of transitivity' is one of three major fallacies involving such conditionals,[19] the other two being the 'fallacy of strengthening the antecedent' and the 'fallacy of contraposition' – these last two being inferences of the following forms respectively:

(F1) $p \ \Box\!\!\rightarrow q \vdash (p \ \& \ r) \ \Box\!\!\rightarrow q$
(F2) $p \ \Box\!\!\rightarrow q \vdash \sim\!q \ \Box\!\!\rightarrow \sim\!p$

(Many of the same writers hold that in the case of indicative conditionals all three forms of inference are valid – though, if I am right in contending that the indicative/subjunctive distinction is of no logical significance, this divided stance on the alleged fallacies cannot be a consistent one.) Let me remark, right away, that definition (D1) does *not* sanction the validity of either (F1) or (F2), but only the validity of the following significantly weakened principles:

(P6) $p \ \Box\!\!\rightarrow q, \ \sim\!(p \ \Box\!\!\rightarrow \sim\!r) \vdash (p \ \& \ r) \ \Box\!\!\rightarrow q$
(P7) $p \ \Box\!\!\rightarrow q, \ \Diamond\!\sim\!q \vdash \sim\!q \ \Box\!\!\rightarrow \sim\!p$

It certainly is true that (D1) sanctions the validity of the transitivity principle, (P4), but – I would urge – this principle has in any case much greater intuitive appeal than either of the others (in their unqualified forms).[20] Nonetheless, apparent counterexamples have been devised, which we need to examine.[21] One of the best known is Robert Stalnaker's Hoover counterexample,[22]

---

[19] Notably, David Lewis: see his *Counterfactuals* (Oxford: Blackwell, 1973), pp. 31 ff.

[20] Hunter defends the validity of contraposition while denying that of both strengthening the antecedent and transitivity: see his 'The Meaning of "If" in Conditional Propositions', p. 285. But even he concedes that the validity of contraposition is still open to debate. Someone who believes that all three principles are valid even for subjunctive conditionals is Peter Urbach: see his 'What Is a Law of Nature? A Humean Answer', *British Journal for the Philosophy of Science* 39 (1988), pp. 193–210.

[21] Hunter offers what seems to me to be a particularly weak 'counterexample' to transitivity involving indicative conditionals, asserting baldly that 'from "If you strike that match it will light, and if it will light then it is not wet" you may not validly infer "If you strike that match then it is not wet"': see his 'The Meaning of "If" in Conditional Propositions', p. 285. Clearly, if the latter conditional is deemed false, the following should be deemed true: 'If you strike that match, it may be wet'. But no one deeming this to be true ought to assert the two conditionals of Hunter's premise. Hunter's conclusion only sounds at all strange if one reads into it some implication that striking a match can cause it not to be wet: but although conditionals are often used to intimate the existence of a causal connection, they don't have to be understood in this way.

[22] See Robert Stalnaker, 'A Theory of Conditionals', in *Studies in Logical Theory, American Philosophical Quarterly Monograph* 2 (Oxford: Blackwell, 1968), reprinted in Jackson (ed.), *Conditionals*.

J. Edgar Hoover being the head of the FBI at the time that Stalnaker was writing: 'If J. Edgar Hoover were today a communist, he would be a traitor' (true), 'If J. Edgar Hoover had been born in the Soviet Union, he would today be a communist' (true), therefore (?) 'If J. Edgar Hoover had been born in the Soviet Union, he would be a traitor' (false, surely). It is worth noting that the alleged counterexample is more persuasive when the premises are presented in this order, rather than in the order dictated by principle (P4). This in itself suggests that some pragmatic effect is in operation. My own view is that what the alleged counterexample demonstrates is not the invalidity of principle (P4), but rather the context-sensitivity of counterfactuals like these. Before I demonstrate how this explanation of the Hoover example works, I need to show in just what sense counterfactuals are context-sensitive.

7 THE CONTEXT-SENSITIVITY OF COUNTERFACTUALS

Quite generally, a sentence (type) is 'context-sensitive' just in case the proposition expressed by (a token of) it is partly determined not merely by the standard meanings of its constituent words but also by its circumstances of utterance. Thus, for instance, the proposition expressed by (a token of) the sentence (type) 'I am hungry' is partly determined by the identity of the speaker and the time of utterance. Consequently, an assertion of the sentence 'I am hungry' can be consistent with a denial of that same sentence, provided the circumstances of the assertion and the denial are appropriately different. This is obvious enough with sentences containing indexical expressions such as 'I', 'here', and 'now'. But I think it is also true of many counterfactual conditionals, quite independently of any indexical expressions which they may contain. That is, even when the references of any such indexical expressions have been fixed by the circumstances of utterance, there may still be a residual context-sensitivity as regards what proposition a counterfactual sentence should be taken to express. This additional sensitivity is a sensitivity to certain conversational intentions of the speaker, as the following example serves to show.[23]

Suppose we are together in a room which we both know to contain a considerable amount of highly flammable gas owing to a gas leak, and we both observe the presence there of a third person, Brown, concerning whom we know the following facts: first, that he has in his hand a box of dry and perfectly sound matches; and second, that he is an extremely cautious

---

[23] See also my 'Jackson on Classifying Conditionals', where this and other examples are discussed in more detail.

176 *Conditionality*

individual who is exceptionally sensitive to the presence of gas and strongly averse to risking its ignition by a naked flame. You may assert, with very good reason, 'If Brown had struck one of those matches just now, then there would have been an explosion'. Your reason is that naked flames in the presence of flammable gas cause explosions. Plausibly, what you say – the proposition that you express – is true. Even so, I may assert, with equally good reason, 'If Brown had struck one of those matches just now, then there would *not* have been an explosion'. My reason is that Brown, being hyper-cautious, only strikes matches when he is sure that flammable gas is not present, and consequently that he would only have struck a match just now if he had first ensured the removal of all such gas. Plausibly, what I say – the proposition that I express – is also true. Yet how can that be so, since you and I appear to contradict each other? What you say is of the form '$p\,\square\!\!\rightarrow q$' and what I say is of the form '$p\,\square\!\!\rightarrow \sim q$', and yet according to principle (P2), from '$p\,\square\!\!\rightarrow q$' one may infer '$\sim(p\,\square\!\!\rightarrow \sim q)$', so that from what you say you should infer, it seems, the negation of what I say.

We appear to disagree with each other. But in fact there need no more be a genuine disagreement between us here than there would be if I were to say 'I am hungry' and you were to say 'I am not hungry'. The difference between us is not a difference concerning the truth-value of any proposition that either of us expresses, but a difference concerning what propositions we take our utterances to express in these circumstances. You are using the counterfactual sentence 'If Brown had struck one of those matches just now, then there would have been an explosion' to convey something about the causal relation between naked flames and explosions in the presence of flammable gas. I am using the counterfactual sentence 'If Brown had struck one of those matches just now, then there would not have been an explosion' to convey something quite different but compatible with what you say – something about Brown's cautiousness in the presence of flammable gas.

8 POSSIBLE-WORLDS INTERPRETATIONS OF COUNTERFACTUALS

One way to render perspicuous the context-sensitivity of counterfactuals is to utilize the language of 'possible worlds' in stating their truth-conditions.[24] (This approach is familiar anyway through the work of

---

[24] Hunter is very scathing about possible-worlds analyses of conditionals: see his 'The Meaning of "If" in Conditional Propositions', pp. 289–90. He objects that we can often determine the truth-value of a conditional even though '[a]bsolutely nothing about ... possible worlds enters our heads' (p. 289). But a possible-worlds semantics for conditionals purports to state their *truth-conditions*, not to describe the psychological processes that we undergo in assessing their truth-values. I myself have no

The truth about counterfactuals 177

Stalnaker and Lewis, although I disagree with the details of their analyses.) Earlier I put forward (D1) as defining the logical form of all conditional sentences, including counterfactual conditionals, but stressed that the interpretation of any particular conditional sentence would depend upon an appropriate reading of the modal operators involved. Now, as is standard, we can give a generic reading of the necessity operator in terms of possible worlds by taking '$\Box A$' to say that 'A' is true in *every* possible world. Likewise we can take '$\Diamond A$' to say that 'A' is true in *some* possible world. But what worlds we take ourselves to be quantifying over in any particular case will depend, first of all, upon what type of modality we have in mind – logical, causal, or deontic, for instance. Thus we may restrict our domain of quantification to all physically possible worlds (worlds in which our actual laws of nature still hold true), or we may restrict it to all deontically possible worlds (worlds in which no actual moral imperative is infringed). Further than this, though, we may impose certain constraints on the *similarity* between the worlds over which we quantify and the actual world. Indeed, it seems that we shall *have* to do this in interpreting counterfactual conditionals, for the simple reason that in many cases not to do so would result either in vacuity or in trivial falsehood.

Consider, for instance, the counterfactual conditional 'If Brown had struck one of those matches just now, then there would have been an explosion'. According to (D1), this has the following possible-worlds interpretation: in every possible world it is not both the case that Brown strikes one of those matches and there is not an explosion, and either in some possible world Brown strikes one of those matches or else in every possible world there is an explosion. Now, even if we restrict the domain of quantification to physically possible worlds, this interpretation will inevitably make an assertion of this counterfactual false unless further constraints are imposed on the range of worlds to be taken into account. For there will of course be *some* physically possible worlds in which Brown strikes one of the matches and there is not an explosion – for instance, worlds in which a super-efficient sprinkler system puts out the lighted match quickly enough to prevent the gas igniting. So we have to specify that the range of worlds to be taken into account must be similar to the actual world in certain relevant respects – for instance, they must not contain such sprinkler systems.

sympathy for the *metaphysics* of possible worlds, as I make clear in Chapter 8, but am happy to exploit them for present purposes purely as a heuristic device with no serious ontological implications.

178 *Conditionality*

But in which respects should similarity be deemed relevant in any given case? That, I contend, depends upon what the speaker intends to convey by asserting a given counterfactual in the circumstances in which he does. For instance, if his intention in asserting the counterfactual just cited is to convey something about the causal relation between naked flames and explosions in the presence of flammable gas, then we need to interpret what he says as restricting the range of possible worlds taken into account to ones which are at least similar to the actual world in having such gas present in the room. However, such worlds will only contain the event of Brown's striking a match if they also differ considerably from the actual world with regard to Brown's psychology. Hence if, conversely, it is appropriate to a speaker's intentions to suppose that the range of relevant worlds is restricted to ones which are similar to the actual world with regard to Brown's psychology, we should not expect a speaker to be prepared to assert the counterfactual 'If Brown had struck one of those matches just now, then there would have been an explosion'. The important point to appreciate is that we cannot accommodate similarity to the actual world *both* in respect of the presence of gas in the room *and* in respect of Brown's psychology, without restricting ourselves to worlds in which *Brown does not strike a match* – under which restriction any counterfactual beginning 'If Brown had struck one of those matches just now, ...' turns out to have, in the relevant sense of 'impossible', an impossible antecedent. And yet, without reference to the speaker's intentions, there is no principled way of deciding which of these aspects of similarity should be accommodated and which disregarded.

The crucial fact to emerge from all this is that a speaker's intentions in asserting a counterfactual can help to determine the propositional content of his assertion by fixing an appropriate measure of similarity across possible worlds for the proper evaluation of the truth or falsity of what he asserts. This should not be seen as making the truth of a counterfactual assertion dependent upon the whims of the speaker: what depends on the speaker's intentions is what measure of similarity is to be deemed appropriate for the evaluation of what he asserts, but whether or not his assertion is to be evaluated as true by that standard is not subject to his whim.

9 THE QUESTION OF TRANSITIVITY

Now we can return to the alleged counterexamples to transitivity – that is, the apparent violations of principle (P4) – such as Stalnaker's Hoover example. My contention is that we are seduced into conceding that this is a

The truth about counterfactuals 179

counterexample by sleight of hand, rendered possible by the context-sensitivity of counterfactuals.[25] Upon being presented with a counterfactual sentence, we naturally endeavour, if possible, to construe it according to a similarity-measure which will make it come out as true, provided that we can think of such a measure which is not unduly strange. This is just an application of a principle of charity in our practice of interpretation: other things being equal, try if you can so to interpret an assertion that it plausibly comes out as expressing a true belief. Now, presented with the first premise of the Hoover example, this principle is easy to honour: we simply adopt a similarity-measure which makes worlds in which Hoover is still head of an FBI serving a capitalist US government relevantly similar – for in all such worlds in which Hoover is a communist, he is also a traitor. We can also easily honour the principle of charity in respect of the second premise of the Hoover example, by adopting a similarity-measure which makes worlds in which Hoover adheres to the ideology of his native country relevantly similar – for in all such worlds in which Hoover is born in a communist-run state, he is a dutiful communist. However, when we come to the *conclusion* of the Hoover example it is no longer so easy to think of a similarity-measure which will, without an undue effort of the imagination, make the counterfactual in question have an interpretation under which it is to be evaluated as true. We are therefore apt to adopt the same similarity-measure as we did in interpreting the second premise – not least because both counterfactuals have the same antecedent – and according to this measure the conclusion comes out as *false*.

But in order to see this sequence of counterfactuals as constituting a genuine counterexample to transitivity, it is obviously imperative that they should all be interpreted according to the same similarity-measure. Otherwise, all that we have on our hands is a fallacy of equivocation. And here we should observe that if we now go back to the first premise and apply the same similarity-measure as was used to evaluate the second premise as true and the conclusion as false, it turns out that according to this similarity-measure the first premise is *also* false – for, of the worlds in which Hoover adheres to the ideology of his native country, there are plainly many in which he is a communist and yet is not a traitor, such as worlds in which he is born in the Soviet Union and remains there all his life. On the other hand, if, in evaluating all three counterfactuals, we adopt the similarity-measure which we originally used to interpret the first premise, then it is

---

[25] See my 'Conditionals, Context and Transitivity', *Analysis* 50 (1990), pp. 80–7, for an earlier version of the explanation which follows. The present version is, I think, rather better.

180   *Conditionality*

the *second* premise which comes out as false, because if the only relevantly similar worlds are ones in which Hoover remains head of an FBI serving a capitalist-run US government, there can plainly be many such worlds in which Hoover is born in the Soviet Union and yet is not a communist – for instance, worlds in which he is a dissident emigrant to the USA. Finally, if we adopt a similarity-measure which makes relevantly similar those worlds in which Hoover *both* adheres to the ideology of his native country *and* remains head of an FBI serving a capitalist US government, then it turns out that the conclusion of the Hoover example should, after all, be evaluated as *true*. For in all such worlds in which Hoover is born in the Soviet Union, he is a committed communist who has come to work in the service of a capitalist US government – work which requires him to have adopted American citizenship – with the consequence that he is indeed a traitor to his adopted country.

Thus we see that however we achieve consistency in applying the same similarity-measure to evaluate all three counterfactuals, we cannot end up with an evaluation which makes both premises true and the conclusion false. We are only lulled into thinking that we have a counterexample to transitivity on our hands because we are tempted to adopt a new similarity-measure to interpret the second premise, since we instinctively look for a measure which will make the assertion come out as true, if this can reasonably be done. Then we forget to review our evaluation of the first premise in the light of this change. But if the premises are presented *in the reverse order*, the impression that we have a counterexample to transitivity gives way to an impression that both premises cannot plausibly be evaluated as true without equivocation (equivocation over the choice of similarity-measure to be adopted in evaluating them).

10 CONCLUSION

Conditionals in general present an extremely perplexing set of linguistic phenomena which often seem to defy a simple, uniform treatment of them for logical purposes. In this chapter I have tried to show how one can defend a relatively simple core theory of the logic of conditionals while respecting the many subtle differences of their interpretation which the complexities of usage demand, especially in the case of counterfactuals. (And here I should stress that the logic of conditionals generated by definition (D1) is, of course, entirely reducible to standard monadic modal logic, whereas this is not so for the systems of Stalnaker and Lewis, in which the counterfactual conditional connective is irreducibly dyadic.)

The truth about counterfactuals 181

Counterfactuals are indeed highly context-sensitive, but provided that this is properly recognized they can still be seen to obey a relatively straightforward underlying logic and to possess determinate truth-values in a wide range of cases. This context-sensitivity is not something that we should deplore, but an inevitable feature of the indispensable communicative role which counterfactuals play in rational discourse.

CHAPTER 10

Conditionals and conditional probability

As I made clear in the previous chapter, my own view – which is contrary to mainstream opinion amongst philosophical logicians – is that, while there is a genuine distinction to be drawn between indicative and counterfactual (or, more generally, subjunctive) conditionals, even if the nomenclature for characterizing this distinction may be called into question, the distinction is not one that arises at the level of the *logical form* of conditionals of the two kinds. In my view, conditionals of both kinds submit to the same logical analysis, both being reducible to propositions involving only truth-functional connectives and (monadic) modal operators. Thus, my contention is that any conditional of the form 'If p, then q' is analysable as being logically equivalent to a proposition of the form '$\Box(p \rightarrow q)$ & $(\Diamond p \lor \Box q)$' – see definition (D1) of Chapter 9 – although in the case of counterfactual conditionals the kind of modality involved is 'alethic', whereas in the case of indicative conditionals it is 'epistemic'. As I say, this is far from being the most widely accepted view, which is that indicative conditionals in natural language are logically equivalent to so-called *material* conditionals – so that an indicative conditional of the form 'If p, then q' is logically equivalent to a proposition of the form '$p \rightarrow q$', where the arrow '$\rightarrow$' symbolizes the truth-functional connective commonly known as *material implication* – whereas counterfactual conditionals require a quite different *possible-worlds* analysis, according to which, roughly speaking, 'If p were the case, then q would be the case' means 'In all the closest possible worlds in which p is the case, q is also the case'. It is important to note that a proposition of the latter form is *not* reducible to one involving only truth-functional connectives and (monadic) modal operators. Thus, according to mainstream philosophical opinion, the word 'if', as it functions in natural language, is *ambiguous* in a very deep sense – something which seems to me to be inherently extremely implausible. But this mainstream view is not the only rival to my own. Another is the view that *indicative* conditionals, at least, are to be analysed in terms of the

182

Conditionals and conditional probability 183

notion of *conditional probability*, as this is understood in the mathematical theory of probability. This view seems to me to be preferable to the mainstream view, since there is some prospect of extending it to embrace also *subjunctive* conditionals and thereby preserving the univocality of 'if'. However, despite this virtue, I think that the view also has insuperable defects which require us to reject it, leaving – I hope – my own view as the most plausible one, all things considered.

Now, much philosophical ink has been spilt on the relationship between conditional statements and conditional probability, including a famous proof by David Lewis that the probability of a conditional's being true cannot on pain of triviality be identified with a conditional probability, and a defence by Dorothy Edgington of the thesis that, for this very reason, conditional statements do not express propositions and so do not have truth-conditions.[1] It is Edgington's position that I particularly wish to examine in this chapter, although I also have more general points to make both about conditionals and about the notion of conditional probability. Above all, I wish to defend the view that the notion of conditionality is *conceptually prior* to that of conditional probability, so that the latter can be explicated in terms of the former, but not vice versa. My own view of conditionals can, of course, happily accept this, but Edgington's view equally obviously cannot. Thus, by attacking Edgington's view – which, I should emphasize, I hold in the highest regard and for that reason take to be all the more worthy of critique – I hope indirectly to garner support for my own, or at least to remove a serious threat to it. But I shall say no more about what I earlier called the mainstream view, which in my opinion is seriously flawed as an account of the semantics of indicative conditionals and far from satisfactory as an account of the semantics of counterfactuals, not to speak of its highly implausible implication that 'if' is ambiguous. I should also make it clear that in the present chapter, in contrast to the previous one, which concentrated on counterfactual conditionals, the focus will be on *indicative* conditionals, since it is this kind of conditional that the probabilistic approach seems best suited to deal with, even if it is in principle extensible to subjunctive conditionals as well. Thus this and the previous chapter, between them, are intended to convey my current views about the semantics of conditionals quite generally, both indicative and subjunctive.

---

[1] David Lewis's results are to be found in his 'Probabilities of Conditionals and Conditional Probabilities', *Philosophical Review* 85 (1976), pp. 297–315, reprinted in F. Jackson (ed.), *Conditionals* (Oxford University Press, 1991). For more on such triviality proofs, see E. Eells and B. Skyrms (eds.), *Probability and Conditionals* (Cambridge University Press, 1994). For Edgington's views, see especially her 'On Conditionals', *Mind* 104 (1995), pp. 235–329, which provides the main target for most of what I have to say here.

184   *Conditionality*

I EDGINGTON ON CONDITIONALS

According to Edgington, probability may be interpreted as *degree of belief* – in the sense that degrees of (rational) belief are held to bear to one another relationships captured by the axioms of the standard probability calculus.[2] Clearly, it cannot plausibly be claimed that it is psychologically impossible for a person actually to possess degrees of belief, or 'partial' beliefs, which do not stand in such relationships – though it can be argued that such a person's belief distribution would not be coherent, in the sense that a 'Dutch book' could be made against him or her. Hence we are dealing with the beliefs of a putatively 'rational' subject, at least in this fairly minimal sense of 'rational'.

Now, standardly, in the mathematical theory of probability (which Edgington has no wish to query on this score), the conditional probability of B given A (where A and B are propositions) is defined as the ratio of the probability of the conjunction of A and B to the probability of A (provided that $p(A) > 0$), as follows:[3]

(1) $p(B|A) = p(A \ \& \ B)/p(A)$

Accordingly, Edgington proposes to endorse the corresponding equivalence, with 'degree of belief' standing in for 'probability' (and with the corresponding proviso that $b(A) > 0$):

(2) $b(B|A) = b(A \ \& \ B)/b(A)$

This is interpreted as meaning: one's degree of belief in B given A equals the ratio of one's degree of belief in the conjunction of A and B to one's degree of belief in A. But *what is* a 'degree of belief in B given A'? According to Edgington, it is just a degree of belief in the conditional 'If A, then B'.[4] (She holds this because of her acceptance of what is sometimes called 'Adams's thesis' – a thesis which I shall examine and criticize later in this chapter.) Then, in the light of Lewis's triviality result, Edgington

---

[2] Compare F. P. Ramsey, 'Truth and Probability', in his *The Foundations of Mathematics and Other Logical Essays* (London: Kegan Paul, 1931).

[3] Note, however, that Bruno de Finetti – with Ramsey held to be one of the founders of the 'subjective' theory of probability – *denied* that (1) should be seen as a definition of conditional probability, holding it to be, rather, 'a theorem derived from the requirement of coherence': see J. von Plato, *Creating Modern Probability* (Cambridge University Press, 1994), p. 270. The proviso that $p(A) \neq 0$ is required, of course, because division by zero is mathematically impossible.

[4] For present purposes, we may take this to be an indicative conditional, although Edgington believes that her approach may be extended to include subjunctive or counterfactual conditionals. For more on the distinction between indicative and subjunctive conditionals, see Chapter 9.

Conditionals and conditional probability 185

contends that 'If *A*, then *B*' *does not express a proposition*, and so does not have truth-conditions nor, consequently, a truth-value. According to her, to assert 'If *A*, then *B*' is not to assert the truth of any proposition: rather, it is *conditionally* to assert the consequent, *B*, under the supposition that, or 'given', the antecedent, *A*.

2 SOME PROBLEMS FOR EDGINGTON'S VIEW

Edgington's doctrine, although superficially attractive, appears – to me, at least – utterly mysterious upon deeper inspection. First of all, we always supposed that belief is a *propositional attitude*: that *what* we believe is always *that* such-and-such, where 'such-and-such' is something propositional in nature. Not so, it seems, on Edgington's theory – or, rather, not always so. Sometimes we believe (that) such-and-such: for instance, we may believe – to some degree, on Edgington's account – (that) *A* or (that) *A* and *B*. But at other times we believe, to some degree, *B* given *A*, or if *A* then *B*, which (allegedly) is not a proposition. Or perhaps not: for in more considered moments Edgington seems to want to say that we have *conditional beliefs* (as opposed to belief in conditionals), so that it is not that '*B* given *A*' is somehow the object of our belief, but rather that we have a degree of belief in *B conditional upon*, or *given*, *A*.[5] On this interpretation, the contents of belief are indeed always propositional, but it is just that in addition to straightforward *beliefs*, we have 'conditional beliefs', which are no more beliefs than conditional assertions are assertions.

Either way, though, difficulties loom. Suppose we take the first interpretation, according to which '*b(B|A)*' expresses a degree of belief in '*B* given *A*', or (equivalently, for Edgington), a degree of belief in the conditional 'If *A*, then *B*'. And remember how '*b(B|A)*' is defined – as a ratio of two degrees of belief; that is, as the ratio between $b(A \& B)$ and $b(A)$. Now, is it not odd to say that a *ratio* between two degrees of belief is itself *a degree of belief*? Surely, this is just as odd as saying that a ratio between two degrees of temperature is itself a degree of temperature. If I say that the ratio between the average winter temperature and the average summer temperature in a certain place is one half, what I am saying is that it is twice as hot in summer as in winter in that place, on average. I am not saying anything at all about what the temperature is at that place at any time. (I shall return to this analogy later.)

---

[5] See Edgington, 'On Conditionals', p. 263.

186 *Conditionality*

The confusion here – if that is what it is – may be traced back to the original 'definition' of 'conditional probability':

(1) $p(B|A) = p(A \ \& \ B)/p(A)$

In particular, we may be misled by the appearance of the symbol 'p' on both sides of the equation. What we need to appreciate is that the significance of 'p' as it appears on the left-hand side of the equation has nothing whatever to do with its significance as it appears on the right-hand side. There is orthographic sleight of hand going on here. For, on the left-hand side, 'p' – or, more exactly, '$p(\ )$' – does not really appear at all, as a well-formed symbol, in the way that it does (twice) on the right-hand side. Rather, what significantly appears on the left-hand side is '$p(\ |\ )$' – which is a quite different symbol from '$p(\ )$'. There is no good reason at all for including 'p' in both of these symbols. '$p(\ )$' no more occurs significantly in '$p(\ |\ )$' than 'rat' occurs significantly in 'Socrates'. In short: conditional probability, so-called, is *not* a kind of probability – not, at least, if (1) is supposed to be taken as defining what it is. The very term 'conditional probability', it now seems, is an oxymoron.

But – it may be asked – why can't the same move be made as was made earlier regarding the notions of conditional assertion and conditional belief? That is, why not just say that 'conditional probability' is the probability of one proposition, *B*, *given* another proposition, *A*? Accordingly, we could write it as '$p(B)/A$', rather than as '$p(B|A)$'. I imagine that Edgington would, in fact, have no objection to this notation, since she has no objection to something very similar to it, namely '$p_A(B)$'.[6] But let us be clear about what this manoeuvre can achieve, which I think is very little. We should not be under any illusion that, by making this move, we have ensured that in talking of 'conditional probability' we really are talking about *probability*. For, just as we should not be under any illusion that 'p' in '$p(\ |\ )$' means the same as 'p' in '$p(\ )$', so too we should not be under any illusion that 'p' in '$p(\ )/$' means the same as 'p' in '$p(\ )$' either. Indeed, 'p' has no independent meaning in any of these symbols. So it is just a cheat to assume that we are talking about the same sort of thing – 'probability' – in both cases. The fact is that the only relation that so-called 'conditional probability', as defined by (1), has to any kind of *probability* – where the latter is understood as a notion explicated by the axioms of the standard probability calculus (Kolmogorov's axioms) – is that the former is defined as a ratio of probabilities. And again I make the

---

[6] See Edgington, 'On Conditionals', p. 263.

Conditionals and conditional probability 187

point that a ratio of two degrees of some quantity is not, in general, itself a degree of that – or indeed any – quantity. This is simply an application of 'dimensional analysis' – the technique which tells us, for instance, that a quantity which is the product of velocity and time has the dimension of length.

Perhaps it may be urged against me here that degrees of probability, and likewise of belief, are 'dimensionless', unlike degrees of temperature, so that this point does not apply to the former. Alternatively, it might be urged that even with degrees of temperature, such a ratio does determine a 'temperature', but one measured according to a different scale. However, all that these objections really appeal to is the fact that a ratio between numerical values is always itself a numerical value, provided that the denominator is not zero (pure numbers are, of course, 'dimensionless'). They do not address my central complaint that the 'p' in '$p(\ |\ )$' and its variants bears a merely orthographic relationship to the 'p' in '$p(\ )$': in short, that the meaning of 'conditional probability' has been left entirely undetermined by (1), even if 'its' numerical value has been fixed – whatever 'it' is. At the very least, then, even if I have not proved that the ratio of probabilities specified in (1) is not a probability, I hope it is clear that those who think otherwise have some explaining to do: they need to explain in what sense such a ratio *is* a probability.

These last remarks, it will be seen, provide the basis of an objection to the alternative way, canvassed above, of understanding the notion of (degree of) conditional belief, according to which '$b(B|A)$' is understood as denoting the degree of belief in B, conditional upon, or given, A (rather than as the degree of belief in 'B given A'). My point would again be that we deceive ourselves if we think that we have articulated here a genuine notion of *belief*, which bears more than a nominal relationship to the standard notion, as expressed by the verb 'believe'. The 'b' in '$b(B|A)$' bears a merely orthographic similarity to the 'b' in '$b(A)$', where the latter is taken to denote degree of belief in a proposition A. In short, theorists like Edgington have done nothing whatever to show that they are entitled to use the expressions 'degree of belief in A' and 'degree of belief in B, conditional upon A' (or 'degree of conditional belief in B, given A') with any expectation that the words 'degree of belief', as they figure in those expressions, bear any significant semantic relationship to one another whatsoever.

There is, however, an obvious response which the devotees of conditional probability can make here. This is to say that these conditional notions are the semantically prior ones, and that the notions of 'absolute'

188   *Conditionality*

probability and 'absolute' belief are to be understood as special cases of the
general notions. Thus, on this view, the 'absolute' probability of A, $p(A)$, is
just the conditional probability of A given the tautology, T:[7]

(3) $p(A) = p(A|T)$

Likewise, then, devotees of the notion of conditional belief could perhaps
say that a degree of belief in a proposition A, $b(A)$, is 'really' just the degree
of conditional belief in A given T, $b(A|T)$. This approach may work,
perhaps, for probability (although even here one might argue that even here it is
merely cosmetic, because '$p(\ |T)$' is effectively just a stylistic variation on
'$p(\ )$', and still represents a function of just one argument). But it is not so
easy to say this about belief, as I shall now explain.

Remember, we canvassed two different construals of the notion of
'conditional belief in B given A', which carry across to the special case
where $A = T$. According to one, to have a degree of belief in A given T is to
believe, to some degree, 'A given T', or 'If T, then A' – where this is not to
have some degree of belief in any *proposition*. So it turns out, on this
construal, that we were wrong to suppose that belief is a propositional
attitude at all. No object of belief has truth-conditions! On the other
construal, to have a degree of belief in A given T is to believe, to some
degree, A, given, or conditional upon, T. On this construal, the object of
belief is always something propositional, with truth-conditions and (potentially, at least) a truth-value. Even so, the suggestion now is that we can
only understand belief in a proposition as an irreducibly conditional
notion: to have a high degree of belief that, say, it will rain tomorrow, is
'really' to have a high degree of *conditional* belief that it will rain, given
some arbitrary tautology – say, given that it will either rain or not rain
tomorrow. (Some might want to go even further than this, and urge that
all belief is 'really' conditional belief given, or relative to, some body of
'background knowledge', K: but such a doctrine has all the disadvantages
of the view now being examined, and more besides.) This suggestion is
frankly incredible. Moreover, the implication is that whenever we make
what *appears* to be an unconditional assertion – for instance, 'It will rain
tomorrow' – we are 'really' making a *conditional* assertion, in this instance
one such as 'If it will either rain or not rain tomorrow, then it will rain
tomorrow'. And, on Edgington's theory, this conditional assertion cannot

---

[7] Compare Richard Swinburne, *An Introduction to Confirmation Theory* (London: Methuen, 1973),
pp. 34 ff.

Conditionals and conditional probability   189

be something with truth-conditions or a truth-value. Remarkably, it turns out that nothing that we assert is ever really *true*.[8]

3 ALTERNATIVE NOTIONS OF CONDITIONAL PROBABILITY

Of course, we can say that there is such a thing as the probability that B will/would have *if A* is/were true – and we could quite intelligibly call *this* 'conditional probability'.[9] But, transparently, this notion of conditional probability cannot be used to explicate conditionals (which is what Edgington wants to do), since it relies on a conditional for its very expression – for instance, if we adopt the following definition:

(4) $p_A(B) = x =_{df}$ If A, then $p(B) = x$

('The conditional probability of B given A is x' means 'If A (is true), then the probability of B is x'.) I might add that, very arguably, we understand 'if' better than we do 'given', so that this approach is preferable to the reverse approach of Edgington, who attempts – in my view – to explain the obscure by the more obscure.

Edgington, however, explicitly denies that one can read 'It is probable that B given A' as 'If A, then it is probable that B': she thinks this is a 'howler'.[10] Her argument is that this would have the absurd consequence that all probabilities are 1 or 0. Why? Because $p(A|A) = 1$ and $p(A|{\sim}A) = 0$: but if we read these as 'If A, then $p(A) = 1$' and 'If $\sim A$, then $p(A) = 0$', then, given the logical truth of '$A \vee \sim A$', we can derive '$p(A) = 1 \vee p(A) = 0$'. She adds: '"I'm sure that A if A" does not have the consequence that if A (is true), then I'm sure that A (is true)'.[11] However, this argument assumes that '$p(A|A)$' is *correctly* defined as '$p(A \ \& \ A)/p(A)$', and consequently *does* $= 1$. We are perfectly at liberty to define 'The conditional probability of A given $A = x$' as meaning 'If A (is true), then the probability of $A = x$', and simply deny that x in this case must $= 1$. Edgington's argument is clearly question-begging. What it does show (at best) is that the two different definitions of conditional probability are incompatible – it doesn't show which, if either of them, is 'right'.

In any case, we could offer yet another definition of conditional probability which would be altogether immune to this argument of

---

[8] I note that Edgington does allow that a conditional with a true antecedent may be said to be true/false according as the consequent is true/false – but this is 'truth' only by courtesy, and not fundamental to her theory of conditionals: see her 'On Conditionals', pp. 290–1.
[9] Compare Donald Nute, *Topics in Conditional Logic* (Dordrecht: Reidel, 1980), p. 109.
[10] See Edgington, 'On Conditionals', p. 269.   [11] Edgington, 'On Conditionals', p. 269.

190 *Conditionality*

Edgington's. According to this definition, 'The conditional probability of B given $A = x$' means 'If the probability of $A = 1$, then the probability of $B = x$':

(5) $p_A(B) = x =_{df}$ If $p(A) = 1$, then $p(B) = x$

According to this definition, $p_A(A) = 1$ just in case: If $p(A) = 1$, then $p(A) = 1$. And since the latter conditional is certainly true – even by Edgington's theory, since it is of the form 'If P, then P' – it follows that, indeed, $p_A(A) = 1$. As for $p_{\sim A}(A)$, this $= 0$ just in case: If $p(\sim A) = 1$, then $p(A) = 0$. And the latter is also certainly true, by the axioms of the probability calculus. However, Edgington can now no longer appeal to the logical truth of '$A \vee \sim A$' to derive the supposedly absurd conclusion '$p(A) = 1 \vee p(A) = 0$'. She would need to appeal, instead, to '$p(A) = 1 \vee p(\sim A) = 1$', which is just equivalent to the very conclusion that she wants to reject. As for her other remark, quoted earlier, the corresponding thing to say now would be this: 'I'm sure that A if A' does not have the consequence that if I am sure that A, then I'm sure that A. But, of course, it precisely *does* have this consequence.

Another way of writing the definition of conditional probability just proposed is this:

(6) $p_A(B) =_{df}$ the probability x such that if $p(A) = 1$, then $p(B) = x$

In words: the conditional probability of B given A is the probability which B has/would have if the probability of A is/were 1. It should be observed that this definition results in the same value for the conditional probability of B given A as does the standard ratio-based definition of conditional probability, (1), when that is taken in conjunction with the usual 'Bayesian' assumption that we should update our subjective probabilities according to the principle of 'conditionalization'. According to the latter principle, the value that $p(B)$ should have when A is discovered to be true is the value that $p(B|A)$ had beforehand.[12] The rationale for this is that upon learning that A – that is, when $p(A) = 1 - p(B|A) = p(B)$, and so, provided that the value of $p(B|A)$ does not change upon learning that A, it follows that the value that $p(B|A)$ has before learning this equals the value that $p(B)$ has or would have after learning this. However, this is just what the newly proposed definition, (6), implies with regard to $p_A(B)$ – namely that its value is equal to the value that $p(B)$ has or would have if $p(A) = 1$.

---

[12] See Colin Howson and Peter Urbach, *Scientific Reasoning: The Bayesian Approach* (La Salle, IL: Open Court, 1989), pp. 284 ff.

Conditionals and conditional probability

But now shouldn't we say that the definition just proposed is, in fact, *much more intuitive* than the standard one which is stated in terms of a ratio of 'absolute' probabilities? (A defender of the latter definition cannot, as we have just seen, complain that the new definition has different and therefore unacceptable implications.) But if that is so, then, precisely because the new definition uses a *conditional* in its statement, one cannot appeal to the notion of conditional probability thus defined in order to explicate conditionals: the notion of conditionality is the conceptually prior notion. My charge, thus, is that an intuitively plausible explication of the concept of conditional probability presupposes the very concept of conditionality which Edgington aspires to explicate in terms of conditional probability. (Here it may be asked why an explication of 'if' which *uses* 'if' should be any more problematic than the Tarskian truth-condition for '*A* and *B*' which uses 'and', namely: '*A* and *B*' is true iff *A* is true *and B* is true. My answer is that the latter is unproblematic precisely because, as one of the base clauses of an inductive truth-definition, it does not pretend to provide an *explication* of the concept of conjunction.)

Edgington may object, however, that when probability is interpreted as degree of belief, it is *not* always the case that the conditional probability of *B* given *A*, as determined by the standard ratio, is equal to the probability that *B* would have if the probability of *A* were 1. For example,[13] she may say that I have a high degree of conditional belief that, given that the CIA are bugging my office, I won't know about it – and yet, if I were to know for sure (have a degree of belief = 1) that the CIA were bugging my office, I would have a *zero* degree of belief that I didn't know about it. However, if this really is so, then one might say, for this very reason, that degrees of belief cannot be interpreted in terms of the probability calculus – that their formal properties do not conform to those of any kind of probability: and that would compromise Edgington's entire approach to conditionals and conditional beliefs. (One might say this, in particular, if one held that the 'Bayesian' principle of 'conditionalization' is central to the project of interpreting degrees of belief in terms of the probability calculus: for, exactly to the extent that the CIA case looks like a counterexample to my proposed definition of conditional probability, (6), it looks like a counterexample to the principle of conditionalization as well.) On the other hand, however, the supposed counterexample can itself be challenged, on the grounds that it depends, illicitly, upon an epistemically irrelevant indexical (first-person) characterization of the belief in question.

---

[13] Compare Edgington, 'On Conditionals', p. 269.

192 *Conditionality*

Clearly, I have a high degree of conditional belief that, given that the CIA are bugging my office, I won't know about it, simply because I have a high degree of conditional belief that, given that the CIA are bugging *any* ordinary citizen's office, that citizen won't know about it – for I don't consider myself to be any exception in this regard. However, if I were to know for sure that the CIA were bugging some ordinary citizen's office, I would indeed have a very high degree of belief that *that citizen* wouldn't know about it – even if that citizen happened to be myself. So it seems that the case in question, when properly unpacked, does not really constitute a counterexample to the claim at issue.[14]

Let me sum up my conclusions so far. I have proposed an intuitively appealing definition of 'conditional probability', according to which the conditional probability of B given A is the probability that B would have if A had a probability of 1. (At the end of the present chapter, however, I shall propose a small modification to this definition, which renders superfluous my response to the problem case discussed in the preceding paragraph.) Now, clearly, it would be *circular* to use the notion of conditional probability, *thus defined*, in order to explicate the notion of a conditional statement or a conditional belief, because the definition itself employs a conditional. Furthermore, while it is true that the *value* of the conditional probability of B given A, as determined by this definition, will equal the value of that probability as determined by the standard definition of conditional probability (the ratio-based definition) – assuming, at least, that we update probabilities according to the principle of 'conditionalization' – nonetheless, there are compelling reasons for thinking that the standard 'definition' cannot properly qualify as a *definition* (that is, explication of the meaning) of the term 'conditional probability', as opposed merely to providing a correct *measure of the value* of a conditional probability. Nor is it plausible to suppose that the notion of conditional probability is just *primitive*, standing in need of no definition or explication.[15] I conclude that we *do* need to define conditional probability and have no real option but to define it in a way which already takes the notion of a conditional statement for granted – and hence that Edgington's attempt to explicate conditional statements and beliefs in terms of conditional probability puts the cart before the horse.

---

[14] For another way of handling such cases, see D. H. Mellor, 'How to Believe a Conditional', *Journal of Philosophy*, 90 (1993), pp. 233–48, 243.

[15] *Pace* Edgington, 'On Conditionals', p. 270.

4 ADAMS'S THESIS

However, whether or not one can explicate conditionals in terms of conditional probability, it is a further question whether or not *Adams's thesis* is correct, this being the thesis that the probability of 'If A, then B' equals the conditional probability of B given A – where probability is construed as degree of (rational) belief.[16] Stated using Edgington's symbolism, we have:[17]

Adams: $b(\text{If } A, \text{ then } B) = b(B|A) = b(A \ \& \ B)/b(A)$, provided that $b(A) > 0$

Of course, given Lewis's proof, Adams's thesis can't easily be true unless conditionals *lack truth-conditions*; that is, *do not express propositions* – although one can get around this in various arcane ways, such as by interpreting conditional sentences as being strongly context-dependent.[18] But that is a consequence which Edgington is happy to embrace. However, it seems plain enough from examples that Adams's thesis is at least highly questionable. The lottery example is perhaps the clearest way of making the point.[19] The conditional probability that I shall not win the lottery, given that I buy just one ticket out of a hundred thousand on sale, is plainly very high – that is (in my terms), if the probability of my buying just one ticket were 1, the probability of my not winning would be very high. Does it follow that I should assign a high probability (degree of belief) to 'If I buy just one ticket, I shall not win the lottery'? Remember, we can make the odds as high as we like, without altering the nature of the example. If Edgington is right, there must be odds which would justify me in believing this conditional with as high a degree of belief as I assign to pretty well any of my very firmest beliefs, such as that the sun will rise tomorrow. But even at these odds, I suggest, someone purchasing just one lottery ticket would in fact *deny* that he believed that he would lose if he bought just one ticket. A very strong belief that one will lose if one buys a ticket ought to be sufficient to deter one from buying a ticket. After all, a very strong belief that one will *win* if one buys a ticket

---

[16] See Ernest Adams, *The Logic of Conditionals* (Dordrecht: Reidel, 1975), p. 3.

[17] See Edgington, 'On Conditionals', p. 263, where she calls this simply 'The Thesis'.

[18] See Edgington, 'On Conditionals', pp. 305 ff. In Chapter 9, I urge that conditionals *are* context-dependent, but not in a way that would automatically give comfort to those who favoured an appeal to their context-dependency in order to evade the implications of Adams's thesis.

[19] In my 'The Truth about Counterfactuals', *Philosophical Quarterly* 45 (1995), pp. 41–59 (see also Chapter 9 of the present book), I used this example to make a point about assertibility, which enabled Edgington to parry it in her 'On Conditionals', p. 287 n. But really the example works equally well with regard to degree of belief.

should suffice to induce one to buy a ticket – and so, by the same token, an equally strong belief that one will *lose* if one buys a ticket should suffice to induce one *not* to buy one. On Edgington's theory, a purchaser of just one ticket ought to have the latter belief, and so ought not to buy a ticket – and yet people do buy lottery tickets, and so either we must charge them with irrationality or else we must deny that they ought to have the belief which Edgington's theory says that they ought to have.

Against me, it may be said that what is to be gained by winning is much greater than what is to be lost by losing, so that the two cases are not parallel. However, we could adjust the example and compare the original lottery case with a gamble in which there is a very high conditional probability of winning a small amount – say, equal to the price of the stake – given that one takes the gamble. In this case, according to Edgington, one has a very high degree of belief that one will win a small amount if one plays, and this, it would seem, should suffice to induce one to play. By the same token, then, if one has an equally strong belief that one will *lose* a similarly small amount if one plays, this should suffice to induce one *not* to play (and this, by Edgington's account, is what obtains in the original lottery case). Yet lottery ticket buyers don't refrain from playing, and so must either be convicted of irrationality or else cannot be credited with a very high degree of belief that they will lose if they play. (What they do believe, of course, and with complete conviction, is that if they were to play, then the probability of their losing would be very high: but that, in my view, is quite another matter.)

Note here that it will not help *Edgington* to point out that, in the original lottery case, one knows that there is a very small but finite chance of winning a great deal of money if one buys a ticket. Of course, *I* can acknowledge that fact and use it to explain why it can be rational to buy a ticket. But 'If I buy a ticket, there will be a small but non-zero chance of my winning a large sum' entails 'If I buy a ticket, I *may* win' – and this is incompatible with 'If I buy a ticket, I *shall not* win'. Edgington, however, says that I ought to believe the latter very strongly, so she cannot allow that I should also believe the former very strongly. In confirmation of my claim that these two conditionals are incompatible, consider the following imaginary conversation between X and Y:

X: If you buy a ticket, you will not win.

Y: Yes I may – somebody has to win and it could be me.

Conditionals and conditional probability

Clearly, *Y* here is *disagreeing* with *X*. Of course, 'Not *A*' is not, in general, incompatible with 'Possibly *A*': but this just goes to show that 'If you buy a ticket, you will not win' and 'If you buy a ticket, you may win' – which are incompatible, as the disagreement between *X* and *Y* indicates – cannot be construed as a pair of conditionals which differ only in that one has a consequent of the form 'Not *A*' and the other a consequent of the form 'Possibly *A*'.[20]

Besides the lottery case, there are other apparent counterexamples to Adams's thesis, such as the following one concerning coin-spinning.[21] Suppose I assert, with complete and justifiable conviction, 'If you spin this coin, it will land heads'. That would be an appropriate thing to assert if I knew for sure that the coin was a two-headed one, or otherwise heavily biased to land heads. Suppose then that I knew, to the contrary, that the coin was perfectly fair: in that case, I surely ought to *deny* what I previously asserted, and with just as much conviction. However, according to Edgington's account, I ought instead to be indifferent in the latter case between the conditional 'If you spin this coin, it will land heads' and 'If you spin this coin, it will land tails' – I should (by Adams's thesis) have the *same* degree of belief (neither high nor low) in each of them, because for a fair coin the conditional probability of its landing *heads* given that it is spun equals the conditional probability of its landing *tails* given that it is spun (a probability of 50%, or 0.5, in each case). But if a high degree of belief in 'If this coin is spun, it will land heads' expresses a strong conviction that the coin is heavily biased to land heads, then a middling degree of belief in that same conditional should apparently express a *moderate* conviction that the coin is heavily biased to land heads – whereas in fact what one has in the hypothesized circumstances is a *strong* conviction that the coin is *unbiased*.

We can restate this argument more formally as follows, letting *B* be the proposition 'This coin is heavily biased to land heads', *S* the proposition 'This coin is spun' and *H* the proposition 'This coin will land heads'. Now, it is plausible to claim that one's degree of belief in 'If *S*, then *H*' should be proportionate to one's degree of belief in *B*, being high when the latter is high and low when the latter is low. (Indeed, some philosophers would make the even stronger claim that the disposition statement *B* is *analytically equivalent* to the conditional 'If *S*, then *H*', in which case one's degree of belief in each should certainly be the same.) However, according to

---

[20] See my 'The Truth about Counterfactuals', p. 47 (and also Chapter 9 of the present book).

[21] Compare A. Hájek and N. Hall, 'The Hypothesis of the Conditional Construal of Conditional Probability', in Eells and Skyrms (eds.), *Probability and Conditionals*.

196 *Conditionality*

Adams's thesis, one's degree of belief in 'If *S*, then *H*' ought to be (approximately) equal to one's degree of belief in 'If *S*, then not-*H*', when one has a high degree of belief that the coin is unbiased and in consequence has a low degree of belief in B. Moreover, these equal degrees of belief must sum to unity, according to Adams's thesis, and so cannot both be low. Therefore, according to Adams's thesis, when one has in such circumstances a low degree of belief in *B*, one should *not* have a low degree of belief in 'If *S*, then *H*', contrary to the plausible claim made previously. Hence Adams's thesis must be mistaken if that claim is correct. In confirmation of its correctness and in further disconfirmation of Adams's thesis, observe that it is in fact perfectly possible for a rational subject to have low degrees of belief in *both* 'If *S*, then *H*' *and* 'If *S*, then not-*H*' – to wit, when the subject strongly believes the coin to be unbiased. In such circumstances, the subject will rightly reject *both* of the conditionals, 'If this coin is spun, it will land heads' and 'If this coin is spun, it will not land heads', in favour of the conditional 'If this coin is spun, it *may or may not* land heads'.

5 EDGINGTON'S RESPONSE

Earlier in this chapter,[22] I raised some questions concerning the standard ratio-based definition of conditional probability. Recall that, according to that definition, the conditional probability of *B* given *A*, written '$p(B|A)$', or alternatively '$p_A(B)$', is defined as follows:[23]

(7) $p(B|A) =_{df} p(A \, \& \, B)/p(A)$, provided that $p(A) > 0$

One question that I raised was the following: what entitles us to suppose that the expression '$p(\ |\ )$', as defined by (7), really signifies any kind of *probability*? Of course, it is easily shown that the *value* of $p(B|A)$ must lie between 0 and 1 and thus within the numerical value range of a probability. But so, too, may the values of many other functions lie within this range. An *absolute* probability function, signified by an expression such as '$p(\ )$', is a function of just one argument – that argument being a proposition – with a numerical value between 0 and 1. In (7), however, we are purportedly introduced to a different kind of probability function, which is a function of *two* arguments – both of them propositions – with a

---

[22] And in the original paper on which those parts of this chapter are based, my 'Conditional Probability and Conditional Beliefs', *Mind* 105 (1996), pp. 603–15.

[23] (7) differs from (1) above only in that I have made it explicit that it is supposed to be a *definition* and have included in it the proviso that $p(A) > 0$.

Conditionals and conditional probability   197

numerical value between 0 and 1. What is such a probability supposed to be a probability *of*? Not the probability of a *proposition*, clearly, since the function takes not a single proposition but a pair of propositions as its arguments. The answer will be offered that such a probability is simply the *conditional* probability of one proposition, *B*, *given* another proposition, *A*. Definition (7), however, throws no light at all on what is meant by saying this, beyond telling us that it is a way of talking about the ratio between the (absolute) probabilities of two propositions, (*A* & *B*) and *A*. Why call this ratio a 'conditional' *probability*?

Dorothy Edgington thinks that she has an answer to this question. This is what she says:

> The question Lowe raises … is a fair one, and it has a straight answer. Let us use the notation '$p_A(B)$' for 'the probability of *B* given *A*'. Take any law of probability, any consequence of the axioms of probability theory, e.g.: $p(\sim B) = 1-p(B)$; $p(B \vee C) = p(B) + p(C) - p(B \ \& \ C)$. Add the standard definition of conditional probability, and we can prove a parallel law: $p_A(\sim B) = 1-p_A(B)$; $p_A(B \vee C) = p_A(B) + p_A(C) - p_A(B \ \& \ C)$, etc. The probability of *B* given *A*, on the standard definition, deserves a name which contains the word 'probability' because, if $p( )$ is a probability function in which $p(A) \neq 0$, then $p_A( )$ [or: $p(|A)$] is a probability function, according to the axioms.[24]

Now, as we have already observed, $p(\mid)$, as defined by (7), is a function of *two* arguments, whereas the 'probability functions' with which the standard axioms of probability are concerned are functions of just *one* argument. Consequently, the mere fact that, when definition (7) is added to those axioms, one can prove various laws governing $p(\mid)$ which 'parallel' (Edgington's expression) the laws governing standard probability functions can by no means imply that $p(\mid)$ itself is such a function, for the very simple reason that $p(\mid)$ is not a function of just one argument. But, given that $p(\mid)$ cannot qualify as a probability function in the standard sense, why should a mere parallelism between the laws of $p(\mid)$ and the laws of probability suffice to warrant our calling $p(\mid)$ a 'probability' function in *any* sense? I shall return to this question in the next section, where I shall try to show that, in fact, such a parallelism provides a *very weak reason indeed* to think of '$p(\mid)$' as signifying any kind of probability.

Before proceeding, however, it is important to appreciate that Edgington's claim in the passage just quoted is *not* that $p(\mid)$ *itself* is a probability function, but rather that 'if $p( )$ is a probability function in which

---

[24] Dorothy Edgington, 'Lowe on Conditional Probability', *Mind* 105 (1996), pp. 617–30: see p. 620. I have adapted her logical symbolism very slightly to bring it into conformity with my own.

198 *Conditionality*

$p(A) \neq 0$, then $p_A(\ )$ [or: $p(\ |A)$] is a probability function, according to the axioms [of probability theory]'. (Note that '[or: $p(\ |A)$]' here is Edgington's own wording, not my interpolation.) What exactly are we to make of this? Presumably, Edgington considers that '$p_A(\ )$', or '$p(\ |A)$', like '$p(\ )$', expresses a probability function of just one argument – as it were, the '*given A* probability' of a proposition. To see the situation in the clearest possible light, let us recast (7) using Edgington's own preferred subscript notation, '$p_A(\ )$', as follows:

(7*) $p_A(B) =_{df} p(A \ \& \ B)/p(A)$, provided that $p(A) > 0$

We could then summarize matters as follows. The standard definition, (7*), treats the 'A' in '$p_A(B)$' as occupying one of two argument-places in a two-place functional expression. But it seems that, in the quoted passage, Edgington implicitly treats the 'A' in '$p_A(B)$' as being, rather, an *index* which distinguishes the putative *one*-argument probability function, $p_A(\ )$, from another such probability function, $p(\ )$ – the latter being a familiar *absolute* probability function. Consequently, it may be objected that the standard definition, (7*), does *not* in fact serve to define what Edgington takes herself to mean by the expression '$p_A(B)$'.

Here, however, it may be pointed out that, quite generally, if $f(x, y)$ is a function of *two* arguments, x and y, then we may define in terms of it a related function of just *one* argument, $f_a(y)$, by letting x have a constant value, $x = a$. And this, it may be said, is all that Edgington is implicitly doing, quite innocuously. Thus it may be conceded that, strictly speaking, (7*) doesn't *itself* serve to define '$p_A(\ )$', as Edgington uses this expression, but it may also be urged that it is a simple matter to construct such a definition from (7*) in the foregoing manner. However, in that case, it would seem that $p_A(\ )$'s entitlement to be called a 'probability' function rests squarely on $p(\ |\ )$'s own entitlement to be so called, since we are now understanding the former to be defined in terms of the latter. So now, by a somewhat circuitous route, we are led back to our earlier question whether a mere parallelism between the laws of $p(\ |\ )$ and the laws of probability suffices to warrant our calling $p(\ |\ )$ a 'probability' function in any sense.

6 CONDITIONAL PROBABILITY AND CONDITIONAL TRUTH-VALUE

At this point, I think it is instructive to explore an analogy between probability and *truth-value*. For this will enable us to see, amongst other things, why a mere parallelism between the laws of probability and those of

Conditionals and conditional probability 199

'conditional probability', as defined by (7) or (7*), does not in fact suffice to warrant a description of the latter as being a kind of probability.

Let $t(\ )$ be a function which takes a single proposition as argument and has one of two numerical values, namely, the value 1 just in case the proposition in question is true and the value 0 just in case the proposition in question is false. We may read the functional expression '$t(A)$' as 'the truth-value of A'. Now, by analogy with definition (7*), let us formulate the following putative definition of what we may be tempted to call *the conditional truth-value of B given A*:

(8) $t_A(B) =_{df} t(A \ \& \ B)/t(A)$, provided that $t(A) \neq 0$

We see that, according to (8), the 'conditional truth-value of B given A' is, quite simply, the ratio of the truth-value of $(A \ \& \ B)$ and the truth-value of A, provided that the latter is not 0. Of course, if $t(A)$ is not 0, then it must be 1. Accordingly, we see that $t_A(B)$ is a function which takes two propositions, A and B, as arguments and has as its value the truth-value of the conjunction $(A \ \& \ B)$ if A is true, and is otherwise undefined (that is, if A is false). So, where it is defined, $t_A(B)$ takes the same value as $t(B)$.

Indeed, we can take the analogy between 'conditional truth-value' and 'conditional probability' even further. As we saw earlier, Edgington herself, following Ernest Adams,[25] has proposed that the probability of a conditional, 'B if A', just *is* the conditional probability of B given A (provided that $p(A) \neq 0$):[26]

(9) $p(B \text{ if } A) = p_A(B)$

As we noted earlier, David Lewis has famously shown that, on pain of triviality, there is no *proposition* that 'B if A' can be taken to express, if (9) is correct.[27] Edgington happily embraces this consequence of (9), and contends that conditionals have neither truth-conditions nor, hence, truth-values (with certain exceptions to be mentioned in a moment). But suppose that one were to propose, by analogy with (9), the following:

(10) $t(B \text{ if } A) = t_A(B)$

This states that the truth-value of a conditional, 'B if A', is simply the *conditional* truth-value of the consequent, B, 'given' the antecedent, A.

---

[25] See again Adams, *The Logic of Conditionals*, p. 3.
[26] See Edgington, 'On Conditionals', p. 263. See further section 4 of the present chapter, on Adams's thesis.
[27] See again Lewis, 'Probabilities of Conditionals and Conditional Probabilities'.

200 *Conditionality*

Now, paralleling Lewis's triviality proof, it is easy to show that there is no *proposition* that '*B* if *A*' can be taken to express, if (10) is correct. This is because, for any proposition X, $t(X)$ must either take the value 1 or else the value 0: but '$t(B$ if $A)$', according to (8) and (10), denotes a value only provided that $t(A)$ is not 0, and is otherwise undefined. Hence $t(B$ if $A)$ cannot be the truth-value of any *proposition*. In fact, ironically enough, I imagine that Edgington herself ought to feel quite sympathetically towards (10), since she herself allows that the conditional '*B* if *A*' has the truth-value of *B* provided that *A* is true, but otherwise lacks a truth-value.[28] And, indeed, there is a quite long-standing tradition which sees the indicative 'if' as having what is sometimes called a 'defective' truth-table, whereby it takes the truth-value of the consequent when the antecedent is true, but otherwise lacks a truth-value.

Now, all of this may be independently quite interesting, but we need to bring matters back to the point. The point was that Edgington suggests that conditional probability, as defined by (7) or (7*), deserves the name 'probability' because the laws of conditional probability parallel those of ordinary, 'absolute' probability. Now, however, it is easy enough to see that, by the same token, the laws of 'conditional truth-value', where the latter is taken as being defined by (8), parallel the laws of ordinary, 'absolute' truth-value. For example, one 'absolute' law is that if $t(B) = 1$ then $t(\sim B) = 0$, and another is that $t(B \lor C) = 1$ iff either $t(B) = 1$ or $t(C) = 1$, and paralleling these we have the 'conditional' laws that if $t_A(B) = 1$, then $t_A(\sim B) = 0$, and that $t_A(B \lor C) = 1$ iff either $t_A(B) = 1$ or $t_A(C) = 1$. What, then, are we entitled to say about the notion of 'conditional truth-value', as purportedly defined by (8)? If Edgington's line of argument (as quoted earlier) is correct, the conclusion should be that we are entitled to think of 'conditional truth-value' as *a kind of truth-value*, the truth-value of one proposition 'given' another proposition. But this, I submit, is manifestly absurd. There is surely not, in addition to ordinary, 'absolute' truth-value – truth or falsehood *simpliciter* – a peculiar kind of 'relative' truth-value. '$t_A(B)$', as defined by (8), cannot be taken to denote a new *kind* of truth-value. If the expression '$t_A(B)$' is to be espoused at all, it is better explained, rather, as denoting the (ordinary) truth-value that *B* has *if A* is true. This, however, is to explain the notion of 'conditional truth-value' in *conditional* terms. And my contention is that, in like manner, we can only make clear sense of the notion of 'conditional probability' if we attempt to explain it, too, in conditional terms – not,

---

[28] See Edgington, 'On Conditionals', pp. 290–1.

Conditionals and conditional probability   201

that is, as a new *kind* of probability, but rather as the (ordinary) probability that a proposition has *if* certain conditions obtain. In short: talk about conditional probability is properly construed not as *talk about a conditional kind of probability*, but rather as *talk of a conditional kind about probability*.

7 A NEW CONDITIONAL DEFINITION OF CONDITIONAL PROBABILITY

Edgington, it must be pointed out, quite explicitly denies that the notion of conditional probability can be adequately explicated or defined in conditional terms. (Understandably so, for to concede this would be to concede that the notion of a conditional judgement is fully intelligible independently of the notion of conditional probability.) The definition that I myself proposed earlier was, in essence, this:[29]

(11) For any proposition B, $p_A(B)$ is the probability that B has if a probability of 1 is assigned to A

Concerning this definition, Edgington maintains, in the light of various putative difficulties which she raises for it, that it is 'inadequate, and beyond repair'.[30] However, it is of considerable interest to note how, according to Edgington herself, the probability function $p_A(\ )$ relates to the probability function $p(\ )$, namely as follows:[31]

Start with $p(\ )$. Now assign zero probability to all the possibilities in which $\sim A$ is true – assign probability 1 to A; keep the relative probabilities of the possibilities in which A is true the same as before; and you have $p_A(\ )$.

But what is said here appears to be fully captured by the following *conditional* statement, which I now propose as a definition replacing (11):

(12) For any proposition B, $p_A(B)$ is the probability that B has if a probability of 1 is assigned to A and, for any propositions C and D which entail A, the ratio $p(C)/p(D)$ is left unaltered in value

Of course, the propositions $(A \mathbin{\&} B)$ and A are *themselves* propositions which entail A, so that it is implicit in the antecedent of (12) that the ratio $p(A \mathbin{\&} B)/p(A)$ is to be left unaltered in value. This enables us to see why the standard definition of $p_A(B)$, (7^*), assigns it precisely the same value that

---

[29] See (6) in section 3 above.   [30] See Edgington, 'Lowe on Conditional Probability', p. 625.
[31] Edgington, 'Lowe on Conditional Probability', p. 620.

202 *Conditionality*

(12) assigns to $p_A(B)$ – that is, why the standard definition is *extensionally* correct. Why? Because if the antecedent of (12) is realized – so that A is assigned a probability of $1 - B$ and $(A \& B)$ will then both have the *same* probability; and the probability that $(A \& B)$ then has will equal the *ratio* between that probability and the probability that A then has, since this last probability will just be 1; but, *ex hypothesi*, the ratio in question will be left unaltered in value from its original value; consequently, if the antecedent of (12) is realized, B will then have a probability equal to the value of the ratio of the probabilities originally assigned to $(A \& B)$ and A – which is precisely the value assigned to $p_A(B)$ by (7*).

All that remains to be asked is what grounds Edgington could possibly have for refusing to allow that (12) constitutes precisely the 'repair' which she claimed (11) to be 'beyond'. Plainly, she cannot object that (12) assigns a different value to $p_A(B)$ from that assigned to it by (7*), which she accepts, since I have just proved otherwise. Moreover, as we have just seen, (12) has the virtue of explaining precisely *why* (7*) assigns the correct value to $p_A(B)$.

8 CONCLUDING REMARKS ON CONDITIONALITY AND OTHER LOGICAL NOTIONS

In this and the previous chapter I have tried to set out and justify my current views concerning the semantics and logic of conditionals, both indicative and subjunctive, partly offering direct defences of my own chief claims and partly presenting arguments against the main rival views. My view has what I take to be the attractive feature of providing a *unitary logic of conditionals*, both indicative and subjunctive, in virtue of assigning the same fundamental logic form to conditionals of both kinds, while at the same time allowing there to be a genuine semantic distinction between them, explicable by appeal to the different types of modality in terms of which propositions of this logical form may be interpreted – 'alethic' modality in the case of subjunctive or counterfactual conditionals, and 'epistemic' modality in the case of indicative conditionals. Thus, 'if' is not fundamentally *ambiguous*, according to my view. I take it to be an additional virtue of my view that it provides a way of analysing the notion of conditionality in terms of the notion of modality, thus reducing the number of fundamental logical notions that we need to recognize. In other words, it turns out, if I am correct, that not all of the five core logical notions examined in this book – *reference, predication, identity, modality,* and *conditionality* – are fundamental. Of course, I have also proposed, in

Chapter 8, an account of *metaphysical* modality which holds that truths regarding what is metaphysically necessary or possible are grounded in truths about *essence*, where the notion of essence is understood in a distinctively Aristotelian way. However, I would not want to represent this view as maintaining that the notion of metaphysical modality is *reducible* to that of essence and, in any case, I have already made it clear that I want to acknowledge types of modality other than metaphysical – or, more generally, *alethic* – modality, notably what I have hitherto called *epistemic* modality. The family of modal notions is, then, much wider, in my view, than the ambit of the notion of essence, which serves as a ground only for modal truths of one specific variety, the metaphysical. Hence I am happy to acknowledge the general notion of modality as being a *fundamental* logical notion, unlike the notion of conditionality.

The notions of reference and predication look likewise to be fundamental. In particular, the idea that predication can be reduced to *identity* – in other words, that every predicative proposition is really an identity proposition, affirming the identity of 'one' thing with 'another', even if only their 'partial' identity, whatever that can exactly be taken to mean – seems to me hopeless, although some philosophers have espoused it. According to this view, to affirm, for instance, that *Mars is red* is to affirm a – presumably only 'partial' – identity between *Mars* and *redness*, a certain particular and a certain universal. But I do not believe that such a view can hope to capture all the distinctions between types of predication that were discussed in Chapters 3 and 4. Rather, I see predications of identity as being just one of these types of predication amongst others. This is not to imply, however, that the notion of identity is, conversely, reducible to that of predication. As I see it, identity is an irreducible and indefinable *formal relation*, unique amongst relations in being truly predicable of anything whatever *and that thing itself* and never truly predicable of any one thing *and anything else*. As can be seen from this very characterization of identity, we have to presuppose the notion of identity even to say *what it is*. For the very words 'itself' and 'else' imply identity and difference, or non-identity.

Equally hopeless, I should say, would be the idea that the notion of *reference* is reducible to one or more other logical notions, such as the notions of predication and identity. Some philosophers might suppose that the statement 'Mars is red', in which reference is seemingly made to the planet Mars, is somehow reducible to a statement affirming that *redness*, the universal, is identical with one of a set of universals, namely all those universals that we would ordinarily think of as being exemplified by Mars and, collectively, only by Mars. This would be to endorse the so-called

204 *Conditionality*

'bundle' theory of particulars, identifying each particular with a 'bundle' of universals. But this theory is unsatisfactory for reasons too well known to be discussed here. In any case, this line of thought, even if successful in the case of reference to particulars, such as Mars, would not provide us with a way of eliminating or reducing reference to *universals*. And the reverse strategy of doing away with universals in favour of particulars, as nominalism proposes, would conversely still leave reference to *particulars* on our hands. A more promising strategy might seem to be to try to eliminate reference in favour of predication and *quantification*, by construing 'Mars is red' as meaning 'There is exactly one thing that is Mars and it is red', in line with Russell's theory of descriptions. However, the predicate '– is Mars' ostensibly means '– is identical with Mars', in which reference is again apparently made to *Mars*. This could be avoided by resorting once more to the bundle theory, but we have already seen that this still leaves reference to *universals* on our hands.

My tentative conclusion, then, is that of the five logical notions that have been the central topics of this book, those of *reference, predication, identity*, and *modality* are truly irreducible and fundamental in character. To these I would add the notions of *negation, existence*, and *truth*, mentioned in the Preface, and also the notion of *generality*, as expressed by the quantifiers 'all' and 'some'. But these are subjects for another occasion.

Bibliography

Adams, E. W. *The Logic of Conditionals* (Dordrecht: Reidel, 1975).
 'Subjunctive and Indicative Conditionals', *Foundations of Language* 6 (1970), pp. 89–94.
Aristotle, *Categories and De Interpretatione*, trans. J. L. Ackrill (Oxford: Clarendon Press, 1963).
Armstrong, D. M. *A Combinatorial Theory of Possibility* (Cambridge University Press, 1989).
 What Is a Law of Nature? (Cambridge University Press, 1983).
Austin, J. L. 'Ifs and Cans', reprinted in his *Philosophical Papers*, 2nd edn (Oxford University Press, 1970).
Bennett, J. 'Farewell to the Phlogiston Theory of Conditionals', *Mind* 97 (1988), pp. 509–27.
Bower, T. G. *Development in Infancy* (San Francisco: Freeman, 1974).
 A Primer of Infant Development (San Francisco: Freeman, 1977).
Brody, B. *Identity and Essence* (Princeton, NJ: Princeton University Press, 1980).
Bryant, C. 'Conditional Murderers', *Analysis* 41 (1981), pp. 209–15.
Davidson, D. 'The Individuation of Events', in his *Essays on Actions and Events* (Oxford: Clarendon Press, 1980).
Dudman, V. H. 'Conditional Interpretations of "If"-Sentences', *Australian Journal of Linguistics* 4 (1984), pp. 143–204.
 'Indicative and Subjunctive', *Analysis* 48 (1988), pp. 113–22.
 'On Conditionals', *Journal of Philosophy* 91 (1994), pp. 113–28.
Dummett, M. *Frege: Philosophy of Language*, 2nd edn (London: Duckworth, 1981).
 The Interpretation of Frege's Philosophy (London: Duckworth, 1981).
Edgington, D. 'Do Conditionals Have Truth-Conditions?', *Critica* 18 (1986), pp. 3–30, reprinted in Jackson (ed.), *Conditionals*.
 'Lowe on Conditional Probability', *Mind* 105 (1996), pp. 617–30.
 'On Conditionals', *Mind* 104 (1995), pp. 235–329.
Eells, E. and Skyrms, B. (eds.), *Probability and Conditionals* (Cambridge University Press, 1994).
Evans, G., 'Can There Be Vague Objects?', *Analysis* 38 (1978), p. 208.
Fine, K. 'Essence and Modality', in James E. Tomberlin (ed.), *Philosophical Perspectives, 8: Logic and Language* (Atascadero, CA: Ridgeview, 1994).
Fodor, J. A. *The Language of Thought* (New York: Crowell, 1975).

Bibliography

Frege, G. 'Function and Concept', in *Translations from the Philosophical Writings of Gottlob Frege*.

Die Grundlagen der Arithmetik [1884], translated as *The Foundations of Arithmetic* by J. L. Austin (Oxford: Blackwell, 1953).

'On Concept and Object', in *Translations from the Philosophical Writings of Gottlob Frege*.

Translations from the Philosophical Writings of Gottlob Frege, 2nd edn, ed. and trans. P. T. Geach and M. Black (Oxford: Blackwell, 1960).

French, S. and Krause, D. *Identity in Physics: A Historical, Philosophical, and Formal Analysis* (Oxford: Clarendon Press, 2006).

Geach, P. T. *Reference and Generality*, 3rd edn (Ithaca, NY: Cornell University Press, 1980).

Grice, H. P. 'Indicative Conditionals', in his *Studies in the Way of Words* (Cambridge, MA: Harvard University Press, 1989).

Hájek, A. and Hall, N. 'The Hypothesis of the Conditional Construal of Conditional Probability', in Eells and Skyrms (eds.), *Probability and Conditionals*.

Howson, C. *Logic with Trees* (London: Routledge, 1997).

Howson, C. and Urbach, P. *Scientific Reasoning: The Bayesian Approach* (La Salle, IL: Open Court, 1989).

Hunter, G. 'The Meaning of "If" in Conditional Propositions', *Philosophical Quarterly* 43 (1993), pp. 279–97.

Jackson, F. *Conditionals* (Oxford: Blackwell, 1987).

(ed.), *Conditionals* (Oxford University Press, 1991).

Keefe, R. 'Contingent Identity and Vague Identity', *Analysis* 55 (1995), pp. 183–90.

Theories of Vagueness (Cambridge University Press, 2000).

Kripke, S. A. 'Identity and Necessity', in M. K. Munitz (ed.), *Identity and Individuation* (New York University Press, 1971).

Naming and Necessity (Oxford: Blackwell, 1980).

LePore, E. and McLaughlin, B. (eds.), *Actions and Events: Perspectives on the Philosophy of Donald Davidson* (Oxford: Blackwell, 1985).

Lewis, D. K. *Counterfactuals* (Oxford: Blackwell, 1973).

On the Plurality of Worlds (Oxford: Blackwell, 1986).

Parts of Classes (Oxford: Blackwell, 1991).

'Probabilities of Conditionals and Conditional Probabilities', *Philosophical Review* 85 (1976), pp. 297–315, reprinted in Jackson (ed.), *Conditionals*.

'Vague Identity: Evans Misunderstood', *Analysis* 48 (1988), pp. 128–30.

Locke, J. *An Essay Concerning Human Understanding* [1690], ed. P. H. Nidditch (Oxford: Clarendon Press, 1975).

Lowe, E. J. 'Conditional Probability and Conditional Beliefs', *Mind* 105 (1996), pp. 603–15.

'Conditionals, Context and Transitivity', *Analysis* 50 (1990), pp. 80–7.

The Four-Category Ontology: A Metaphysical Foundation for Natural Science (Oxford: Clarendon Press, 2006).

'Identity, Individuality and Unity', *Philosophy* 78 (2003), pp. 321–36.

Bibliography

'Impredicative Identity Criteria and Davidson's Criterion of Event Identity', *Analysis* 49 (1989), pp. 178–81.

'Indicative and Counterfactual Conditionals', *Analysis* 39 (1979), pp. 139–41.

'Individuation', in M. J. Loux and D. W. Zimmerman (eds.), *The Oxford Handbook of Metaphysics* (Oxford University Press, 2003).

'Jackson on Classifying Conditionals', *Analysis* 51 (1991), pp. 126–30.

Kinds of Being: A Study of Individuation, Identity and the Logic of Sortal Terms (Oxford: Blackwell, 1989).

'Locke on Real Essence and Water as a Natural Kind: A Qualified Defence', *Proceedings of the Aristotelian Society*, Supplementary Volume 85 (2011), pp. 1–19.

'The Metaphysics of Abstract Objects', *Journal of Philosophy* 92 (1995), pp. 509–24.

More Kinds of Being: A Further Study of Individuation, Identity and the Logic of Sortal Terms (Malden, MA and Oxford: Wiley-Blackwell, 2009).

'Not a Counterexample to Modus Ponens', *Analysis* 47 (1987), pp. 44–7.

'Noun Phrases, Quantifiers and Generic Names', *Philosophical Quarterly* 41 (1991), pp. 287–300.

'On the Alleged Necessity of True Identity Statements', *Mind* 91 (1982), pp. 579–84.

'On the Identity of Artifacts', *Journal of Philosophy* 80 (1983), pp. 220–32.

'One-Level versus Two-Level Identity Criteria', *Analysis* 51 (1991), pp. 192–4.

The Possibility of Metaphysics: Substance, Identity, and Time (Oxford: Clarendon Press, 1998).

'Rationality, Deduction and Mental Models', in K. Manktelow and D. E. Over (eds.), *Rationality* (London: Routledge, 1993).

'Reply to Noonan on Vague Identity', *Analysis* 57 (1997), pp. 88–91.

'A Simplification of the Logic of Conditionals', *Notre Dame Journal of Formal Logic* 24 (1983), pp. 357–66.

'Sortals and the Individuation of Objects', *Mind and Language* 22 (2007), pp. 514–33.

Subjects of Experience (Cambridge University Press, 1996).

A Survey of Metaphysics (Oxford University Press, 2002).

'The Truth about Counterfactuals', *Philosophical Quarterly* 45 (1995), pp. 41–59.

'Two Notions of Being: Entity and Essence', in Robin Le Poidevin (ed.), *Being: Developments in Contemporary Metaphysics* (Cambridge University Press, 2008).

'Vague Identity and Quantum Indeterminacy', *Analysis* 54 (1994), pp. 110–14.

'What Is a Criterion of Identity?', *Philosophical Quarterly* 39 (1989), pp. 1–21.

Mackie, J. L. *Truth, Probability and Paradox* (Oxford: Clarendon Press, 1973).

Mellor, D. H. 'How to Believe a Conditional', *Journal of Philosophy*, 90 (1993), pp. 233–48.

Noonan, H. 'E. J. Lowe on Vague Identity and Quantum Indeterminacy', *Analysis* 55 (1995), pp. 14–19.

Nute, D. *Topics in Conditional Logic* (Dordrecht: Reidel, 1980).

Bibliography

Olson, E. T. 'Material Coincidence and the Indiscernibility Problem', *Philosophical Quarterly* 51 (2001), pp. 337–55.

Parsons, T. *Indeterminate Identity: Metaphysics and Semantics* (Oxford: Clarendon Press, 2000).

Plantinga, A. *The Nature of Necessity* (Oxford: Clarendon Press, 1974).

Putnam, H. 'The Meaning of "Meaning"', in his *Mind, Language and Reality: Philosophical Papers, Volume 2* (Cambridge University Press, 1975).

'Why There Isn't a Ready-Made World', in his *Realism and Reason: Philosophical Papers, Volume 3* (Cambridge University Press, 1983).

Quine, W. V. 'Existence and Quantification', in his *Ontological Relativity and Other Essays* (New York: Columbia University Press, 1969).

'On What There Is', in his *From a Logical Point of View*, 2nd edn (Cambridge, MA: Harvard University Press, 1961).

'Speaking of Objects', in his *Ontological Relativity and Other Essays*.

Ramsey, F. P. *The Foundations of Mathematics and Other Logical Essays* (London: Kegan Paul, 1931).

'Truth and Probability', in his *The Foundations of Mathematics and Other Logical Essays*.

'Universals', in his *The Foundations of Mathematics and Other Logical Essays*.

Rosen, G. 'Modal Fictionalism', *Mind* 99 (1990), pp. 327–54.

Russell, B. *Our Knowledge of the External World* (London: George Allen and Unwin, 1922).

'Propositional Functions', in his *Introduction to Mathematical Philosophy* (London: George Allen and Unwin, 1919).

Salmon, N. *Reference and Essence* (Oxford: Blackwell, 1982).

Smith, B. 'Against Fantology', in M. E. Reicher and J. C. Marek (eds.), *Experience and Analysis* (Vienna: HPT & ÖBV, 2005).

'Of Substances, Accidents and Universals: In Defence of a Constituent Ontology', *Philosophical Papers* 26 (1997), pp. 105–27.

Stalnaker, R. C. 'A Theory of Conditionals', in *Studies in Logical Theory, American Philosophical Quarterly Monograph 2* (Oxford: Blackwell, 1968), reprinted in Jackson (ed.), *Conditionals*.

Strawson, P. F. 'Entity and Identity', in H. D. Lewis (ed.), *Contemporary British Philosophy, Fourth Series* (London: George Allen and Unwin, 1976), reprinted in his *Entity and Identity and Other Essays* (Oxford: Clarendon Press, 1997).

Individuals: An Essay in Descriptive Metaphysics (London: Methuen, 1959).

Suppes, P. *Axiomatic Set Theory* (New York: Dover, 1972).

Swinburne, R. *An Introduction to Confirmation Theory* (London: Methuen, 1973).

Tiles, J. E. *Things That Happen* (Aberdeen University Press, 1981).

Urbach, P. 'What Is a Law of Nature? A Humean Answer', *British Journal for the Philosophy of Science* 39 (1988), pp. 193–210.

Van Fraassen, B. C. *Laws and Symmetry* (Oxford: Clarendon Press, 1989).

Von Plato, J. *Creating Modern Probability* (Cambridge University Press, 1994).

Wiggins, D. *Sameness and Substance Renewed* (Cambridge University Press, 2001).

Williams, B. *Descartes: The Project of Pure Enquiry* (Harmondsworth: Penguin, 1978).

Williamson, T. 'Criteria of Identity and the Axiom of Choice', *Journal of Philosophy* 83 (1986), pp. 380–94.

Wittgenstein, L. *Philosophical Investigations*, trans. G. E. M. Anscombe (Oxford: Blackwell, 1958).

Index

abstract objects, 15, 21, 54, 74, 92, 99, 109, 113, 142, 146
activities, 32
actual world, the, 142, 159, 177–8
Adams, E. W., 199
Adams's thesis, 184, 193, 195–6
adherence, 102, 107, 113
aggregates, 100–1, 113
amorphous lump, 89, 91, 93, 108
animals, 16–18, 23, 25, 29
anti-essentialism, 145
anti-realism, 108, 116, 146
Aristotle, 5–6, 55–7
Armstrong, D. M., 40, 44
aspect, 31
assertibility, 167
assertibility-conditions, 165–6
attention, 22–3
attributes, 32–3, 56–8, 60–1
axiom of extensionality, 14, 74
axiom of regularity, 76

Barcan–Kripke proof, 120, 123, 128–30
Barcan–Kripke step, 129–31
belief, 185, 188
  degrees of, 184–5, 187–8, 191, 193, 195
Bower, T. G., 86, 88
box-arrow symbol, 169
brittleness, 104
Brody, B., 73
Butler, J., 146

categorial concepts, 11, 19, 21, 23, 25, 27–8
categorial ontology, 3, 31, 39, 55, 62
categorial terms, 13–14, 16, 27
categorial uniqueness, problem of, 39
categorialism, 2, 11–12, 19, 21–4, 26–30
  perceptual, 21
category mistakes, 57, 61
causal powers, 112–15
characterization, 31, 33, 35

chemical compounds, 151
conceptions, 97
  adequate, 97–8, 101, 107
concepts, 97–8, 107–9, 153–6
conceptual truths, 153–4
conceptualism, 107–9, 116, 153–4
concrete objects, 15, 75, 91, 109
conditional connective, 169
conditional logic, 7, 168–9, 180, 202
conditional probability, 7, 166–7, 182–4, 187, 189–90, 192–4, 198, 201
  ratio-based definition of, 184, 186, 191–2, 196
conditional truth-value, 199–200
conditionalization, 190–2
conditionals, 6, 167–8, 182
  Austinian, 172–3
  context-sensitivity of, 163, 175–6, 179, 181
  counterfactual, 163–4, 172, 175–8, 180
  Dutchman, 164, 173
  with impossible antecedents, 171
  indicative, 163–5, 167, 172, 183
  logical form of, 171
  material, 165, 173, 182
  possible-worlds interpretations of, 176–7
  subjunctive, 25, 163–4, 166, 183
  transitivity of, 174, 178–80
consistency, 142, 158
constants, 34, 51
count nouns, 12
counterfactual fallacies, 173
counting, 12–13
criteria of application, 12
criteria of identity, 2, 4, 11–20, 25, 27, 69–71, 73–4, 79, 84, 87, 89, 91, 94–5, 98, 100–2, 115
  impredicative, 69
  primitive, 84, 87, 89–90
  type-(A), 80–1, 93
  type-(B), 75, 77–8, 80–2, 84, 92–3
criterial relations, 14, 16, 19, 77, 81–2
cross-categorial terms, 34

210

Index

Davidson, D., 76–7, 81, 91
de Finetti, B., 184
definite descriptions, 28, 149–50, 204
definitions, 80
demonstratives, 80, 85–7
directions, 71–2, 75, 78, 80
dispositions, 32, 41, 104–5, 195
  accidental, 43–4
  essential, 43
  idiosyncratic, 41–2
Dretske, F., 40
Dudman, V. H., 164
Dummett, M., 71, 84–8, 93, 108

Edgington, D., 7, 183–9, 191–4, 197–202
electrons, 38, 112, 114–15, 135–6
empirical evidence, 155
empty set, 76
essence precedes existence, 99, 148–9, 152, 155, 157
essences, 5–6, 56–7, 97, 99–102, 105–15, 144–5,
  147–8, 150–4, 156–7, 203
  general, 97, 145
  individual, 98, 145
  real, 147
essential dependence, 114–15, 146
essential truths, 153–4
essentialism, 144
  serious, 144, 158, 160
Evans, G., 5, 119–24, 126–9, 131–2, 135–7
events, 65, 76, 81, 152
exemplification, 31, 36–7
  dispositional, 36–7
  occurrent, 36
existence, 4, 51, 54, 60, 64, 66, 116, 204
existential dependence
  strong, 37–8
  weak, 37–8
external world, the, 155

facts, 121–2, 125, 157
Fantology, 51, 54–5, 57
feature-placing language, 86, 89, 93
Fine, K., 6
forms of thought, 1
four-category ontology, the, 31–5, 37, 39, 45
Frege, G., 3–4, 51–5, 57, 70, 72–5, 78, 80–2
Fregean thesis, the, 70–1, 73, 78–9, 82–4, 87,
  89–90, 93
functional expressions, 71–2
functions, 54
fuzzy boundaries, 120–1, 135

Geach, P. T., 74, 95
generality, 204
God, 148

H_2O, 147, 149–52
hierarchies of subsumption, 13
hunks of matter, 17–18, 24–5, 29, 90
Hunter, G., 169–70, 174, 176
hydrogen atoms, 112, 114

identity, 4–5, 14, 35, 37–8, 51, 60, 92, 95, 119, 146,
  150, 203–4
  indeterminate, 134–7
  of indiscernibles, 73
  necessity of, 119–20, 123, 128–9, 133, 150
  non-contingency of, 128–34, 138
  personal, 72
  primitive, 115
  relative, 95–6
  substitutivity of, 132–4
  vague, 120
identity conditions, 5, 81, 92, 94, 103, 106, 115–16,
  141, 153
indeterminacy, 121
indexical expressions, 175
individual accidents, 56
individual substances, 33, 39
individuation, 11, 19, 52, 86–90, 93, 108
  principles of, 19–20
individuative concepts, 94, 98, 107, 116
individuators, 20
inference problem, 40
inference to the best explanation, 143
infinity, 62
inherence, 56, 58, 60
innateness, 86, 88–9, 93
instantiation, 31, 33, 35, 40
islands, 18

Jackson, F., 165
Jansen, L., 41

Kant, I., 4
kinds, 12, 14, 27, 32–3, 38, 40–1, 75, 104, 111
  natural, 19, 149
Kripke, S. A., 5–6, 133, 147, 149
Kuratowski, K., 96–8

lambda symbol, 122
language of thought, 89
Leibniz, G. W., 73
Leibniz's law, 95, 103, 122, 125, 127–8, 132, 134
Lewis, D. K., 6, 113, 142, 158, 166, 177, 180, 183–4,
  193, 199
life, 16, 18
  sameness of, 16, 19
lines, 71–2
living organisms, 105
Locke, J., 5, 12, 16–17, 70, 97, 100, 144, 146–7

Index

logic, 34, 119
formal, 55, 63, 134
free, 130
laws of, 130–1
second-order, 57, 62
lotteries, 167, 193–4
lumps, 100–7, 110, 113–14, 153

manifestations, 32
Marcus, R. B., 5
material composition, 103–5
material constitution, 105–6, 109, 116
material implication, 182
material objects, 16
mereological sums, 112–13
metamorphosis, 14, 16, 18
metaphysical possibility, 98, 110–11, 115, 139, 151–2
modal combinatorialism, 143
modal logic, 6–7, 124, 139–40, 180
modal operators, 171, 182
modal primitivism, 144
modality, 6, 119, 139, 156–7, 160, 166, 177, 203–4
alethic, 165, 172, 182, 202
epistemic, 165, 172, 182, 202
modes, 32–3, 37, 40, 56, 58, 60–1
modus ponens, 168, 170, 173
mountains, 15, 17–18, 20, 121

naming, 29–30
natural kind terms, 26–30, 149
natural laws, 32, 40–2
conditional, 42, 44–5
natural necessitation, 40
NCI. *See* identity:non-contingency of
necessary self-identity, 130–1
necessary truths, 130
Nef, F., 43
negation, 204
numbers, 79

objects, 32–3, 39, 51–4
Ockham, William of, 39
Oderberg, D. S., 41
ontological categories, 2–3, 34, 37, 39, 50, 62–3, 145
ontological commitment, 51, 141, 148
ontological dependency, 37, 39, 56, 72, 81
ontological square, the, 34, 36–9
ontology, 51
pure, 65

parallelism, 71–2
paraphrase, 148
particulars, 31–2, 34, 57
bundle theory of, 204

perception, 21–2
persistence conditions, 104–6, 116
individual, 106
sortal, 11, 13–14, 18–19, 106
person-stages, 72
phase changes, 19, 42
philosophical logic, 1
planets, 150
possible worlds, 6, 54, 110–11, 139–41, 144, 156, 158
abstractionism concerning, 142–3, 158–60
accessibility relations between, 140
concretism concerning, 142–3, 157–8, 160
fictionalism concerning, 143, 160
similarity between, 177–9
precisifications, 124, 137
predicables, 56–7, 63
predicate logic, 34, 50–1, 57, 141
predicates, 52–3, 98, 131, 133
predications, 56, 58, 63–4, 203
categorial, 3, 50, 63–5
dispositional, 3, 31
formal, 2–3
material, 2
occurrent, 3, 31
primary substances, 52, 55–6, 58, 60–1, 72
principle of charity, 179
principle of instantiation, the, 44–5
principles of composition, 112
probability calculus, 184, 186, 190–1
probability functions, 196–8, 201
proper names, 26–30, 51, 72, 79, 149
properties, 34, 51, 53–4, 57, 62, 122, 127, 130–3
property abstraction, 131, 133–4
propositional attitudes, 185, 188
propositions, 142, 157, 159, 175–6, 183, 185, 193, 197, 200
atomic, 51, 60
protons, 112, 114
Putnam, H., 108, 147, 149

quantification, 140–1, 204
quantifiers, 4, 28, 51, 60
restricted, 60
unrestricted, 65
quantities of matter, 100
quantum entanglement, 135
Quine, W. V., 4, 51–3, 141, 148

Ramsey, F. P., 39
rationality, 99, 115, 184
reference, singular, 2, 12, 26–8, 70, 80–5, 88–9, 203
vague, 136
Russell, B., 1, 3–4, 28, 51, 55, 143, 204
Russell's paradox, 52, 98–9

Index

scepticism, 155
secondary substances, 56–8, 60–1
semantic values, 52–4
set membership, 96
set theory, 76
sets, 15, 20, 53, 74–6, 95, 98, 101, 113–14,
    146, 159
  ordered, 95–6, 98
ship of Theseus, 91
ships, 92
singular terms, 70–3, 78–80, 82–4, 87, 89–91,
    93, 136–7
Smith, B., 50
sortal concepts, 11
sortal logic, 40, 42
sortal terms, 12–13, 15, 42, 74, 79–80, 82–3, 85, 87,
    90, 92
  artefactual, 91
  criterionless, 83–4, 87–8, 90–1
sortalism, 2, 11
species, 56–7, 59, 61, 63
Stalnaker, R. C., 174, 177–8, 180
states of affairs
  dispositional, 40–1
  occurrent, 40
statues, 100, 102–4, 106, 110, 113, 153–4
Strawson, P. F., 86
subjects, 34, 57, 61

tense, 31
thoughts, singular, 2, 19–20, 23–30, 89
Tooley, M., 40
tracking, perceptual, 22–5, 87–8, 90, 93
transcategorial terms, 13, 16–17, 27
transuranic elements, 148
tropes, 32, 39, 57
truth, 204
truthmakers, 50, 65, 110

universal generalizations, 40, 61
universals, 2–4, 31–4, 37, 40, 45, 57, 203

vague objects, 119–20
vagueness, 5, 15–17, 102, 119
  ontic, 120
  semantic, 120, 124, 136
van Fraassen, B. C., 40–1
variables, 28, 34, 40, 60–1, 65

Wason selection task, 168
Wasserman, R., 41
water, 41–2, 147, 149–51
Wiener, N., 96
Wiggins, D., 108
Williams, B., 108
Williamson, T., 72
Wittgenstein, L., 65, 70, 85, 87

CPSIA information can be obtained at www.ICGtesting.com
Printed in the USA
LVOW12*0457170614

390309LV00002B/8/P